DATE DUE

PRINTED IN U.S.A.

PRESUMED GUILTY

PRESUMED GUILTY
WHEN INNOCENT PEOPLE ARE WRONGLY CONVICTED

MARTIN YANT

PROMETHEUS BOOKS
BUFFALO, NEW YORK

FEB 1 9 1992

PRESUMED GUILTY: WHEN INNOCENT PEOPLE ARE WRONGLY CONVICTED. Copyright © 1991 by Martin Yant. All rights reserved. No part of this book may be reproduced in any manner whatsoever without written permission, except in the case of brief quotations embodied in critical articles and reviews. Inquiries should be addressed to Prometheus Books, 700 E. Amherst Street, Buffalo, New York 14215, 716-837-2475.

95 94 93 92 91   5 4 3 2 1

Yant, Martin, 1949-
    Presumed guilty : when innocent people are wrongly convicted / Martin Yant.
        p.   cm.
    Includes bibliographical references and index.
    ISBN 0-87975-643-8
    1. Judicial error—United States—Cases. 2. Trials—United States. I. Title.
KF9756.Y36   1991
347.73'12—dc20
[347.30712]   90-26301
                                                                            CIP

Printed in the United States of America on acid-free paper.

For my parents, whose sense of justice aroused me;
for my children, whose sweet innocence inspired me;
and for Pamela Ellinger-Dixon, whose spirit showed me the way.

I realize I am a voice crying in the wilderness, but I believe that the innocent are convicted far more frequently than the public cares to believe, and far more frequently than those who operate the system dare to believe. An innocent person in prison, in my view, is about as rare as a pigeon in the park.

—The Reverend James McCloskey

Contents

Acknowledgments

I could almost write a book about the many fine people who helped make this book possible. But I will limit myself to naming those to whom I am most indebted.

First and foremost are my editors at Prometheus Books: Bob Basil, who gave me the opportunity, and Mary Beth Gehrman, who helped translate it into a reality.

For the benefit of their insights on the tragedy of wrongful convictions, I am grateful to criminologist C. Ronald Huff of Ohio State University; Edith and Lewis Crosley, mother and stepfather of Todd Neely; and the family of Randall Dale Adams.

In addition to my understanding boss at the *Columbus Dispatch*, editorial page editor and raconteur extraordinaire Dick Carson, I would like to thank my colleagues Mary Ann Edwards, Steve Berry, Bob Bloom, Jim Hunter, Susan Kelly, George Myers Jr., Lisa Reuter-May, Phil Rudell and Cathy Weaver for their encouragement and assistance.

Finally, I would like to express admiration for all those from within and without the system who have exposed the too-frequent injustice of justice; and, most of all, those who have endured this indignity with a dignity that may spur the reforms needed to spare others the same fate.

Introduction

Justice Denied

The American criminal-justice system is far too often a source of injustice for the innocent rather than of justice for the guilty.

Despite all the alleged protections built into the trial process, the sad fact is that a person facing criminal charges is actually presumed guilty until proved innocent rather than presumed innocent until proved guilty.

As a result, it is conservatively estimated that several thousand Americans a year are convicted of serious crimes they did not commit. Some are convicted of crimes that didn't even occur.

And for every innocent person convicted, several others are unjustly arrested and put through needless trauma before being released.

Many of those wrongly convicted end up paying for someone else's crime with several years of their lives.

Some have even paid *with* their lives. According to a study by Hugo Adam Bedau and Michael L. Radelet published in the *Stanford Law Review* in 1987, of the 350 Americans mistakenly convicted of a potentially capital offense between 1900 and 1985, twenty-three were executed. Several others were saved with only minutes to spare.

And for almost every innocent person sent to prison or put to death, a guilty person goes free to commit more crimes—including murder.

In the following chapters, you will see how and why such outrageous miscarriages of justice occur and what can be done to avoid them.

You will also see how most of these egregious errors are the result of mere chance and could happen to anyone—including you.

Find that hard to believe?

Then wait till you see how engineer Lenell Geter ended up with a life sentence for armed robbery because he read books and fed the ducks in a park during his lunch hour.

Wait till you see how Randall Dale Adams came within three days of being executed for the murder of a police officer he had nothing to do with because he ran out of gas at the wrong place and the wrong time.

Wait till you see how William Jackson Marion was executed for the murder of a man found to be alive four years later.

Wait till you see how a desperately poor couple who abandoned their seriously ill daughter in hopes she would receive the care they couldn't afford were convicted of her murder, only to have her discovered alive and well twenty months later.

Wait till you see how Joyce Ann Brown ended up in prison for almost ten years because the car used in a robbery-murder was rented by *another* Joyce Ann Brown.

Wait till you see how innocent people are convicted or sentenced to death largely because of the testimony of inexpert "expert witnesses" for hire, faulty forensics tests, and inaccurate polygraph exams.

Wait till you see what it cost the Reverend Bernard Pagano before another man confessed to the crimes with which the Roman Catholic priest was charged.

Wait till you see the cross that Bible-college student Steven Linscott has had to bear because he believed a nightmare he had might have been a spiritual sign that could help police solve a murder.

Wait till you see how Larry Hicks was almost executed for a murder he didn't commit because he helped some neighbors move and had a lazy court-appointed attorney who didn't even bother to appeal his conviction.

Wait till you see how Julius Krause broke out of prison and got the man who actually committed the crime Krause was jailed for to confess to authorities—then was reincarcerated for eleven more years because he had escaped.

Wait till you see the tragedy endured by young Todd Neely because a neighbor was assaulted by a teenager while Neely was dining with his family several miles away—and he had a time-stamped receipt to prove it.

Wait till you see how Clarence Boggie was convicted not once, not twice, but *three times* for crimes he did not commit; he probably would have spent the rest of his life in prison if he hadn't been cleared by mystery writer Erle Stanley Gardner's "Court of Last Resort."

Wait till you see how Nicola Sacco and Bartolomeo Vanzetti were executed for a robbery-murder they didn't commit because, in the words of their supposedly impartial trial judge, they were "anarchist bastards."

Wait till you see how eight of the nine "Scottsboro Boys" were sentenced to death for rapes that never occurred, because they were black.

Wait till you see how industrialist Leo Frank was convicted of a murder he didn't commit, then lynched after his death sentence was commuted to life in prison, because he was Jewish.

Wait till you see how carpenter Bruno Richard Hauptmann was unjustly executed for "the crime of the century"—the kidnapping-murder of the Lindbergh baby—because he was German and the victim of a con artist.

Wait till you see how people facing serious charges have been poorly defended by lawyers who were drunk or on drugs; how one defendant was convicted because his attorney slept through most of his trial and another was convicted while his attorney secretly slept with the prosecutor; and how one attorney neglected to note that a client convicted of rape was impotent and another overlooked proof that a client's blood type was different from the rapist's.

Wait till you see how so many unsuspecting suspects are still beaten or browbeaten into confessing to crimes they didn't commit.

And wait till you see how so many others are deliberately framed by unscrupulous police, ambitious prosecutors, vindictive "victims," or the real perpetrators.

Still don't think it could happen to you? Then read on.

1

Trials and Errors in Dallas

Our procedure has been always haunted by the ghost of the innocent man convicted. It is an unreal dream.

—Judge Learned Hand

Lenell Geter lived that "unreal dream," and it was a nightmare. He would probably still be living it, too, if it weren't for his friends and lawyers. Outraged when Geter was convicted of a crime he did not commit, they took his case to the court of public opinion and finally got him freed—but not until he had served sixteen months of a life sentence.

Geter's ordeal began in August 1982, when he was arrested by police investigating a series of armed robberies in several Dallas suburbs. One of those communities was Greenville, where the 24-year-old black engineer worked.

Geter would be considered an unlikely suspect in most towns. He had recently graduated from South Carolina State College and had a good job with E-Systems, a large military and electronics contractor. He was a religious, nonsmoking teetotaler known for his soft-spokenness and hard work.

But Greenville wasn't a typical town when it came to race. Until the late 1960s, motorists entering the city of twenty-two thousand were greeted with a sign boasting that it had "The Blackest Land—

The Whitest People."[1]

Blacks there were still viewed with enough trepidation in 1982 that Geter's habit of spending his lunch hour reading books and feeding the ducks at a local park aroused the suspicion of a 68-year-old neighborhood busybody who took it upon herself to write down his car license-plate number.

When a fast-food restaurant on the other side of town was robbed, the woman informed the police of Geter's supposedly suspicious behavior. That was enough reason for investigators to show his photo to witnesses to the heist. All agreed he wasn't the robber. But that didn't stop police from passing on Geter's photo to officers investigating similar robberies in neighboring towns, where witnesses to two of the crimes identified him as the holdup man. Based solely on such notoriously inaccurate evidence, police charged Geter with one of the two heists, a $615 robbery of a Kentucky Fried Chicken outlet in Balsch Springs.

Geter's private attorney quickly exhausted his limited funds and withdrew from the case. He was replaced by a court-appointed attorney who put forth the kind of effort you would expect for a $200 fee. What little time the lawyer spent on the case was devoted to trying to get Geter to plead guilty to a lesser charge. Geter adamantly refused.

At the last minute, the attorney asked for more time to prepare his case. But the judge refused. As a result, several of Geter's co-workers who were prepared to testify he was at work when the crime occurred couldn't be located in time for the trial, and Geter was found guilty by an all-white jury. To add insult to injury, the attorney also missed the deadline for filing for a retrial based on the would-be witnesses' affidavits.[2]

Things got even worse at the sentencing hearing, where Detective James Fortenberry testified that the sheriff in Geter's home county had told him that Geter, who had no prior arrest record, was "probably an outlaw" and was suspected of several robberies there. Sheriff Ed Darnell of Bamberg County, South Carolina, later said Fortenberry had "misunderstood" him—a nice way to say he was lying. He added that he wouldn't have known the alleged outlaw "if he were to walk through my door."[3]

By then, however, Geter already had been sentenced to life in prison. But that, fortunately, wasn't the end of the story. Geter's irate co-workers, most of them white, started a defense committee and raised $11,000 for Geter's appeal. They also began telling anyone who would listen about the travesty of justice that had befallen him. The National Association for the Advancement of Colored People also entered the picture.

Before long, the local news media became convinced that the case should be looked into. After a revealing article appeared in the *Dallas Times Herald*, Geter's plight attracted the attention of the *New York Times*, ABC News, *People* magazine, the Phil Donahue show, and Cable News Network. But the coup de grace was an award-winning segment that the CBS News program "60 Minutes" aired on December 4, 1983; it ripped the prosecution's case to shreds as only that show could.

Ten days later, a joyful Geter was released on $10,000 bond put up by his co-workers and was greeted by cheers from a crowd of supporters and a chorus of questions from a crush of reporters. But Dallas County's hard-nosed district attorney, Henry Wade, always a man of his convictions, vowed that Geter wasn't out of the woods until he passed the polygraph test he had agreed to take.

"If he fails the test, he will have a new trial," the longtime DA said.[4]

But Geter was no longer so trusting. He apparently realized that polygraph test results are wrong as often as they are right—especially if conducted by a biased examiner. So Geter refused to take one administered by Wade's agent. Instead he took—and passed—tests conducted by two independent examiners. But Wade's office said the results were "not worth the paper they're printed on" and scheduled a new trial for April 9, 1984.

Wade's eagerness subsided, however, after the testimony of two new defense witnesses. The first, an employee of the first restaurant Geter was accused of robbing, said she never heard from police again after giving a description of the bandit that didn't match Geter's. The second, a victim of the second robbery in which Geter had been implicated, testified that a detective "became frustrated" when she wouldn't identify anyone in two photo lineups that included Geter. "That's okay—I've got my man anyway," she quoted him as saying.[5]

Shortly after their testimony, Wade abruptly announced at a press conference that the charges against Geter were being dropped because four of the five witnesses who had identified Geter in court as the holdup man had since fingered a two-time convict already facing charges in several other chicken-restaurant robberies.

"As a result of this investigation and as a result of our office finding who we feel committed the robbery, we feel like Geter is innocent and that this office has found the guilty party," Wade told reporters as he tried to put the best face possible on his office's original error. "Therefore, the Lenell Geter case will be dismissed."

But, in a prelude to performances to come, the notoriously bullheaded Wade refused to apologize for the two years of hell his office had put Geter through.

"He'd still be down there in the penitentiary if it hadn't been for me," he said. "I'm the one who offered him a new trial. I offered to let him take a lie-detector test, and we found the person who we think did it."

Wade admitted, however, that the man he had just declared guilty would not be charged with the offenses because the prosecution's case had been weakened by the witnesses' changing stories.

The new suspect, needless to say, didn't appreciate being all but tried and convicted in a press conference. "He's trying to get a scapegoat," Curtis Eugene Mason said. "Those witnesses—what makes them so reliable? They put Geter in prison, then they turn around and put me in prison."[6]

A jubilant Geter, on the other hand, expressed delight with Wade's decision, and added that he was looking forward to marrying his long-patient fiancée. But he also expressed fears that there were many others in similar situations who would never have the benefit of the kind of publicity and support that had won him his freedom.

"People expect our judicial system to work in a one-hundred-percent efficiency mode," the engineer said. "I know it doesn't, and

I'm a prime example. There are other Lenell Geters out there."

Geter's supervisor, who helped organize support for his employee, agreed. "The law-enforcement people and the district attorney didn't try to find the truth; they just tried to get a conviction," Charles Hartford said. "My feeling about law and order has kind of changed after watching this. You keep wondering how many other times something like this happens."[7]

The unfortunate answer is that it happens a lot more often than most people imagine—as an award-winning documentary film and several other controversial Dallas County cases were about to show.

Crossing the Thin Blue Line

The first of those cases eventually eclipsed Geter's in prominence and controversy. Ironically, the incident that prompted the furor actually preceded Geter's case by several years.

The date, to be precise, was Sunday, November 28, 1976—one of the coldest nights in Dallas history. It was twenty-nine degrees. Police officers Robert Wood, an American Indian and decorated three-year veteran, and Teresa Turko had just started the graveyard shift.

At 12:38 A.M., Wood and Turko were at the drive-in window of a West Dallas Burger King. Wood bought a cup of coffee and Turko a milkshake. As they prepared to leave, a dirty blue compact car drove by on Hampton Road with only its parking lights on. Wood turned onto the street, put on his flashing lights, and pulled the car over. The 27-year-old officer parked a few feet behind on the shoulder of the road. Because Wood apparently planned only to remind the driver to turn the car's headlights on, neither he nor Turko followed the prescribed procedure of calling in the car's license-plate number.

That was a fatal mistake. If they had, they would have been told the car had been reported stolen and that the suspected thief was also believed to have stolen a nine-shot, .22-caliber pistol loaded with lethal hollow-point bullets.

Wood knew none of this as he approached the driver, who suddenly shot him several times—twice after he was lying motionless on the ground. He was pronounced dead at a nearby hospital a short time later.

As the killer sped away, the 24-year-old Turko threw her milkshake aside and fired five shots at the car. She later said she might have hit it once, but wasn't sure. The hysterical Turko then radioed such confusing information about the shooting and her location that responding squad cars were told to drive down Hampton Road until they found her. When they did, Turko proved to be highly confused and short on details. She couldn't recall the car's license-plate number. She hadn't gotten a close look at the driver. She couldn't identify the make of the car, but thought it might be a Chevrolet Vega. All she could say for sure was that the driver was the only person in the car, and that he was wearing a coat with a heavy collar.

With that small amount of information to go on, Dallas police began one of the most intense manhunts in Texas history. Thousands of hours were spent checking on the nearly ten thousand Chevrolet Vegas registered in the state. Police interviewed several witnesses who had been driving by at the time of the shooting. But none—including three who would later provide crucial, detailed trial testimony—were able to give a good description of the driver.

Turko, meanwhile, was hypnotized by an expert from California. But she still could recall practically nothing. Almost a month later, police still had little to go on.

Then came their first break. The police chief of Vidor, a tiny swamp town on the Texas-Louisiana border, called to say he had been told a local 16-year-old juvenile delinquent, David Harris, had been bragging to friends that he had "offed a Dallas pig." On the day before Wood's killing, the chief said, Harris had stolen his father's gun and a neighbor's blue Mercury Comet.

Harris had apparently skipped town the day of the Dallas killing, but was back the next day boasting of his cop-killing adventure in the big city. Harris bragged to at least six people in the next few days that he had gunned down Wood. "He stood up and said if he was lying God could strike him dead," one friend was later quoted as saying.

The detectives working on the Wood case were ecstatic. They asked that Harris be brought to Dallas as soon as he could be found. When Vidor police finally caught up with the troubled teenager a short time later, he admitted to the car and gun thefts, but denied having anything to do with the Dallas murder.

Later, Harris led officers to a small swamp, where he showed them how he had hidden the stolen pistol underwater after spraying it with boot oil and wrapping it in a sock. The weapon was sent to Dallas, where ballistics tests identified it as the gun used to kill Wood.

When he was taken to Dallas for questioning on December 21, Harris admitted to having been in the car when Wood was shot, but said he hadn't pulled the trigger. He said he had only told his friends that to impress them, and that the killer was actually a factory worker he had picked up earlier that day by the name of Randall Dale Adams. Harris said they had spent the day together drinking beer and smoking pot. That night, they drove to the 183 Drive-In and watched two soft-core porno movies, *The Student Body* and *Swinging Cheerleaders*.

When they decided to leave shortly after midnight, Harris said, Adams drove because he knew how to get to the motel he and his brother had been living in since they had come to Dallas in search of work a few weeks earlier. Along the way, a cop pulled the car over. Harris said Adams had told him to hunch down so he couldn't be seen. As the officer approached the window, he said, Adams calmly gunned him down and sped away before Harris realized what had happened.

"He told me not to worry about it, to forget I ever saw it," Harris testified later.[8]

Adams then drove to his motel and got out. Harris said he was so scared he got behind the wheel and drove aimlessly for some time before heading back to Vidor.

At the same time Harris was talking his way out of trouble, Adams was busy working at the pallet company where he been hired his first day in Dallas. It was hard work, but he liked it. In time, he thought he could build a good life for himself in the booming city. The 28-year-old Ohioan had no reason to think otherwise. He had no criminal record. He had an honorable discharge from the Army. He had a good work history. And, most of all, he and the brother who had come South with him, Kenzo Ray, had a strongly religious and supportive family back in Columbus.

But all that meant nothing to the two police officers, backed up by several others outside the building, who suddenly approached Adams and told him he was wanted for questioning at the police station downtown. When they got there, Adams was taken into a small room, where he was questioned at length about the fateful day he spent with David Harris.

Adams told how he had gone to work that Saturday with the hope that overtime work would be available, but the plant was closed. As he drove back toward the motel, he ran out of gas. He said he was walking down the road toward a gas station when Harris pulled up and offered his help.

Adams said they ended up spending the day together, and his version of their activities matched Harris's almost perfectly—except for a two-and-a-half-hour difference on when they left the movie. Adams put the time at about 9:30 instead of midnight. He said he was back in his hotel room a little before 10 P.M. His brother was already asleep, so he watched the last part of the "Carol Burnett Show" and the beginning of the ten o'clock news, then turned in—two-and-a-half hours before Wood was killed.

But the police weren't impressed. They grilled Adams for several more hours without an attorney present, trying to get him to confess to Wood's murder. At one point, Adams claims, a detective threw the murder weapon on the table and demanded that Adams pick it up. When he refused, Adams says the officer pulled out his gun and threatened to shoot him if he didn't do as he was told. Adams told him to go ahead and shoot, because he wasn't picking up the gun. He knew he was as good as dead anyway if his fingerprints turned up on the weapon.

As the hours wore on, a weary Adams finally agreed to sign a statement—later identified to the press as a "confession"—in which he admitted spending the day with Harris before driving the car to his motel and getting out. Unfortunately, Adams ended his account with a vague sentence—"I do not remember anything after I took a right turn on Inwood until I was turning left on Fort Worth Avenue"— that would come to haunt him.

Despite Adams's insistence that he had only meant he remembered nothing of significance, least of all a killing, while driving that stretch of road, First Assistant District Attorney Doug Mulder claimed Adams didn't want to remember what happened at that point because it was then that he killed Wood.

Courtroom observers were used to Mulder making so much out of so little. He was notorious for doing anything he could get away with to obtain a conviction. And it worked. The ambitious prosecutor had an unbroken chain of murder convictions, some of them despite the flimsiest of evidence. ("It takes a good prosecutor to convict a guilty defendant. But it takes a *great one* to convict an innocent defendant," Dallas prosecutors supposedly were fond of jesting at the time.) And for each of those convicted Mulder had also won the maximum sentence—either life in prison or, preferably, the death penalty.

That's why many believe Mulder chose to prosecute Adams rather than Harris to begin with, even though the evidence overwhelmingly pointed to the latter. Harris, after all, was a good old Texas boy— with the emphasis on "boy." At age sixteen, Harris could not, under the law at that time, get the death penalty. Adams, on the other hand, was the odd man out—with the emphasis on "man." He was not only a hippie-looking Northerner, he was also eligible for the execution the public had been demanding for Wood's killer.

With so much at stake, Adams needed a crack criminal-defense attorney. But that would cost a fortune he didn't have. So he ended up instead with two well-meaning lawyers who had had limited criminal-trial experience. Dennis White had a good record in the criminal cases he had handled, but he was primarily a real-estate attorney. Edith James knew the law well, but had trouble using it to her advantage in the tense atmosphere of a courtroom.

But Mulder still had his work cut out for him. The case against Adams was weak, and he knew it. He had no physical evidence, and the murder came in the middle of an incredible crime spree by Harris: First he had stolen the gun and car. Then, after returning to Vidor from Dallas, he had committed a series of armed robberies, burglaries, and assaults, for which the charges were to be quietly dropped later in return for his testimony. At sixteen, in fact, Harris already had a rap sheet as long as Wilt Chamberlain's arm.

Adams, on the other hand, had no criminal record at all and no real motive to kill Wood—especially if you believed his claim that he didn't even know the car was stolen.

Mulder also had a serious problem with his other key witness. Officer Turko had observed little and remembered even less. Investigators also suspected that, contrary to what she said, Turko didn't follow procedure and get out of the squad car while Wood approached the other vehicle. That would explain why she didn't get the license-plate number, couldn't describe the car, and her bullets failed to hit it as it sped away. Even worse for Mulder, Turko had said the driver was the only person in the car. That fit Adams's story and not Harris's. She also said the driver was wearing a coat with a fur collar, like the one Harris was wearing when he was arrested. Adams apparently had no such coat.

But Mulder also had an ace up his sleeve in District Judge Don Metcalfe, a prominent participant in Dallas's criminal (in)justice system. And it wasn't long before Metcalfe came to Mulder's rescue. After allowing the defense to present the friends to whom Harris had bragged about killing a Dallas cop, Metcalfe issued a crucial ruling that prohibited the jury from hearing about Harris's entire crime spree, into which Wood's murder seemed logically to fit.

Adams's attorneys nonetheless remained naively confident, since the prosecution had only two weak witnesses, one of whom had bragged about committing the murder himself.

But on the last day of the trial, Mulder sprang a big, ethically questionable surprise. The devious DA produced three mystery witnesses: Emily Miller and her husband, R. L. Miller, and Michael Randell. In suspiciously similar wording, all three claimed they had driven past the crime scene before the shooting, the Millers in one car and Randell in another. Randell and Mrs. Miller both identified the killer's car as "a Ford product," and said they had watched closely what was going on because they were "nosy." Finally, all three identified Adams as the man with "bushy hair" they had seen in the car that had been pulled over. But Mrs. Miller did it with the most emphasis.

"He's the man. He's the man right there," she said with crushing certainty as she pointed at Adams. Mrs. Miller also said she had previously picked Adams out of a police lineup, then out of a photo lineup.[9]

Adams's lawyers, White and James, appeared to be in a state of shock. Adams could tell by the expression on their faces that his cause was lost.

Mulder had pulled a fast one on them by holding his best witnesses until the "rebuttal" stage. That freed him from the obligation of informing the defense attorneys of their names beforehand, because the prosecutor theoretically doesn't know what he has to rebut until the defense has presented its case. It was a dirty trick to introduce such crucial witnesses at this stage, but Judge Metcalfe let Mulder get away with it.

White made things worse when he cross-examined Emily Miller, by asking her what she was doing in a black neighborhood at that time of night—he didn't realize that one of the other witnesses, a black, was her husband. If he didn't look like a racist, he at least looked like a fool, and Texans don't suffer fools gladly (unless they have money, that is). At the end, White was so flustered that he forgot to reserve the right to recall the trio when the trial resumed the following week.

Over the weekend, however, White began picking up information that indicated the three witnesses had lied in order to win part of the $21,000 reward that had been offered to anyone aiding in the arrest and conviction of Wood's killer. On Monday, White asked that all three be recalled. But Mulder said they had checked out of their motel and that he didn't know where they were. At that point, White demanded to see any affidavits signed by the increasingly enigmatic witnesses. They proved to be quite revealing. Only Emily

Miller's had been signed before Adams's arrest, and it described the killer as a "light-skinned Negro or Mexican." Adams is white with fair features. Randell's affidavit was written the day *after* the newspapers had printed Harris's version of the murder and Adams's photo. And R. L. Miller's affidavit hadn't been written until the trial was already underway.

But Judge Metcalfe came to Mulder's rescue once again. He refused to have the affidavits made known to the jury. It would be unfair, he said, because the witnesses weren't there to explain them. He didn't seem concerned about being unfair to Adams, however, whose life was on the line.

Closing arguments were heard on May 2, 1977. And it was then that Mulder gave an emotional speech so good that the supposedly objective Judge Metcalfe would later admit it caused tears to well up in his eyes, perhaps further blinding him to the truth. The appeal was so dramatic, in fact, that it would later inspire the title of a movie that would undo the gross injustice Mulder and Metcalfe were about to complete. But that wasn't on Mulder's mind then. Apparently, the only thing he cared about was winning the death sentence of Randall Dale Adams. And he tugged very hard on the jury members' heartstrings to do just that:

> In the sterile, well-lit, almost laboratory conditions of the courtroom, we forget what really has caused our paths to cross. But you see, we are all here because Robert Wood, a name that has kind of drifted by the side, is dead—gun downed and shot down by Randall Adams. We know very little about Robert Wood. We know he left a widow, he left a family. He died as a soldier fighting a war against crime. Our laws are enforced and protected by that thin blue line of men and women who daily risk their lives by walking into the jaws of death, sometimes to walk back out again and sometimes to perish.
>
> Have you ever stopped and thought who protects the police officer? Who picks up their banner when they fall in battle? You see, their faith and their trust rests with your conscience and your courage. Don't give this man a life sentence when he has earned death. And I ask you: Don't turn your back on Robert Wood.[10]

Early the next morning, the jury found a bewildered Randall Dale Adams guilty of capital murder. Then came the crucial penalty phase of the trial, when the jury must determine whether the defendant is likely to be such a threat to society that he should be put to death.

In Dallas at that time, that would often be when psychiatrist James Grigson would enter the picture. Almost without fail, "Dr. Death," as Grigson was known, would testify—for a fee, of course—that the defendant was an incurable "sociopath" who, he could predict with "one-hundred-percent certainty," would kill again.

As will be detailed in a later chapter, by 1988 Grigson's predictable testimony would become so controversial that, in one eventful week, the U.S. Supreme Court would rule he had infringed on a prisoner's constitutional rights, the American Civil Liberties Union would condemn him as "a menace," and the American Psychiatric Association would publicly question his professional ethics.

Grigson's handling of the Adams case was a good example why. Just before the trial, Grigson spent a total of twenty minutes with the frightened and confused defendant. First, he had Adams replicate some drawings on a sheet of paper. Then he asked him what it meant to say "a rolling stone gathers no moss" and "a bird in the hand is worth two in the bush." Then he asked Adams if he had any remorse for killing Robert Wood. Adams said he couldn't have remorse for a crime he didn't commit. He calmly explained for what seemed like the thousandth time that he had been framed, and that David Harris was the one who should be remorseful, because David Harris had to be the killer.

Based on that paltry examination, Grigson testified that Adams was the most virulent kind of sociopathic killer: the kind who had no remorse, pity or regret; the kind who would kill again and again if given the chance; the kind who was a definite danger to society. The fact that Adams had not tried to flee Dallas or change his appearance and had gone to work every day after the murder, Grigson said, was only further proof that he did not have normal human emotions: He was the type of person who "could work all day and creep all night."

Grigson's "expert" testimony proved deadly. Later that day, Adams was sentenced to death by electrocution.

Meanwhile, disturbing rumors about the surprise witnesses continued to arise. So did questions about their testimony: Could they really have seen the killer in the driver's seat? It was, after all, dark and cold. Emily Miller had even said there might have been frost on the windows. They had also had to look across three lanes of traffic. In fact, Mrs. Miller had had to look across her husband *and* three lanes of traffic. But if she hadn't seen Adams, how could she have picked him out of the lineup?

Answers to some of those questions began to come in a few days after the verdict, when attorney White received a call from Elba Jean Carr. Carr said she had worked with the Millers at a South Dallas gas station. She told him that the day after the shooting, Mr. Miller had told her he "hadn't seen anything" that night but was willing to say he had for the $21,000 reward.

Carr also said Mrs. Miller had lied when she testified that she had been working as the station's manager that night. Mrs. Miller had been fired ten days before for cash-register shortages. More pieces of the puzzle began to fit together when White learned that the district attorney's office had dropped armed-robbery charges against Mrs. Miller's daughter by a previous marriage two days after Adams's trial ended, apparently as a reward for Mrs. Miller's crucial testimony.

Based on that information and his suspicions that Mulder had withheld other crucial evidence, White filed a motion for a new trial. But Metcalfe, after listening to Carr's testimony, quickly dismissed the motion.

White wasn't through yet, however. He requested an FBI investigation of Mulder's conduct and filed a $5 million civil-rights suit against the Dallas County district attorney's office. But the FBI refused to launch a probe and the civil-rights suit was dismissed. That was the end of the line for a disgusted White. An admitted idealist, White was so outraged by the case that he decided to give up his law practice altogether. "If you're trying to be ethical, and you feel that the people you're up against are not ethical, then you can't give your clients a fair shake," White explained later. "You have to be unethical to deal in an unethical system. I couldn't in good conscience continue in a system like that."[11]

White was so distraught, in fact, that he could never get up the nerve to visit Adams after the trial. "I was too embarrassed to face him," he said.[12]

Shortly after Adams's conviction, when the Texas legislature voted to change the state's form of execution to death by lethal injection, Mulder said it wouldn't alter Adams's sentence because he was already "dead meat on the table."[13]

But Mulder was wrong. In 1980, Adams's fortunes took their first favorable turn when the U.S. Supreme Court ruled that the jury in his case had been improperly selected. The court said Metcalfe had erred when he had allowed Mulder to exclude potential jurors who couldn't say for certain that the possibility of a death sentence would not influence their view of guilt or innocence. White, who had called the panel a "hanging jury," didn't know how accurate he was until he later learned that several of its members were related to police officers.

The attorney assigned to the appeal as part of an automatic process in capital cases was Melvyn Carson Bruder, who had won a landmark case in the Supreme Court in 1972. When the Texas Court of Criminal Appeals unanimously upheld Adams's conviction, Bruder appealed to the Supreme Court. Three days before Adams's scheduled execution, Justice Lewis Powell issued a stay. When arguments were later heard by the full court, eight of the justices listened attentively. But the ninth appeared distracted. That justice was William Rehnquist, the sole dissenter in the eight-to-one ruling that saved Adams's life. It is that same William Rehnquist who, as chief justice, is now pushing to limit death-penalty appeals.

Adams's case was remanded for retrial, and Mulder's boss, DA Henry Wade, predicted Adams would "probably get the death sentence" once again in the trial Wade vowed to quickly pursue. But Wade, apparently fearful that Adams might be acquitted in a second trial, later changed his mind. Instead, he and Dallas Police Chief Glenn

King successfully petitioned Governor William Clements Jr. to com-
mute Adams's sentence to life in prison.

Adams immediately filed a petition demanding a retrial. He said
the only reason Wade had sought the commutation was that he knew
information about the witnesses for the prosecution uncovered by
Adams's attorneys—including the fact that Turko had changed her
version of events after being hypnotized, when subjects are highly vulnerable to suggestion—would have made it impossible to get a conviction. But the Texas Court of Criminal Appeals turned Adams down
by a six-to-three vote.

Bruder at this point decided he had done all he could for Adams
and withdrew from the case. It was just a job, and the job was done.

Things were looking bleak for Adams at the very time they were
looking very lucrative for Mulder, who had tired of waiting for Wade
to retire. Bobby Lee Manzell Jr., the son of a wealthy Texas oil baron,
was facing charges in a case in which four men had killed a homeowner
during a burglary.

When one of the four agreed to testify for the prosecution, legend
has it that the senior Manzell enticed Mulder into leaving the DA's
office and defending his son in return for a $100,000 retainer and
a piece of valuable land in downtown Dallas. Mulder took the bait.
And almost before anyone realized it, he had arranged to have the
strong case against young Manzell dismissed. That launched Mulder
on his way to one of the most remunerative criminal-law practices
in Texas.[14]

But things weren't going quite as well for David Harris. All the
charges facing him at the time of Adams's trial had been dropped
in return for his testimony, even though he had said at the trial that
no deals had been made.

It wasn't long, however, before he was in trouble once again. After
a series of minor scrapes with the law both before and after joining
the Army, Harris ended up serving eight months in the brig at Fort
Leavenworth for a violent assault on his commanding officer in West
Germany, as well as a series of burglaries and an armed robbery in
1978. After his release on June 29, 1979, Harris stole a Camaro and

headed for California. There, he joined forces with another small-time crook and went on a binge of robberies and burglaries.

In San Bernardino County, they picked up a hitchhiker named James Filaan. Filaan had been arrested in the past for forgery and passing bad checks. But he had no history of violence—until he got into the Camaro. Over the next twenty-four hours, Harris and his accomplice forced Filaan to participate in a series of thefts and robberies the likes of which he had probably never dreamed. When they were finally caught in the act of robbing an electronics store, Harris aimed his gun at one of the cops who had them surrounded and pulled the trigger. But this cop was luckier than Officer Wood. The gun misfired, and the trio was taken into custody.

When Harris was put on trial for armed robbery and kidnapping, he resorted to a tactic Randall Dale Adams knew all too well: He blamed the crimes on the hitchhiker, Filaan. But the strategy didn't work this time around. Harris was found guilty and sentenced to six years in prison. He was paroled from San Quentin in early December 1984 and allowed to return to Vidor through special arrangements— no doubt motivated by California's delight at getting rid of him.[15]

The following September 1, however, Harris got into bigger trouble than ever when he broke into the apartment of Beaumont car salesman Mark Mays and kidnapped Mays's girlfriend. As the then-24-year-old hardened criminal dragged the woman toward a pickup, Mays grabbed a gun and followed in hot pursuit. After the two exchanged shots, Mays lay on the ground wounded.

Harris then walked over to Mays and calmly pumped three more bullets into him at close range. Mays died instantly. After his arrest a few days later, Harris tried to blame Mays for the fatal gun battle. None of it would have happened, he told police, if Mays had stayed in the apartment as he had been told. "That man was crazy," he said. "He tried to kill me."

On April 19, 1986, a Beaumont jury found Harris guilty of capital murder and sentenced him to death.

In the interim, a bespectacled filmmaker and sometimes–private investigator named Errol Morris had come across Randall Dale Adams

while interviewing prisoners sentenced to death based on the testimony of Dr. James Grigson, about whom Morris had hoped to make
a documentary.

Of the twenty-seven prisoners Morris interviewed, Adams stood
out because of the intensity with which he claimed he had been framed.
"He insisted on his innocence, but I knew little about the case and
was in no position to judge," Morris said later. "At first I didn't
really believe him."

But the more the thin, articulate Adams talked about how he
had been set up by a teenager driving a stolen car, the more Morris
listened. "I was twenty-eight years old," Adams told Morris. "I'd never
been in trouble. I was nonviolent before, I was nonviolent after. But
for five seconds, Dallas County said I went crazy and . . . shot one
of their police officers because my Ohio driver's license had expired.
That's garbage."[16]

Morris was intrigued, and decided to look into the case. Before
long, he had changed the focus of his film from "Dr. Death" to Randall
Dale Adams. The result was a film that borrowed Mulder's graphic
description of police as the "thin blue line" and used it to expose
his deliberate miscarriage of justice. Accentuated by a haunting score
by minimalist composer Philip Glass, The Thin Blue Line presented
Morris's findings through riveting reenactments and revealing interviews—including a spellbinding one with Harris at the end in which
he admitted Adams was innocent.

The film's impact was so stunning that one critic called it "perhaps
the most stylish documentary ever made."[17]

Morris himself described it as "a story of greed, delusion, self-
deception and a misguided certainty that led to a death sentence for
an innocent man, freedom for a killer (who would kill again), and
fame and fortune for an ex-prosecutor who was willing to gamble
a man's life to advance his career."

But Morris came to that conclusion only after countless hours
of investigation and dozens of interviews. His probe began with the
district attorney's files in Dallas, where he found several inconsistencies
with the case presented in court. The first of these inconsistencies

was typical of what was to follow. Adams and Harris had agreed that they had gone to a drive-in that fateful night, but disagreed on when they left. Adams said they departed at 9:30 and that Harris dropped him off at the motel just before ten—two-and-a-half hours before Wood was killed. Harris said they left the movie around midnight, just before the murder. In the files, Morris found an investigator's report that said the theater had closed well before midnight and the movie both men said they left in the middle of started at 8:40—all of which seemed to support Adams's version of events.

When Morris interviewed the theater's owners, they not only verified that the drive-in had closed long before midnight, but also discounted Harris's claim that he had bought popcorn just before leaving. That would be impossible, they said, because the stand always closed at 10:30.

Morris found something else of great interest in the files: telephone receipts from the Alamo Plaza Motel indicating that the DA's office had paid for phone calls placed by the Millers at the very time Mulder was saying in court that the couple couldn't be found for further cross-examination.

Also of interest were the lineup sheets. The one for Harris, showing he had been able to pick out Adams, was there. The one for the Millers was not.[18]

Morris decided he had to interview the mystery witnesses. It took him several months to track them down, but it was worth it. All three agreed to talk on camera, perhaps thrilled by the attention.

Emily Miller, after a rambling prologue about how she often fantasized about being a detective, finally admitted she had at first picked out "the wrong man" at the lineup and selected Adams only after prodding by the police. Her now-former husband admitted he "really didn't see anything that night" and that, contrary to his testimony, he also had failed to pick out Adams in the lineup. Michael Randell admitted he was drunk "out of my mind" as he passed the cars and was preoccupied with a woman other than his wife who was in the car with him.

Greatly relying on the new evidence developed by Morris, attorney

Randy Schaffer of Houston took on Adams's case for expenses only. He presented his justification for a new trial on December 6, 1986. The hearing was conducted by U.S. Magistrate John Tolle even though Tolle had defended the district attorney's office in Adams's civil-rights suit. It wasn't until Tolle denied Adams's motion after a frustrating seventeen-month delay that Morris learned of Tolle's conflict of interest. When Schaffer challenged the decision on those grounds, Tolle sheepishly withdrew his ruling, claiming his prior involvement in the case had slipped his mind.

By then, however, the action had switched to the court of public opinion, thanks to the premiere of *The Thin Blue Line* at the Dallas Film Festival two weeks earlier.

Morris had wrapped up his interviews in grand fashion the day after Tolle's hearing, when he finally got Harris on camera after several delays. Ironically, when Morris finally was able to interview Harris, the camera broke during the most crucial part of the session. Fortunately, Morris had a tape recorder that captured the following conversation, which he placed at the end of the film:

> Morris: Is Randall Adams an innocent man?
> Harris: I'm sure he is.
> Morris: How can you be sure?
> Harris: Because I'm the one that knows.
> Morris: Were you surprised the police blamed him?
> Harris: They didn't blame him. I did. A scared 16-year-old kid who sure would like to get out of it if he can. . . . They didn't have nothing else, you know, until I gave them something, so I guess when they got something, they run with it.

When Morris asked Harris if he was alone in the car when Wood was shot, he says Harris "smiled—a broad, open, frightening smile— and nodded his head." That was as far as Harris would go at that time. But at the end of Morris's skillful portrayal of the tragedy's events and its equally tragic aftermath, that was plenty far enough.

When *The Thin Blue Line* opened to rave reviews across the nation in August 1988, the cocky Harris showed an amazingly compassionate side of his personality when he wrote the following in a letter—a copy of which I later obtained from a news source—to explain to his mother why he had all but confessed to Morris during the interview:

> It seems like my whole life is surrounded by "wrongs" of some kind, and it seems like I've never done the right thing when I could and should have. Absolving Randall Dale Adams of any guilt is a difficult thing for me to do, but I must try to do so, because he is innocent. That is the truth.
>
> This may be hard for you to believe; and you are asking how I could have done this. It's a question I've asked myself for many years. The only thing I can say is that I didn't really and fully understand the injustice I had done to Adams. I couldn't except [sic] and face the truth of what I had done, nor could I face the possibility of losing the love of you and Dad because that was the only love I had ever known. I knew I couldn't be a failure at the age of sixteen. I, like any other kid, wanted you all to be proud of me, which is something I felt had eluded me for some reason. I needed to be accepted and gain approval by somebody. It's hard to explain because I can't even understand some of the things I've done, etc. . . .
>
> I'm truly sorry for the hurt and problems I've caused you all. I can't do anything about the publicity or I would, because the last thing I want is for you all to suffer for what I've done. Maybe you can understand, maybe not, but I can't carry this burden any longer; if the truth hurts me, the falsehoods hurt even more.

Pressure mounted for the case to be reopened, and Schaffer took advantage of it to demand action in the state courts that previously had been so reluctant. This time they weren't. In early December 1988, a courageous State District Judge Larry Baraka recommended to the Texas Court of Criminal Appeals that Adams be granted a new trial.

"I'm numb," Adams said after the ruling. "I don't know what to say. Right now I'm in shock."

A delighted Morris said, "I'm very happy about the judge's decision. I deeply believe in Randall Adams's innocence. Obviously, the man should not be in jail."

The feisty Schaffer, always the picture of self-confidence, predicted that no retrial would ever take place if the appeals court ordered one. "The state will not prosecute Adams again because they lack evidence and credible witnesses," he said.[19]

After a lot of bluster and unpardonable delaying tactics from the DA's office, Schaffer was finally proved right. One such delay occurred after the appeals court upheld Judge Baraka's order for Adams's release pending retrial. Instead of complying, the DA's office got the court's supervising judge to suspend Baraka's order.

In a hastily scheduled hearing, assistant DA Winfield Scott argued that if Adams was released, "you will be putting a man on the streets who is a cold-blooded killer who would easily kill again." He also shocked observers by directly attacking Baraka, saying he was "afraid" to be in Baraka's courtroom and that the case should be transferred to an unbiased judge.[20]

Scott also said the appeals court judge who had written the retrial order was, of all horrible things, "a liberal." Then he condemned Morris as "an underground cult movie maker." Finally, and incredibly, he attacked the other assistant DA working on the case for her support of an unsuccessful motion for Adams's release filed with the state parole board after Baraka's December decision.[21]

Scott's broadside was too much, even for vengeful Dallas. The *Dallas Times Herald* said his antics could only "be viewed as vindictive and of dubious legality." The newspaper also condemned the overall conduct of the office of District Attorney John Vance, who had replaced Wade in 1987, as "shameful" even by Dallas's distorted standards.

"We do not understand why District Attorney Vance permits this disgraceful activity," the paper's editorial concluded. "There should be no place in his office or in the criminal-justice system for individuals who used the power of the state to wage personal crusades."

For once Vance actually listened to someone else's opinion. Scott was fired a few days later.

After Scott's tirade, as Adams was led away to await the supervising judge's decision, he said, "I hope the people of Dallas will take a very close look at what is happening right now. This is your court system, people."

The people had indeed taken a close look, and many didn't like what they had seen. Neither did the supervising judge. The following day, he released Adams on $50,000 personal recognizance bond, under which he didn't have to put up any cash. Adams was soon a free man for the first time in twelve-and-a-half years.

Surrounded by well-wishers and reporters from across the nation, Adams said the fresh air smelled pretty good, but he was holding his breath until he was out of Dallas. "I feel fantastic, but I'm not out of Dallas yet," he said. "They may try to stop me from doing that."[22]

Vance verified those fears when he announced that prosecutors were still examining the evidence to determine whether Adams should be retried.

In the interim, Adams had the right to leave Dallas, and he wasted little time doing so. His first stop on the way to his home state was Houston, where he conferred with Schaffer and then held a press conference. "I'll be glad to get back to Ohio," he said with a smile. "No offense, but I hate Texas." Adams added, however, that he didn't blame all Texans for "the actions of a few."

Adams also repeated his wish to return to Dallas and clear his name in a new trial. "I believe that if the retrial happens, we may be able to receive some answers as to why all of this happened, and I would like that," he said.[23]

But such was not to be the case. Shortly after Adams's plane landed in Columbus the next afternoon, where he and a beaming Morris were greeted by Adams's mother and sisters, the mayor, and a large crowd of supporters, word came from Dallas that the charges that had cast a cloud over his head for thirteen years were being dropped because of lack of evidence.

"Thank God if it's true," said a somewhat distrusting Adams. His mother, who had lost her home and life savings paying for her son's long defense, was more believing. "You're supposed to have a resurrection around Easter," Mildred Adams said. "I guess this is it."[24]

About all Adams was to get for the twelve-and-a-half years Texas took away from him, unfortunately, was the college diploma he earned behind bars. Adams learned, as Lenell Geter did before him, that it is virtually impossible to win any damages in Texas, because the laws there are tightly designed to protect the state and its officials.

In Geter's case, his $28 million federal lawsuit claiming violation of his civil rights went nowhere until the City of Greenville settled one of his few remaining claims, for $50,000, in November 1990. Randy Ty Senegar, who was jailed for fourteen months after a 1986 rape victim wrongly identified him as the masked man who attacked her, didn't even try to sue for damages, because his attorney told him it would be a waste of time and money and the state might then sue *him* for filing a "frivolous" lawsuit.

The most Adams decided he could hope for was a maximum of $50,000 in compensation from the state legislature. A bill authorizing such a payment failed, however, as such bills virtually always do. Being the state of Texas, after all, means never having to say you're sorry.

But some of Adams's jurors did express their regrets. "Based on everything I have seen and read, . . . I just don't believe the man is guilty," said jury forewoman Bette Fain. "If he had gone to the death chamber and all of this had come out later, that would have been a horrible thing to have on my conscience."

Elliott Rammey was equally upset. "It makes you wonder sometimes about the judicial system," he said. "If somebody as powerful as the DA's office can manipulate witnesses, it seems to me there's something wrong."[25]

The Floodgate Opens

The people of Dallas were soon to find out just how wrong the system could be, when four other individuals there were freed within the next year after serving up to ten years for crimes they also were found not to have committed.

The first was Joyce Ann Brown, who was released in November 1989, shortly after her case was featured on "60 Minutes." Brown had been convicted of aggravated robbery on October 8, 1980, and served more than nine years of a life sentence in prison before the Texas Court of Criminal Appeals ordered that she be retried or the charges be dropped after new evidence came to light.

That new evidence showed that Joyce Ann Brown's only crime was having the same name as a woman who leased the car used in the robbery of a fur store. During the stickup, one of the two women robbers, Rene Michelle Taylor, gunned down owner Rubin Danzinger as his wife, Ala, watched. Taylor avoided a possible death sentence by pleading guilty to murder in exchange for a life term. Despite Taylor's insistence that Brown was not her accomplice, and her employer's assurance that Brown was at work at the time of the robbery, Brown was arrested after a distraught Ala Danzinger identified her from a mug shot as the second robber.

To obtain her conviction, prosecutors relied on the often-used but long-discredited testimony of a cellmate. In return for a reduced sentence she denied she had been promised, Martha Jean Bruce told the jury Brown had confessed to the crime during a conversation in their cell. Brown's conviction was thrown out and a new trial ordered because Bruce's previous conviction for lying to the police had not been made known to the defense. But instead of retrying Brown, prosecutors announced they were dropping the charges against her on February 14, 1990, because, they said, they had confirmed reports on the existence of a second Joyce Ann Brown who, it turned out, had a history of committing armed robberies with Taylor.[26]

That same day, Governor William Clements Jr. pardoned former paramedic Michael Anthony Woten, who had served almost eight years of a fifty-five-year sentence for a robbery in which he had not been involved. Woten had been identified by three eyewitnesses as being one of two "cowboy bandits" who, wielding a pistol and a submachine gun, robbed a Dallas grocery store in 1982. But, in a casual conversation in prison in November 1989, inmate Russell Everett Chamberlain told Woten that he had robbed the store with Charles Hardin, who was killed in a shootout with police in Irving, Texas, later that year. An excited Woten then sent a letter and a statement signed by Chamberlain to the *Dallas Times Herald*.

Woten pleaded with the paper to find the truck driver with the citizens-band radio handle of "Kangaroo," with whom he had always claimed he had hitchhiked a ride to St. Louis on the day of the crime.

Although a private investigator hired by Woten's court-appointed attorney had said he could find no such man, it turned out he didn't try very hard—if he had tried at all. With a little effort, *Times Herald* reporters found Don "Kangaroo" Fainter, and he confirmed Woten's story. After Fainter picked Woten out of a photo lineup and officials found records to confirm that Fainter had driven to St. Louis that day, they decided to seek the pardon for Woten.[27]

University of Washington psychologist Elizabeth Loftus, a leading authority on eyewitness testimony, told the *Times Herald* that putting Woten in a lineup to be identified by two people who had seen him at the store two days earlier was a "stupid" thing for police to do, since it was almost assured they would pick out Woten. A third witness now admits he discussed Woten's physical characteristics with the other two witnesses. But all three witnesses denied during the trial that they had been influenced in any way by discussion with the others or previous sightings.

If an expert like Loftus had been able to testify—which Texas law does not permit—she could have told the jurors of the growing evidence that eyewitnesses are wrong as often as they are right. She could have told them of "feedback factor," through which witnesses who discuss a case reinforce one another's incorrect impressions. She also could have told them of the "assimilation factor," through which witnesses add inaccurate information gained after the crime, as well as "unconscious transference," through which witnesses confuse a person seen in one situation with someone seen in a second situation.

The releases of Brown and Woten came just one week after charges were dropped against Martin Kimsey, who had served five years of a life sentence for a robbery he didn't commit. Kimsey's road to freedom started in 1987, when he read a newspaper account of robberies similar to the one he allegedly had committed. Kimsey knew it was a long shot, but he wrote a letter to one of the men convicted of the crimes and asked if he had been involved in the one Kimsey was doing time for.

Kimsey was disappointed but not surprised when he got no response. Several months later, however, the wife of one of the men convicted of the other robberies informed prosecutors that her husband wanted to confess to Kimsey's "robbery."

When James Clayton Garret was interviewed by investigators, he gave details to the crime that only the robber could know. He and Kimsey also passed polygraph exams before the pardon for which Kimsey was recommended. "I used to think everybody in prison was guilty and just saying they were innocent until it happened to me," Kimsey said after his release.[28]

The last to be released during the year after Adams was freed was Stephen Lynn Russell, who was pardoned after serving ten years for a robbery to which another man finally confessed.[29]

As bad as Dallas may seem, its criminal-justice system probably isn't much worse than many others. It just has seemed that way because of the unusual publicity the Geter and Adams cases received—thanks largely to the lengths to which officials went before finally admitting their mistakes.

The Reverend James McCloskey is a minister who has made it his mission to free wrongfully convicted prisoners, in Dallas and elsewhere. He put it this way after Adams's release: "Dallas has been notorious for wrongful convictions in recent years, but I don't think it's different than other communities. Randall Dale Adams met Errol Morris by a stroke of luck. If he hadn't, you would never have heard of him. He would have been one of those anonymous souls convicted and buried for life. The criminal-justice system in the United States is the best in the world. But it's a far leakier cistern, where many people slip through a wide crack, than the public would care to believe."[30]

Just how many slip through that crack is open to conjecture. McCloskey estimates that 10 percent of the people convicted of serious crimes each year are innocent. George Hairston, a lawyer for the National Association for the Advancement of Colored People, puts the number at 5 percent. And a study by Ohio State University criminologist C. Ronald Huff and two associates produced a "conservative" estimate of one-half of one percent. That may not sound like many until you consider that, with an annual conviction rate of roughly a million and a half, you're talking about more than seventy-five hundred innocent people being convicted *every year*.

How and why does it happen?

We've seen most, but not all, of the answers to that question in the Dallas cases: bigotry, prosecutorial and police misconduct, eyewitness error, false testimony, poor legal representation, improper interrogations, investigative errors, public pressure, frame-ups, and inexpert "expert testimony." And, perhaps most important, an adversary system that stresses the pursuit of victory over the pursuit of truth.

Can such tragedies be greatly curtailed, if not eliminated?

What are the chances of an innocent person being executed?

The answers to these and a lot of other questions start just across the thin blue line.

Notes

1. " 'Some Doubt Has Been Raised,' " *Time*, December 26, 1983, p. 14.
2. "The Wrong Man in Jail?" *Newsweek*, December 19, 1983, p. 51.
3. *Time*, p. 14.
4. Ibid.
5. Associated Press, March 17, 1984.
6. Ibid., March 22, 1984.
7. "Wedding on Again After Mistaken Life Sentence," *New York Times*, March 23, 1984, p. 7.
8. "Guilty Until Proven Innocent," *Dallas Times Herald*, October 23, 1988, p. A-16.
9. Synopsis, *The Thin Blue Line*, Miramax Films, p. 8.
10. Ibid., p. 10.
11. *Dallas Times Herald*, p. A-18.
12. Synopsis, *The Thin Blue Line*, p. 14.
13. Ibid., p. 12.
14. Ibid., p. 19.
15. *Dallas Times Herald*, p. A-16.
16. Synopsis, *The Thin Blue Line*, p. 21.
17. "Director Turns Investigator for 'Thin Blue Line,' " *Dallas Times Herald*, April 30, 1988, p. F-1.

18. Synopsis, *The Thin Blue Line*, p. 23.

19. Associated Press, December 2, 1988.

20. "Dallas Prosecutors Resist Freeing Murder Figure Who Won Appeal," *New York Times*, March 21, 1989, p. 1.

21. "Prosecutor's Fight A Shock? Not to Adams," *Dallas Times Herald*, March 21, 1989, p. B-1.

22. Associated Press, March 21, 1989.

23. Ibid.

24. Author's notes.

25. Associated Press, March 24, 1989.

26. Associated Press, February 15, 1990.

27. "Full Pardon Frees Man After 8 Years," *Dallas Times Herald*, February 15, 1990, p. A-1.

28. Associated Press, February 6, 1990.

29. Associated Press, July 1, 1990.

30. "Prosecutors Are Faulted In Dallas Murder Case," *New York Times*, March 23, 1989, p. 9.

2

The Keystone: Cops

There is nothing more deceptive than an obvious fact. . . . It is a capital mistake to theorize before you have all the evidence. Insensibly, one begins to twist facts to fit theories, instead of theories to fit facts.
— *Sherlock Holmes*

Former U.S. Attorney General Edwin Meese III may have been on shaky constitutional ground when he said that criminal suspects wouldn't be under investigation if they weren't guilty of something. But he probably also reflected the attitude of Americans in general and those in law enforcement in particular when he made the statement.

As one conservative reporter told me after Randall Dale Adams's release, "He may not have been guilty of murder, but he must have been guilty of something or the police wouldn't have arrested him."

That, unfortunately, is the kind of blind loyalty most Americans give their police. To them, the police are the keystone of an otherwise unstable society and the chief protectors of truth, justice, and the American way of life. Most of the people police deal with, on the other hand, are symbols of everything that ails America: drugs, crime, violence, and disrespect for property and even for human life.

So if the police arrest one of these characters, it must be with just cause. That, in fact, is generally the case. But not always. Cops are human. They make mistakes. They are also under immense pressure.

"Arrest totals still are a big fact in evaluating cops," Robert diGrazia, former police chief in Boston told *U.S. News & World Report* in 1984. "Officers are out to make arrests, and nobody usually checks up on whether they are good ones or bad ones."

Colorado lawyer Lance Springs told the same publication, "When you have an us-versus-them mentality, people become suspects all too quickly. Once law enforcement gets locked in on someone, alternative arguments get lost."[1]

An all-too-perfect example of this occurred in a highly publicized Boston case in which a woman and her unborn child apparently were killed by the woman's husband, who blamed the crime on a supposed black assailant. While many were quick to blame the acceptance by police and reporters of Charles Stuart's story on racial bias, Professors J. Edward Russo and J. H. Schoemaker, authors of the book *Decision Traps*, say it actually had more to do with "cognitive bias."

They define such biases as pervasive shortcomings in our judgment that are deeply rooted in our minds. "Although we might expect experienced professionals such as detectives and reporters to overcome most cognitive biases, our studies with other professionals suggest the opposite," they wrote after Stuart's plot was exposed by his brother and Stuart had committed suicide.[2]

The two professors say that perhaps the biggest failure was that police fell victim to "confirmation bias"—the tendency to seek evidence in support of, rather than against, one's initial explanation. "The appeal of the confirming evidence is that it signals that we are on the right track, that our initial guess was right," they write. "This ego support is especially comforting when an entire city is pressing for progress on a horrifying crime."

Sure enough, Boston police soon found evidence to back up their original mistake in the person of William Bennett, a 39-year-old unemployed black with a long criminal record. When Charles Stuart identified Bennett as the assailant, the confirming evidence had been found.

Bennett's involvement made sense to the news media and the public at large because of the "availability bias," which the two psychologists define as "the tendency to believe that what comes to mind most easily or quickly is truly the most common—or what is perceived to be the most common. In urban crime, that is erroneously perceived as black-on-white crime because that is what the news media focus on, when intraracial crime is actually far more common."

The final bias Boston police and reporters fell into, the authors say, is the "concreteness bias"—the tendency to pay undue attention to concrete, vivid information instead of tedious statistics. In the Stuart case, this allowed police to focus on the "concrete facts" of Stuart's frantic calls for help from his car phone that were recorded, no less, by a national television program; a black-on-white crime; and the destruction of a supposedly perfect upper-middle-class white family.

In the process, police ignored the drab statistics showing that roughly a third of the women who are murdered are killed by their boyfriends or husbands. They also failed to note that Charles Stuart had been driving in the opposite direction from their house after leaving a prenatal class at the downtown hospital, and that Stuart's wounds were superficial compared with those that killed his wife. Generally, a robber is more interested in disabling the male, who is more threatening than the female.

But all that mattered to panicky police was that Stuart had said the couple had been attacked by a black man. So they set about finding one who matched the description Stuart gave and—apparently with some coaching, since it turned out there had been no black assailant—Stuart picked out of a lineup the man police had wanted him to pick.

So, thanks to a series of cognitive biases or "decision traps," police almost let Charles Stuart get away with killing his pregnant wife and pinning the murder on an innocent man. Only his brother's guilty conscience stopped the wheels of justice in time.

The lesson to be learned from this case, Russo and Schoemaker suggest, is that "all professionals, not only police and reporters, [must] guard against the hidden cognitive biases that made matters worse in the Stuart case."

To do so, they recommend that investigators:

• Prevent the "confirmation bias" by entertaining multiple explanations and seeking at least some evidence for and against each.

• Avoid the "availability bias" by challenging their preconceptions.

• Dodge the "concreteness bias" by bringing to bear the statistical patterns of similar situations.

"The lessons from the Boston case are not only about the sociopathic mind of Charles Stuart but about the minds of all of us," the psychologists write. "They remind us that even experienced professionals who usually know better succumb to cognitive biases—flaws in judgment that may never be revealed. Would we *even now* know who the murderer was without his brother's guilty conscience?"

The sad thing is that America's police have ample evidence of such logical shortcomings in the number of false arrests and convictions that occur in this crime-ridden nation. They just don't have time to worry about it. They have a job to do. And that is putting people in jail. The fact that some of those people may be innocent is the breaks of the game.

This can reach such absurdities that, in one Philadelphia case, police managed over the years to obtain confessions to the murder of a fellow officer from three different innocent men, two of whom were convicted and sentenced to life in prison before being exonerated.

After Patrolman James T. Morrow was murdered in 1936 while trying to track down a youth he suspected might be the bandit who had been terrorizing the northeast section of Philadelphia, police quickly extracted a confession from a man named Joseph Broderick. When Broderick recanted a few days later, however, it soon became clear to police officials that the confession had been coerced, and Broderick was released.

In May 1937, police tracked down George Bilger—Morrow's top suspect at the time of his murder—at a school for the mentally impaired. A short time later, police had their second confession, which implicated a Philadelphia patrolman as Bilger's accomplice. During Bilger's trial, he was identified by two victims as the bandit Morrow was trying to track down when he was murdered. After Bilger repeated his confession on the stand, the jury promptly found him guilty of first-degree murder and recommended the death penalty. The patrolman Bilger had implicated, however, was acquitted a few days later after the case against him rapidly fell apart.

That caused the judge who presided over Bilger's trial to reconsider the youth's conviction as well, and he eventually set aside the jury's verdict and ordered a new trial. He also asked police to continue their investigation. But Bilger pleaded guilty at a second trial, and the judge, who still had doubts about Bilger's guilt, sentenced him to life in prison rather than to death.

In 1938, however, the robberies resumed, and one victim, school-teacher Edward Tamkin, was murdered. In January 1939, police received a tip that the robber was a man named Jack Batton, whose real name turned out to be Jack Howard, a known criminal. When Howard sensed he was being tailed a few days later, he pulled a gun on the officers following him and was mortally wounded during the gun battle that followed. Police later said they had found several weapons on Howard, including the weapon used to kill Patrolman Morrow.

When Howard was rushed to a nearby hospital, an attendant identified him as a regular visitor of patient Elizabeth Morgan. Although there was no reason to believe Howard had an accomplice, police staked out Morgan's room. When Rudolph Sheeler of New York arrived to visit Morgan, who was his sister, he was arrested and taken to police headquarters, where he was beaten for hours at a time over a two-week period, after which he finally confessed to aiding his onetime friend Howard in the murder of Patrolman Morrow. At his trial a month later, Sheeler, a thoroughly broken man, pleaded guilty and was sentenced to life in prison. Bilger, after two years in prison, was pardoned and transferred to a mental hospital.

Twelve long years later, proof surfaced that showed Sheeler was at work in New York at the time of Patrolman Morrow's murder. When a judge reviewed the case, he found that his confession and court statements contradicted each other as well as key details of the case. After further investigation, he concluded that Sheeler had been forced to confess because police were eager to free Bilger in order to clear the reputation of the officer he had implicated, even though the officer had been acquitted.

Calling the case "a black and shameful page in the history of the Philadelphia police department [which is really saying something, given the department's long and continuing history of abuse], the state supreme court overruled Sheeler's conviction in March 1951 and ordered his immediate release. All told, four detectives and two superior officers were suspended for their roles in the frame-up.[3]

Police in Columbus, Ohio, went to similar lengths to solve the ambush death of a police officer in 1972. Apparently desperate to make someone pay for the crime, police charged Allan E. Thrower even though Thrower had no motive and produced three alibi witnesses who placed him in Detroit at the time of the killing. The only eyewitness to the crime was the slain officer's partner, who identified Thrower as the man who approached the officers' slow-moving squad car and shot the victim. Thrower was convicted and sentenced to life in prison. The case seemed closed for good after the conviction was upheld on appeal.

In 1978, however, an internal affairs investigation was launched after one of the first officers at the scene of the shooting said the surviving officer had told him he had not seen the assailant. Evidence was eventually uncovered that a homicide detective, apparently to enhance his reputation for solving tough cases as well as to make someone pay for the murder, had persuaded the witness to pick Thrower's photo out of a lineup. The officer admitted to investigators that he had perjured himself when he identified Thrower as the killer during the trial, and was suspended from the force until the police chief quickly suspended the suspension.

Tapes also revealed that police had made leading statements that maneuvered two other witnesses, both of whom had criminal records, into linking Thrower to the killing. The homicide detective who had developed the misleading evidence against Thrower also admitted he had committed perjury when he testified at the trial that he had overheard the alibi witnesses conspiring to lie about Thrower's whereabouts at the time of the murder. The detective, who had been suspended a month earlier while the internal affairs department investigated charges that he had manufactured evidence in another murder case, then resigned—*under medical disability!*

At the request of the prosecutor, Thrower—who told the judge he had been "unjustly done" after he was convicted—was released pending a new trial. But all charges against him were formally dropped in 1979. The prosecutor said there was insufficient evidence, however, to prosecute the officers who had framed him.[4]

Such is life in the big city. But such is life in the small city, too.

"Overzealousness by police is a real danger," says the attorney for one small-town man who turned out to be innocent of the crime for which he was initially convicted. Attorney Gerald Glinsek cites "pressure on officers in a small town to charge someone with a horrible murder. Weak people threatened by the police might say anything."[5]

That is exactly what a witness did against Glinsek's client, Ohio farm worker Ernest Holbrook, who was sentenced to life in prison in 1982 for the murder of a 12-year-old girl from a small town near Akron, Ohio. Even though the friend accused of helping Holbrook commit the crime was acquitted and the key witness against them, who claimed he was pressured into making false statements, recanted and was sent to prison for perjury, Holbrook remained in prison. He might still be there, except that after he was jailed another girl was killed and the carpet fibers found on her body matched those found on the body of the girl Holbrook had allegedly killed.

The fibers were eventually traced to the van of Robert A. Buell, who was convicted of murdering the second girl and sentenced to death. Citing the new evidence, the acquittal of Holbrook's alleged accomplice, and the recantation of the key witness, Holbrook's prosecutor asked in 1984 that the charges against Holbrook be dropped. "The state now in good conscience cannot maintain that the fiber evidence, which was of major importance in the conviction of Robert Buell, has no significance in this case," the prosecutor admitted.[6]

Thanks greatly to the increasing availability of computer information—and misinformation—no one is immune from the kind of official overzealousness that caused Holbrook's false conviction, either.

The government now starts computer dossiers on Americans at age five, and along the way adds a lot of confusing, misleading, and inaccurate information that sometimes proves all but impossible to get expunged.

The most controversial government databank is the FBI's National Crime Information Center, which contains approximately twenty million files on fugitives, stolen vehicles, and criminal histories. Police use NCIC routinely whenever they come into contact with an individual, even for a traffic violation or some other misdemeanor. The system usually works well. But if the information is erroneous, it can lead to false arrest—sometimes repeatedly. That was what happened to Terry Dean Rogan, who was arrested five times—twice at gunpoint—in Michigan and Texas for crimes he did not commit. A disgusted Rogan finally went to court, where a U.S. District judge ruled that the Los Angeles Police Department had violated his constitutional rights by continuing to list him in NCIC as wanted for murder and robbery even after the real suspect using his name was identified. In 1987, the city of Los Angeles agreed to pay Rogan $55,000 in damages.[7]

The police had removed Rogan's name prior to his suit, but only after a *Saginaw News* reporter persuaded police that the person they were looking for was Bernard McKandes, who apparently had assumed Rogan's identity after Rogan inadvertently discarded a copy of his birth certificate. McKandes, who was later located in an Alabama prison, where he was serving a sentence for other crimes, was subsequently convicted of the California offenses that had haunted Rogan.[8]

Roberto Hernandez faced much the same fate when he admittedly was driving drunk on February 24, 1986, and was pulled over by California police. But in addition to being charged with driving under the influence, Hernandez was also arrested for charges of an attempted burglary for which police said he was wanted in Chicago. The only problem was, Hernandez had never been to Chicago in his life. "That's what they all say," a cynical cop replied.

It turned out that the Roberto Hernandez wanted by Chicago police matched the California Hernandez right down to the same birth date, and the latter was jailed for eleven days pending extradition proceedings before his attorneys convinced police of the mistake. Two years later, however, Hernandez was arrested for the same Chicago charge.[9]

Airline stewardess Sheila Jackson discovered the pitfalls of misidentification when she was jailed for two-and-a-half days after U.S. Customs agents—checking against computerized files with only a few identifying characteristics—mistook her for a Shirley Jackson named in a fugitive warrant.

"I recently testified before a congressional committee that is trying to stop this kind of abuse, and to my surprise I learned there are hundreds of other cases similar to mine," Jackson said later. "It can happen to anyone whose ID has ever been lost or stolen." Another woman who spoke before the same committee, Jackson said, had been arrested *ten times* on charges falsely attributed to her by NCIC.[10]

Some of these computer-based mistakes would be comical if they weren't so traumatic for their victims. In New Orleans, for example, police arrested a woman who was seventy pounds lighter and six inches shorter than the woman described in the computer. In Los Angeles, police arrested a black man even though the fugitive listed in the computer was identified as being white.[11]

But some computer errors aren't the least bit funny. Take the case of Nick Donald Bagley. Bagley's misfortunes began in 1962, when he was convicted of a murder that the victim's insurance company had determined to be a suicide.

As detailed by *New York Times* columnist Tom Wicker, Bagley presented five witnesses at his trial who testified that he was in North Carolina the entire week the Maryland "murder" occurred. But Bagley, an 18-year-old black, was convicted by an all-white jury anyway, apparently because he had originally confessed to the crime after a full week of intense interrogation.

So Bagley spent eleven years of a life sentence in prison for a crime that may not have even occurred. In 1973, however, he walked away from a work-release program and headed for New York, where he moved in with relatives, got a good job, and began helping his family. When Maryland sought his return, a deal was struck that transferred Bagley's supervision to New York officials, and Maryland agreed to erase the escape charge against him. Bagley lived a clean and productive life for the next eleven years.

In 1986, however, Bagley was arrested while visiting California on an outstanding warrant for failure to appear in court. Bagley contended, correctly, that the warrant was for a look-alike brother. But when his fingerprints were run through the computer, up popped the escape warrant that was supposed to have been expunged.

On the advice of his public defender, Bagley agreed to be extradited to Maryland, where he expected the matter to be quickly cleared up. No such luck. With Bagley back in their hands, Maryland officials reneged on their deal with New York and threw Bagley back in the slammer for his dubious murder conviction of 1962.

"Sometimes," columnist Wicker opined, " 'justice' for Bagley seems blind indeed."

And it may get blinder yet as moves are being made to vastly expand the inaccurate NCIC database so that police would be able to track individuals merely *suspected* of crimes and tap into individual Social Security and income-tax records. When you consider NCIC's error rate, that is a frightening proposition indeed.

According to Kenneth Laudon, a New York University computer scientist who studied criminal-record files for the highly respected congressional Office of Technology Assessment, one of every five warrants listed were found to be wrong or outdated. He estimated in 1984 that 14,000 Americans each year are subject to arrest based on such invalid information. Because of the limited physical descriptions of wanted individuals in the computer files, he added, many others face arrest for bearing only the slightest resemblance to them. "Lots of people match the same descriptions," Laudon told *U.S. News & World Report*.

The FBI itself admits that about 5 percent of the most sensitive information now in NCIC is either incorrect or incomplete. The biggest problem is that the FBI gets most of its information from local agencies, whose accuracy varies widely. An FBI audit of information from Alabama in 1985, for example, found that 13 percent of the information on wanted persons was invalid and that another questionable 17 percent was dropped just before the audit. One particular oddity discovered was that 75 percent of all the wanted persons recorded by the city of Mobile were listed as weighing 499 pounds and standing 7 feet 11 inches tall—which happened to be the maximum entries for the height and weight categories.

As it turned out, the Mobile Police Department "had a knucklehead adding information into the system," an FBI spokesman told the *Wall*

Street Journal. "He didn't think you had to have anything in the system except names," in which case the computer automatically inserted the maximum height and weight. One wonders how many other "knuckleheads" are out there.

But even if the record is accurate, or partially so, for each person questioned, that doesn't mean they committed the crime they are currently suspected of. Evidence suggests, however, that you'd have a hard time convincing a cop, prosecutor, judge, or jury of that. As Ohio State's C. Ronald Huff writes in his study:

> The old adage, "Where there's smoke there's fire," seems alive and well in the minds of the public and some criminal-justice personnel. Where the accused has a history of prior arrest (not necessarily even a conviction), many would more readily believe the current accusations. This becomes a factor in wrongful conviction insofar as the police and other criminal-justice personnel are likely to believe the worst about such suspects and perhaps ignore other leads. Also the accused's past criminal record may be made known when the defendant voluntarily takes the stand or may be brought out through the questioning of other defense witnesses. It is sometimes common knowledge in the community that the accused has "a record." Where any of these factors is present, it makes more difficult the task of confining the verdict to the present facts. If one is conceived of as evil, there is no loss, it is reasoned, and there may be social good, in punishment.[12]

One such victim of this attitude was Leonard Proite, a repeat offender who was found guilty of robbing a gasoline station despite testimony that placed him at a christening forty-five miles away at the time. Proite was later cleared after presenting evidence that he could not have looked through his victim's wallet with his right hand, as charged, because he was partially paralyzed.

"The jury's attitude seemed to be, 'Maybe he didn't commit this crime, but he's a bad guy and he has probably committed ten others and had not been caught,' " Proite's attorney said.[13]

Several of the recently revealed mistaken convictions in Dallas County were greatly affected by the fact that the victims had previous records, which, to make matters even worse, are often misinterpreted.

In the case of alleged supermarket robber Michael Woten, for example, it was the investigating detective's false belief that after a failed attempt to extort money from a Houston market, Woten was arrested when he returned to the store, just as he supposedly had been in this case. Woten was actually caught elsewhere, but the impression based on false information was lasting—and pervasive. Both Woten's court-appointed attorney and his chief accuser had had the same impression.

That's the unfortunate truth people with prior convictions have to face the rest of their lives.

Alfred Blumstein, a Carnegie-Mellon University professor who has been studying crime and punishment for three decades, told the *Dallas Times Herald*, "If you expect the slate will be wiped clean, that's not true. Punishment is part of the debt, but there is a history you have to live with as an ex-con."

As is so often the case, poverty—a common plight of ex-cons—also played an important role in Woten's conviction. Because Woten couldn't afford his own attorney, for example, he had to wait three weeks for a court-appointed one to become available. By then, he had been identified in a lineup and arraigned, in apparent violation of the U.S. Supreme Court's Miranda decision.[14]

But Woten's ordeal was relatively minor compared with what a prior record did to Charles Bernstein, who spent seventeen years in prison on two false convictions prompted by the fact that he had a record. When Bernstein was eighteen, he was convicted in New York of a drugstore burglary and sent to Elmira Reformatory. Bernstein learned his lesson well, and stayed out of trouble after his release. In 1919, he was on business in St. Paul, Minnesota, on the same day a gang of bandits held up a bank in nearby Hopkins. After Bernstein had returned to New York, police checking on hotel visitors for leads discovered that he had a record. So they got his mug shot from New York police and showed it to witnesses. When two identified his photo, Bernstein was arrested in New York and returned to Minnesota. During his trial, two hotel detectives and a clerk testified that Bernstein was in the hotel lobby in St. Paul at the time the bank was robbed, and two bank customers testified that he wasn't one of the bandits. But the two positive identifications by the witnesses who had picked out his photo proved to be enough to earn Bernstein an unjust conviction and a forty-year sentence.

He was released in 1928 and pardoned later when the prosecutor became convinced Bernstein was the victim of mistaken identification.

But Bernstein's troubles were far from over. Some four years after his release, he was once again at the wrong place at the wrong time—in this case Philadelphia, where W. C. Fields said there was never a right time to be. Police looking in the City of Brotherly Love for a man named Charlie in connection with the Washington murder of a major gambling figure soon came across Charles Bernstein. With both a criminal record and a first name going against him, Bernstein was taken to Washington, where he was misidentified by a man who claimed to have witnessed the murder.

Although Bernstein produced six alibi witnesses and only one of the eyewitnesses at the scene of the murder could identify him—and even he admitted he had seen the murderer at a distance—Bernstein was convicted and sentenced to death. Slowly, however, questions began to arise about the veracity of the man who identified Bernstein under less-than-ideal-conditions. Finally, just minutes before his scheduled execution, President Franklin D. Roosevelt commuted Bernstein's sentence to life. He was released in 1940 on a conditional pardon after serving eight years for a murder everyone seemed to agree he had nothing to do with. In 1945, President Harry S. Truman more or less admitted as much by giving Bernstein an unconditional pardon.[15]

With the help of precise scientific techniques, police investigations have grown a lot more sophisticated since then, of course. Or have they?

Notes

1. "When Nightmare of False Arrest Comes True," U.S. News & World Report, December 17, 1984, p. 45.

2. "Racial Bias Was Not the Only Bias in the Boston Murder Hoax,"

Cornell University News Service, 1990.

3. E. D. Radin, *The Innocents* (New York: William Morrow, 1964), pp. 27–33.

4. "Mistakes Aren't New to Ohio Police, Courts," *Columbus Dispatch*, August 26, 1990, p. D-1.

5. *U.S. News & World Report*, p. 45.

6. Associated Press, April 10, 1984.

7. "Wrong Suspect Settles His Case for $55,000," *New York Times*, March 6, 1988, p. 13.

8. "Computer Snafu Ruled a Rights Violation," *Los Angeles Times*, August 13, 1987, p. 41.

9. "Roberto Hernandez Battles His Arresting Similarities to a Wanted Man with Same Name," *People Weekly*, July 17, 1989, p. 95.

10. "A Computer Sent Me to Jail," *Good Housekeeping*, November 1985, p. 124.

11. "Abusive Computers: As Government Keeps More Tabs on People, False Accusations Rise," *Wall Street Journal*, August 20, 1987, p. 1.

12. C. Ronald Huff, et al., *Guilty Until Proved Innocent: Wrongful Conviction and Public Policy*, Ohio State University, 1984.

13. *U.S. News & World Report*, p. 46.

14. "Poverty, Past Sins Made Woten Prisoner of System," *Dallas Times Herald*, February 25, 1990, p. A-1.

15. *The Innocents*, pp. 105–110.

3

Police Pseudoscience

Detection is, or ought to be, an exact science and should be treated in the same cold and unemotional manner.
—Sherlock Holmes

Sir Arthur Conan Doyle's famed fictional detective would be dismayed to see how, in some respects, little real progress has been made in police science since he gave that advice a century ago. To be sure, the technology of crime detection has advanced tremendously since then. But police frequently fail to use that technology or evaluate its effectiveness in the "cold and unemotional manner" Holmes recommended, and, as a result, serious errors often are cloaked in scientific certainty.

Floyd "Buzz" Fay would swear to that—but not on a polygraph. He tried that once before when he was sure he was right, and was rewarded with a life sentence for a murder he didn't commit.

Fay's journey through the labyrinths of truth and falsehood began with a knock on the door of his home in Perrysburg, Ohio, on March 28, 1978. Fay, a valued Conrail employee, knew he was in trouble as soon as he opened that door. "There must have been a dozen cops standing there with shotguns and revolvers pointed at my head," Fay said later. The reason for the friendly call was the murder of Fred Ery, co-owner of a Perrysburg beverage center, earlier that evening.

Ery was working alone in the store when a man wearing a ski mask and carrying a gun walked in. Minutes later, Ery lay dying of a gunshot wound in the shoulder. Before he died, Ery said, "It looked like Buzz, but it couldn't have been." But police ignored the second half of Ery's declaration and concentrated on the first: "It looked like Buzz." That was good enough for them.

Fay, then twenty-six, was charged with aggravated murder and convicted five months later after a trial that relied on two pieces of evidence against him: Ery's alleged identification and a failed polygraph exam. The latter was admitted as evidence because Fay had agreed it could be before taking the exam. Fay knew he was telling the truth, and had expected the polygraph to prove it. It didn't. Fay had just learned that lie detectors lie.

But when Fay was locked up, he knew it wouldn't be for life. "I knew from Day One that I'd get out," he said. "The system just couldn't work that way. One way or another, I'd walk out of there."

Thirty months later, Fay did just that. But it took a lot of hard work on the part of Fay and his public defender, Adrian Cimeran, as well as a lot of luck. Fay's break came when Cimeran got a tip that a former Perrysburg resident who had joined the Army and was stationed in West Germany knew who really killed Ery. When Cimeran was able to persuade detectives to go to Germany to interrogate the soldier, he admitted to driving the getaway car in the robbery-murder. After the serviceman was given immunity from prosecution in return for his testimony, his two accomplices decided to plead guilty to Ery's murder.

While in prison, Fay had pursued the mystery of how the lie detector had indicated he was lying when he knew he had been telling the truth. He read everything he could find on the subject, then sent out the results of his test to a number of supposed experts. "When the results came back, I knew I was onto something," Fay said. "Every opinion I got back was different. None of the so-called experts agreed."[1]

That launched Fay on a crusade against polygraphs that continues to this day. But it's not a one-man crusade by any stretch of the imagination.

David T. Lykken, professor of psychology and psychiatry at the University of Minnesota, has studied the polygraph for more than two decades. In his book *A Tremor in the Blood,* Lykken contends that the innocent will fail lie-detector tests almost 50 percent of the time. "You'd do as well flipping a coin," Lykken says. "In particular, people with strong consciences and religious beliefs can be easily made to feel guilt and anxiety."[2]

The congressional Office of Technology Assessment came to the same conclusion in a comprehensive 1983 study. "There is very poor evidence that polygraph tests can do any more than slightly better than chance in determining whether an individual is truthful or untruthful about specific allegations," Leonard Saxe, senior author of the report, later wrote in the *Washington Post*.

Saxe noted that "psychological and physiological theory suggest that there are many reasons why the responses measured in a polygraph test—heart rate, breathing and sweating—are imperfectly related to whether a person is lying or not. Human beings are not quite as transparent mentally and physiologically as some would have us believe. What we know about human behavior tells us that lie detection is based more on science fiction than science fact."[3]

In reaction to mounting evidence against their once-vaunted reliability, Congress passed a bill in 1988 that prohibited the use of polygraph exams in the private sector but, oddly enough, not in the public sector. That means police can still use them in criminal investigations, and most do, with frightening regularity. And a person's having passed or failed a polygraph exam still has great influence on investigating officers and the public at large. But such widespread acceptance of the polygraph is almost exclusively an American phenomenon. Western European police agencies, including Scotland Yard, remain particularly skeptical of the polygraph's value and accuracy, as does the general population there.[4]

The polygraph, which theoretically measures the presence of deception in subjects by recording respiration rate, the electrical response of the skin, pulse rate, and blood pressure, was invented in the United States and apparently gained its widespread popularity here because of Americans' traditionally eager acceptance of almost any innovation attributed to "science."

Despite the scientific claims of its proponents, however, Lykken notes that none of the polygraph's developers or major proponents have had credentials as scientists. Moreover, the journals that have attested to its accuracy have not been scientific journals, whose stringent standards of peer review result in the rejection of about 80 percent of submitted manuscripts and the revision of most of those that are accepted.[5]

Most truly scientific analyses of the polygraph have raised serious questions about its purported accuracy, which is why its test results generally are not admissible in court. Yet polygraph exams remain a crucial part of criminal investigations in the United States. And that often leads to tragedies like Fay's.

Poorly administered polygraph exams, for example, caused police to focus on four friends as suspects in the gruesome rape and murder of a woman in New Mexico in 1974. Convinced of their involvement in the crime, police pressured witnesses to provide perjured identification of the four men in court, and they were all convicted and sentenced to death. Because three of the four men were from Michigan, the *Detroit News* became interested in their plight and investigated the case—proving, among other things, that the four were in California on the day of the crime. Sixteen months after their convictions, a drifter confessed to the crime, and the murder weapon and auto used in the crime were conclusively linked to him. After spending eighteen months on death row, the four young men were released, fortunately, as living examples of the pitfalls of the polygraph as an investigative tool in the hands of poorly trained police.

So why do police still insist on using it? Elie A. Shneour, director of the Biosystems Research Institute in La Jolla, California, provides the answer in the Spring 1990 issue of *Skeptical Inquirer,* in which he points out that the polygraph exam's "main justification for existence is that it *can* be effective at getting at the truth through *intimidation.*"[6] And intimidation, the next chapter will show, is still part and parcel of police criminal investigations, regardless of what the Supreme Court says about the issue.

Shneour echoes the conclusions of many that the polygraph is less the product of science than of pseudoscience. But it is hardly the only investigative tool—in the hands of police at least—that qualifies for that classification.

Another technique coming under increasing attack is hypnotic interrogation, on which many police departments rely when witnesses exhibit poor recall.

The use of hypnosis to enhance the memories of witnesses is based on the theory that human memory is like a videotape machine that records every perception. Hypnosis advocates contend that these perceptions are then stored in the subconscious, and that the brain accurately replays them on request when the witness is placed under hypnosis, a state resembling normal sleep, by a trained hypnotist.[7]

Yet several recent studies have raised serious doubts about the effectiveness and accuracy of the technique. In one influential study, a panel of the Council on Scientific Matters of the American Medical Association concluded that although subjects generally reveal more information while they are hypnotized, the recollections include many inaccurate details. In one study reviewed by the panel, hypnotized subjects seemed to remember passages of poetry they had learned many years ago but were unable to quote when not hypnotized. But —and it's a *big* but—researchers found that the subjects had also improvised freely or filled in forgotten sections by fabricating passages in the style of the author. The panel also found that hypnotized subjects are more easily swayed by leading questions than are subjects who are not hypnotized. As a result, the panel recommended that hypnotism in the judicial process be limited to the investigative stage, where it should be used with great caution.[8]

A later study published in *Science* magazine went even further. Concerned about increasing doubts regarding anecdotal accounts with which police were supporting their conclusions about hypnotism, Jane Dywan and Kenneth Bowers of the University of Waterloo in Ontario presented fifty-four subjects with sixty slides of simple black-and-white drawings of common objects. Each was viewed for three-and-a-half seconds. Subjects were then given a recall sheet and asked to write the name of the line drawing in each of the sixty blank spaces provided—indicating which items were memories and which were guesses. The subjects were then asked to recall as many of the line drawings as they could on each day of the subsequent week and deposit the sheets daily in a handy drop-box.

The mean number of items recalled on the first trial was thirty. By trial nine, the mean had risen to thirty-eight—an increase of 27 percent. But the number of errors also increased from an average of less than one to an average of four. Then some of the subjects were hypnotized and some were not. All were asked again to recall the sixty objects. The hypnotized were able to recall considerable new material, but most of the newly recalled material was incorrect.

The researchers concluded that this raises considerable doubt about the dependability of the recall of hypnotized witnesses. They also warned that the hypnotized subjects showed a surprising certainty about the accuracy of what they recalled—even when they were wrong.[9]

While many law-enforcement officials view hypnosis as an objective device with which one can retrieve many of the forty trillion to fifty trillion bits of information the mind contains, critics like Martin Orne, professor of psychology at the University of Pennsylvania, see it as a technique with an extremely high likelihood of sending innocent people to prison. Orne contends that some subjects can simulate a hypnotic trance and others can lie willfully under hypnosis. He also says that subjects, in addition to picking up verbal suggestions from the hypnotist or investigator, can also subliminally pick up information from the moment they walk into the police station, and incorporate it into their hypnotic memory of the crime.[10]

We have already seen the dangers of permitting the introduction of hypnotically enhanced testimony in the case of Randall Dale Adams, where Officer Teresa Turko's recollections were radically altered from being favorable to the defense to being favorable to the prosecution.

The same thing happened in the controversial 1984 Ohio mutilation-murder conviction of Dale N. Johnston, in which the only eyewitness, Steven R. Rine, gave hypnosis-enhanced testimony that he saw Johnston force his step-daughter and her boyfriend into a car on Oct. 4, 1982, the last day they were seen alive. An appeals court later overruled Johnston's conviction, based in part on a ruling that the three judges who heard the case should not have allowed Rine's testimony, because of the questionable methods used during his hypnosis. The appeals court's ruling was upheld in 1988 by the Ohio Supreme Court, which laid down strict guidelines on the admission of testimony by hypnotized witnesses.

Ohio thus joined at least nine other states that have either banned or severely limited the use of witnesses who have been hypnotized to aid their recollection.[11]

The reasons for these states' concern was demonstrated during a pretrial hearing in 1989 on whether Rine should be allowed to testify in a new trial, when a psychologist who reviewed tape recordings of Rine's hypnosis sessions testified that investigators had "brainwashed" him with leading questions and suggestions that planted false memories in his mind.

Clinical psychologist Bruce J. Goldsmith of Columbus, Ohio, said that in the first hypnosis session, Rine recalled seeing two teenagers apparently being forced into a car, but he did not identify the couple as the murder victims. Goldsmith also said Rine did not describe anyone matching Johnston's description. By the end of the suggestion-filled second session five days later, however, Rine had "identified" all three individuals.

The presiding judge ruled that Rine could testify on his pre-hypnosis recollections. But he excluded enough other evidence as having been illegally obtained that the charges were dropped and Johnston was freed.

Analysis of physical evidence by police crime labs and medical examiners is generally deemed to be on more solid footing than that developed by the polygraph and hypnosis. Labs, after all, deal in facts, whereas the polygraph and hypnosis deal in interpretations. But lab work, too, is far from perfect.

A *Stanford Law Review* article detailing the wrongful conviction of 350 people for potentially capital offenses, for example, states that sixteen of those convictions were based solely on erroneous diagnoses of the cause of death. (It also attributes eleven of the miscarriages of justice to police negligence and twenty-two to investigative over-zealousness. But by far the most frequent cause of wrongful convictions, with forty-nine instances, were coerced or false confessions, the subject of the next chapter.)

The case books list enough false convictions caused by faulty crime-lab analyses to raise serious questions about the tremendous trust now placed in them by the courts.

In fact, Benjamin W. Grunbaum, a biochemist and environmental physiologist at the University of California at Berkeley, concluded after studying a sampling of crime-lab reports that a surprising number exhibited "negligence, incompetence and outright bias." If a similar percentage of such reports eventually result in wrongful convictions, Grunbaum says, "the total number must be substantial."

Grunbaum has also argued that the lack of any licensing standards for forensic serologists and other forensic scientists is one of several reasons crime-lab analyses of physiological stain evidence, among other things, are unreliable and should not be admissible in courts.

At a 1985 symposium on forensic chemistry, Grunbaum said that the limited number of samples analysts must often work with in crime cases is an open invitation to error unless analysts are required to meet stringent standards, which they now are not. He cited the example of a murder case in which five different analysts reached three different conclusions with regard to the ABO antigens present in a bloodstain. "It's possible that one, two, three, four, or all of the analysts were wrong," Grunbaum said. In another instance, he said a crime lab reported finding sperm in what was later determined to be aspermic semen.

In addition to the lack of licensing standards and the poor condition of many samples, Grunbaum also cited the lack of specialization among criminologists. Analysts at many labs are expected to be expert in several diverse areas, he said, rendering their analyses "potentially more damaging than if no analysis had been performed."

He criticized the "widespread use of novel and unvalidated methods," and the labs' resistance to recognize the need for standardized methodology. Grunbaum also deplored the "orientation of the analyst within the criminal-justice system," whose pro-prosecution bias "makes it difficult to maintain scientific objectivity."

"There is undoubtedly a high degree of proficiency and a strict enforcement of quality control in some public crime laboratories," Grunbaum said. "But there are also laboratories that tolerate careless work, fundamental errors, and faulty or inappropriate methodology."[12]

A nationwide study cited in the New York Times in 1983 seemed to confirm Grunbaum's thesis. The study found that 51 percent of police crime labs misidentified paint samples, 71 percent erred in conducting blood tests, and 28 percent misidentified firearms.[13]

The situation apparently was no better in 1987, when the Times reported that, "as laboratory analysis plays an increasingly important role in law enforcement, there is growing concern about the professionalism and impartiality of the laboratory scientists whose testimony in court can often mean conviction or acquittal."

"To critics," the paper continued, "the work of the 3,500 or so forensic scientists in police crime labs is plagued by uneven training, a lack of certification and professional standards, and questionable objectivity."[14]

The Times noted that forensic scientists usually have bachelor's degrees and training at professional institutes. But critics complain that there are no accreditation requirements, academic degree programs, or recognized standards. Nor, they add, are there national guidelines for resolving different conclusions reached by different experts. Nonetheless, forensic scientists have tremendous influence when they testify on their analyses of specimens of hair, clothing, fibers, drugs, blood, semen, and other materials. Because of the complexity of their work, courts tend to rubber-stamp what the experts say.

A recent National Institute of Justice study cited by the Times, for instance, said jurors ranked forensic experts as the most persuasive witnesses. The study also indicated that the experts are equally influential with others. It found, for example, that prosecutors are less likely to enter into plea bargaining if they have strong forensic evidence, and that sentences tend to be more severe when forensic evidence is used in a trial—which is now the case in one-fourth to one-third of all felony cases and virtually all murder cases.[15]

Unfortunately, such credibility does not take into account the likelihood of bias, perjury, fabrication, or human error. The chances of such lapses being discovered, however, are slight, as are the repercussions when they are discovered. One encouraging exception to that occurred in 1987, when Delbert Lacefield, former supervisor of forensic toxicology at a Federal Aviation Administration research laboratory in Oklahoma City, Oklahoma, pleaded guilty in federal court to having falsified drug-test results on personnel involved in train crashes. What made Lacefield's case different from most, though, is that he had damaged the case of *the government*, not a poor defendant.

Forensic scientists also have been known to enhance their credentials.

"In several instances, some of them widely publicized, forensic experts have exaggerated or fabricated their educational or professional background," the *Times* reported.

"Also in question is the objectivity of forensic testimony, since the vast majority of crime laboratories are part of police agencies. Experts often work hand in hand with prosecutors, while defense attorneys seldom have the resources to do their own forensic work."

After helping to free an innocent inmate while serving an internship as a prison chaplain, the Reverend James McCloskey became interested in wrongful convictions and became involved in cases like that of Joyce Ann Brown. In the process, he came to this conclusion about the work of crime labs:

> We see instance after instance where the prosecutor's crime laboratory experts cross the line from science to advocacy. They exaggerate the results of their analysis of hairs, fibers, blood, or semen in such a manner that it is absolutely devastating to the defendant. To put the defendants at a further disadvantage, the defense attorneys do not educate themselves in the forensic science in question, and therefore conduct a weak cross-examination. Also, in many cases, the defense does not call in its own forensic experts, whose testimony in numerous instances could severely damage the state's scientific analysis.[16]

In the same article, McCloskey cites the "unjust" murder conviction of Roger Coleman as an example of the influence of improper forensic testimony:

> Roger Coleman sits on Virginia's death row today primarily because the Commonwealth's Bureau of Forensic Science expert testified that two foreign pubic hairs found on the murdered victim were "consistent" with Mr. Coleman's, and that it was "unlikely" that these hairs came from someone other than Mr. Coleman. The defense offered nothing in rebuttal, so the testimony stood unchallenged. In a post-conviction hearing, Mr. Coleman's new lawyer introduced the testimony of a forensic hair specialist who had 25 years of experience with the FBI. He testified that, "It is improper to conclude that it is likely that hairs came from a particular person simply because they are consistent with that person's hair because hairs belonging to different people are often consistent with each other, especially pubic hairs."

Another problem McCloskey says he has often encountered is "the phenomenon of lost and untested physical evidence." If the evidence potentially could exonerate the defendant, he says, it often is not tested and is eventually misplaced. "At best this is gross negligence on the part of both the police technician and the defense attorney in not ensuring that tests be done," he writes.

None of this would come as a surprise to Jay Cameron Hall. The nationally recognized forensic scientist warns in his 1974 book, *Inside the Crime Lab*, that the avalanche of drug cases, incompetent evidence collection, and over-reliance on eyewitnesses are crippling labs' crime-solving potential. Hall notes,

> The temptation in an open-and-shut investigation is to let well enough alone and accept the obvious facts, including a confession of guilt. For this reason, many cases never see the inside of a crime lab, but cry for a search for truth. Regardless of how many witnesses observed an event, the existence of overpowering motive, the full and free confession of the [suspect], the physical evidence ought to receive the same attention as if the [suspect] were unknown.

Hall also stresses what too many crime-lab experts seem to have forgotten: "The chief goal of criminalistics is to pin the criminal to the scene of the crime—if guilty—or to exonerate him if innocent."[17]

Arkansas Democrat reporter Mike Masterson revealed a good example of how little Hall's advice on keeping an open mind is followed in 1983, when his investigative articles led to the release of one man convicted on the strength of an inaccurate state crime-lab analysis and the arrest of another for murder on evidence overlooked by a medical examiner's office.

In the first case, a series of six articles showed that the prosecution used inaccurate evidence to convict Ronald Darden for the rape and murder of a 19-year-old Little Rock woman. When Masterson pressed for further analysis of a hair sample taken from Darden's coat, the national FBI lab contradicted the state lab's conclusion that the hair was the victim's. After a new trial was granted, the prosecutor dropped the charges because of "insufficient evidence."

In the second case, Masterson sought to determine the cause of death in November 1982 of a 21-year-old man. Masterson was contacted by the victim's parents after the medical examiner, who had first ruled homicide, issued a second death certificate that concluded the victim had died accidentally as a result of "indeterminant" blows to the head. After Masterson turned up a witness the police had failed to question and a rifle authorities had confiscated but never examined, a suspect was eventually arrested and charged with murder.[18]

Even highly vaunted crime labs like that of the Los Angeles Police Department can make serious mistakes. That became clear in May 1989, when Rickey Ross, a Los Angeles County sheriff's deputy, was arrested in the company of a prostitute. Twelve hours later, police released a ballistics report linking Ross's gun to the bullets that had killed three prostitutes the previous year. Unfortunately for Los Angeles police, the tests leading to that much-publicized conclusion were later found to be dead wrong.

Even worse, it was the third high-profile murder case since 1984 in which LAPD firearms experts were forced to admit that they had reached the wrong forensic conclusion.

A reconstruction of the latest faulty investigation offered two key lessons, the *Los Angeles Times* said. One is that "firearms examination is at times more art than science." The other, it quoted critics as saying, "is that the cockiness of some examiners . . . periodically leads to gross mistakes."[19]

Ironically, the LAPD was in the process of trying to replace police officers with civilian professionals in its firearms lab at the time of the latest error. That is an approach supported by Charles Morton, a nationally respected forensics expert who helped unravel the latest case. Because of their training and background, Morton said, police criminalists "too often get caught up in doing the work of the prosecution," and, as a result, can fail to look at all sides of a case.

That certainly seemed to be true in this case, in which the ballistics determination was made in less than three hours. But because of the national reputation of the examiner, even the deputy's court-appointed attorneys seemed ready to accept the conclusion. "I suppose I was like the average citizen," co-counsel Guy O'Brien told the *Times*. "They said it was a match. I thought it was like a fingerprint."

But Morton, who has worked on some of the nation's major murder trials, changed O'Brien's mind when he was hired to double-check the police lab's findings.

According to the *Times*, Morton often reminds himself of an old Orange County, California, case to keep in mind that mistakes do occur.

In that case, a catering-truck driver named William DePalma had been convicted of holding up a local savings and loan in 1968 even though he produced a dozen witnesses who swore he was serving them lunch fifteen miles away at the time. But one small fingerprint taken from the teller's counter weighed more heavily with the jury, and DePalma was packed off to prison.

Two-and-a-half years later, however, a forensics student studying the case discovered that a police sergeant had fabricated the fingerprint by using a photocopy of a print previously taken from the defendant. DePalma's conviction was overturned, and the sergeant ended up in jail for doing the same thing in yet another case.

That memory always makes Morton suspicious when a case hinges on one piece of evidence, which is just what the current case did. Although Morton didn't discover fraud in the ballistics analysis, he did discover incredible incompetence and/or wishful thinking. When his conclusion was confirmed by a second expert, the charges against Ross were dropped, and the district attorney's office announced that it would begin using outside firearms examiners to double-check the LAPD lab's results. In some cases, the DA's office added, it would bypass the police lab altogether.

It is the human element in any lab procedure that still makes many people dubious about the rapid acceptance of DNA fingerprints taken from body fluids or tissue as a "foolproof" scientific method of detection.

Even if DNA meets with the legal standard of "general acceptance" by the relevant scientific community—which it has not yet done —the human element will still be there to generate error or fraud even if national standards for the tests are established and enforced.

As criminalist Morton stresses, people make mistakes and perpetrate fraud all the time; that is something for the courts to keep in mind, too. Justice is supposed to be blind, but not dumb.

Notes

1. *Columbus Dispatch*, January 29, 1981, p. 1; also, Associated Press, September 26, 1983.

2. "The Truth About Lie Detectors, Says David Lykken, Is That They Can't Detect a Lie," *People Weekly*, May 11, 1981, p. 75.

3. Leonard Saxe, "Business Has No Business With Lie Detectors," *Washington Post*, December 29, 1988, p. 23 A.

4. David T. Lykken, *A Tremor in the Blood* (New York: McGraw-Hill, 1981), p. 45.

5. Ibid., pp. 42–44.

6. "Lying About Polygraph Tests," *Skeptical Inquirer*, Spring 1990, p. 292.

7. Paul B. Weston and Kenneth M. Wells, *Criminal Investigation* (Englewood Cliffs, N.J.: Prentice-Hall, 1984), p. 140.

8. R. Bruce McColm, "Hypnotic Witnesses," *Omni*, February 1981, p. 24.

9. "Hypnosis in Doubt," *Fate*, February 1984, p. 12.

10. *Omni*, p. 25.

11. The other states are Arizona, California, Maryland, Michigan, Minnesota, Nebraska, New York, North Carolina, and Pennsylvania.

12. "Crime Labs Not Reliable, Criminalist Claims," *Chemical & Engineering News*, May 20, 1985, p. 40.

13. "Experts' Day In Court," *New York Times Magazine*, December 11, 1983, p. 103.

14. "As Influence of Police Laboratories Grows, So Does Call for Higher Standards," *New York Times*, December 22, 1987, p. 20A.

15. Ibid.

16. "Convicting the Innocent," *Voice for the Defense*, December 1989, pp. 20–24.

17. Jay Cameron Hall, *Inside the Crime Lab* (Englewood Cliffs, N.J.: Prentice-Hall Inc., 1974), p. 239.

18. M. K. Guzda, "Reporter Helps Free Wrongly Convicted Man," *Editor & Publisher*, December 24, 1983, p. 16.

19. "Eagerness to 'Make' Gun Cited in LAPD Lab Error," *Los Angeles Times*, May 22, 1989, p. 1.

4

Miranda Wrongs

You have a right to remain silent. If you talk, anything you say can and will be used against you in court. You have the right to consult with a lawyer before you are questioned, and may have him with you during questioning. If you cannot afford a lawyer, one will be appointed for you, if you wish, before any questioning. If you wish to answer questions, you have the right to stop answering at any time. You may stop answering questions at any time if you wish to talk to a lawyer, and may have him with you during any further questioning.

—Miranda Rights

Next to the warning label on cigarette packs, Miranda is the most widely ignored piece of official advice in our society.

—Attorney Patrick A. Malone

We certainly *haven't* come a long way since the U.S. Supreme Court's controversial *Miranda* v. *Arizona* decision of 1966 that required police to inform suspects of their Fifth Amendment rights against self-incrimination.

We may no longer have forced confessions quite as outrageous as those extracted from Walter Fowler and Heywood Pugh, two black men police in Illinois persuaded to confess, after several days of beatings, to a 1936 murder known to have been committed by a white man.[1]

Nor do we have such oddities as the 1931 confession to a robbery-murder by Ohioan Julius Krause after police convinced him there was no way he could be acquitted. Four years later, however, Krause's supposed accomplice gave a deathbed statement in which he named his actual partner.

When officials failed to act on the information, Krause decided to do it for them. In 1940, he escaped, tracked the man down, and convinced him to confess to authorities. After the man was convicted and sentenced to prison, Krause voluntarily returned to the Ohio Penitentiary in Columbus, fully expecting to be released. But because Krause had broken the law by escaping, he was kept in custody for another eleven years.[2]

His stay might have been even longer if he had not been assigned to the governor's mansion as a gardener and chauffeur for the governor's wife, Jane Lausche. The state's first lady took an interest in Krause's plight after first being impressed by his talents as an artist. Of those abilities, Lausche, an art school graduate with additional training in architecture, said, "Without training, he does better than I can do. He's extraordinary in everything he undertakes." With a recommendation like that, Governor Frank Lausche commuted Krause's sentence to the twenty years he had already served, and he was released in 1951.

And you certainly don't have cases today like that of Ahmad Kassim, whose 1958 first-degree manslaughter conviction was vacated seven years later when it was determined the confession he signed could not have been his because he couldn't speak or write English. It turned out that the district attorney had written up his own version of events relating to the crime and had had an unsuspecting Kassim sign it.[3]

Police these days are so much more respectful of suspects' rights that they do everything but confess for them. Physical abuse and threats to harm suspects' loved ones are pretty much passé. The new tricks of the trade are real tricks. Like convincing the suspects the cops are on their side. Like conducting phony polygraph exams to convince suspects there is proof they're lying. Like asking suspects to help the detective "think through" details of the crime by playing the role of the criminal. Like telling suspects they have already been linked to the crime by eyewitnesses who don't exist, or by physical evidence that hasn't even been tested yet.

And such tricks are all considered quite kosher. Fred E. Inbau, longtime editor of the *Journal of Criminal Law, Criminology and Police*

Science, and John E. Reid, founder of the Reid College of Detection and Deception, give their imprimatur in their widely used textbook, *Criminal Investigations and Confessions*. Rather bluntly they write: "We do approve of such psychological tactics and techniques as trickery and deceit that are not only helpful but frequently necessary in order to secure incriminating information from the guilty." They ignore, of course, that such techniques often secure incriminating information from the innocent, too.

It was precisely for this reason that the U.S. Supreme Court issued its Miranda decision, in which Chief Justice Earl Warren, referring to texts like the one by Inbau and Reid, wrote:

> By considering these texts and other data, it is possible to describe procedures observed and noted around the country. . . . In essence it is this: To be alone with the subject is essential to prevent distraction and to deprive him of any outside support. The aura of confidence in his guilt undermines his will to resist. He merely confirms the preconceived story the police seek to have him describe. Patience and persistence, at times relentless questioning, are employed. To obtain a confession, the interrogator must "patiently maneuver himself or his quarry into a position from which the desired object may be obtained." When normal procedures fail to produce the needed result, the police may resort to deceptive stratagems such as giving false legal advise. It is important to keep the subject off balance, for example, by trading on his insecurity about himself or his surroundings. The police then persuade, trick, or cajole him out of exercising his constitutional rights.
>
> Even without employing brutality, the "third degree," or the specific stratagems described above, the very fact of custodial interrogation exacts a heavy toll on individual liberty and trades on the weakness of individuals.

The remarkable 292-page transcript of the interrogation of Tom Sawyer provides a rare glimpse into how these techniques were still being effectively employed with impunity in 1986, 20 years after the Miranda decision was issued to protect suspects like Sawyer from such abuses.[4] And this Tom Sawyer wasn't in trouble for a trick he played on his girlfriend Becky or for conning kids into paying him for the privilege of whitewashing his front fence. And his inquisitor wasn't any nice old Aunt Polly.

This Tom Sawyer was a suspect in a murder that took place in Clearwater, Florida, in 1986. A recovering alcoholic, the 36-year-old Sawyer was a groundskeeper at a local golf course. On Halloween weekend of that year, Sawyer's next-door neighbor, 25-year-old Janet L. Staschak, was found strangled in her bed.

Because of his nervous bearing and muscular arms, which looked like they could strangle just about anyone, police decided one afternoon to take Sawyer in for a friendly little 16-hour voyage of self-discovery that would make that of the fictional Tom Sawyer's friend Huckleberry Finn seem like a luxury cruise. The two detectives who questioned Sawyer started with the flattering technique of asking for the suspect's help in figuring out how the crime was committed:

> Detective John Dean: Let me ask you something. I think you're a pretty sharp guy. I think you watch a lot of cop shows. . . . Okay, you got a young girl. She's not bad looking. You know, I only know by pictures. Everybody likes her that she works with.
> Sawyer: Uh-huh.
> Dean: She don't have a boyfriend. She turns up dead in her apartment.
> Sawyer: Uh-huh.
> Dean: What do you think? Given those sets of circumstances, what do you think? . . .
> Sawyer: What did she die of? You can't tell me that?
> Detective Peter Fire: You tell me what you think. You be a homicide investigator.
> Dean: Some theory.
> Fire: Give us your theory. . . .
> Sawyer: At first I figured it has to be someone who knows her. . . .

The game was afoot. But Sawyer wasn't too good a player. He seemed appalled at the scenario the detectives had him developing.

> Fire: Okay. How? Why? What is your opinion of what happened? . . .
> Sawyer: I don't know how he'd kill her. 'Cause you wouldn't have sex with a girl and then kill her unless you were crazy.
> Fire: Well, it's not nutty. Maybe he's upset. That's all.
> Sawyer: Yeah, he's probably pissed off.

Fire: That's right. He doesn't have to be nutty. She could set him off
  wrong, you know. Don't have to be his fault.
Sawyer: Yeah, right, yeah.
Fire: Right? She could have caused the problem.
Dean: There have been several women in the past that have been known
  to piss off guys.
Sawyer: Yeah, okay. He's got the attitude I'm gonna get this bitch,
  right?
Fire: Because he's been rejected.
Sawyer: So then he rapes her, but he's got to kill her now or he's
  gonna get put in court for rape. . . . But he likes her, so how could
  he kill her? Oh, well. . . .

Oh, well, indeed. It took a total of four hours for Dean and
Fire to get Sawyer where they wanted him, after correcting him on
several key details, such as how the woman was killed and how the
body was found.

That's when they finally read him his rights. Then they resorted
to the ploy of the polygraph exam, which Sawyer jumped at the chance
of taking to prove his innocence. The test was shoddily conducted
in violation of polygraphers' codes. Needless to say, Sawyer failed,
and the detectives convinced him it would be better to confess, now
that they had proof he was lying. A later test taken under proper
conditions indicated Sawyer was telling the truth. But by then police
had gotten Sawyer's "confession" after running through the scenario
again. It was then about 1 A.M., and Sawyer had been awake for
about 24 hours.

Dean: Is that reality, what you just described to me now? Is that what
  happened, Tom?
Sawyer: It still says I didn't do it. I don't know.
Dean: You didn't *want* to do it, did you?
Sawyer: No, I don't think I *did* do it.
Dean: Is that what happened, though? . . . Tom, you know the answer.
Sawyer: The only reason I . . . believe I did it is if my hairs were in
  her car and on her body and in her apartment [as he incorrectly
  had been led to believe].
Dean: Is that part of what happened Saturday night? . . . Are you getting
  different pictures?

Sawyer: No. . . .
Dean: Isn't it clearer now that you talked about it? Isn't it? Isn't it
    clear now that you got it out? Is that part of what happened Satur-
    day night?
Sawyer: Yes.
Dean: Yes? Let me shake your hand. Shake my hand.
Fire: It's about time. That's it. That's it. There you go.
Dean: Do you want to go on?
Sawyer: I want to lay down.

After allowing Sawyer a short nap, they resumed the interrogation. It continued for several more hours because of Sawyer's renewed
resistance to confessing to the murder.

"The truth is, and this is going to piss you off," a timid Sawyer
said after his nap, "The truth is . . . the only reason I'm telling this
stuff is because you got evidence to get me. I don't believe I did
it. That's why I want to talk to somebody. I'm going fucking bananas."

Despite his plea to talk to somebody, no attorney was called and
the questioning intensified. Then, at approximately 8 A.M., Sawyer
was charged with first-degree murder.

But Sawyer's statement that the only reason he was telling the
cops what they wanted to hear was that they had the evidence to
convict him anyway became a significant point. Because it turned out
that the police only had evidence to the contrary. The blood and
hair samples taken from Staschak's body and bedclothes did not match
Sawyer's. And forensic analysis determined that the "rape" police had
persuaded Sawyer to confess to hadn't even occurred.

After spending fourteen months in jail, Sawyer was released by
Judge Gerald J. O'Brien pending a pretrial hearing on the validity of
his confession. In the summer of 1988, O'Brien threw the confession
out. He said the enforced sleeplessness, the use of an improper polygraph test, the leading questions, and the endless inquisition had, as
the Supreme Court ruled in a similar case in 1987, drained the suspect's
"powers of resistance and self control . . . and [critically hampered]
his capacity for self-determination."

What makes the transcripts of Sawyer's interrogation even more

frightening is that they are remarkably similar to those of the controversial eight-hour interrogation of 18-year-old high school senior Peter
Reilly of Falls Village, Connecticut, in 1973,[5] during which Reilly
confessed to killing his mother, Barbara Gibbons—but only after police
told him a (faulty) polygraph exam proved his guilt and that they
had enough physical evidence to convict him with or without his
confession. Doesn't this sound familiar?

> Sgt. Tim Kelly: Well, I think we got a little problem here, Pete.
> Peter Reilly: What do you mean?
> Kelly: About hurting your mother last night.
> Reilly: I didn't do it. . . .
> Lt. Lawrence Shay: Don't be afraid to say "I did it."
> Reilly: Yeah, but I'm incriminating myself by saying I did.
> Shay: We have, right now, without any word out of your mouth, proof
>   positive—
> Reilly: That I did it?
> Shay: That you did it.
> Reilly: So, okay, then I may as well say I did it.

Then came a two-hour polygraph exam that Reilly was told showed
he was the likely killer. Kelly then speculated that Reilly might have
hit his mother with his car outside the house and then "set it up
to look like something really violent happened in the house."

But Reilly said that "wouldn't have been like me. Honestly, if
I had hit my mom, the first thing I would have done was call the
ambulance."

But Kelly persisted. "These charts say you hurt your mother last
night," he said. He suggested a second time that the youth may have
hit her with his car, but Reilly insisted he hadn't.

> Kelly: Then if you didn't, then you killed your mother deliberately.
> Reilly: I didn't, though. I don't remember it.
> Kelly: Then why does the lie chart say you did?
> Reilly: I can't give you a definite answer.
> Kelly: You see? But you don't know for sure if you did this thing,
>   do you?
> Reilly: No, I don't.

Kelly: Why?
Reilly: I just don't. I mean, like your chart and everything say I did.
Kelly: Okay.
Reilly: But *I* say I didn't.

After the terrifying experience of finding his badly beaten mother lying on the floor of their home taking her dying breaths, though, and the additional stress of eight hours of grueling questioning, Reilly *did* say he did it.

But young Reilly's many friends in Canaan, Connecticut, never believed that for a moment. They knew him to be too gentle a young man. With no father and an abusive alcoholic mother, Reilly was always eager to please—almost too eager at times, which they suspected was how he was persuaded to sign a confession. Reilly's best friend's parents took him into their house without the slightest fear that they would end up like his mother. Then they and others started a defense fund for the orphan, got him one of the best attorneys in town, and looked forward to his exoneration.

Try as his attorney might, though, she was never able to live up to her advance billing. She let many discrepancies in the prosecution's case go by, and failed to present all the evidence in Reilly's favor. She also failed to challenge the confession itself, which the tapes showed was obtained through falsehood, deception, and the physical and psychological wearing-down of the defendant.

Reilly and his many friends were shocked when he was convicted of first-degree manslaughter and sentenced to six to sixteen years in prison. That's when playwright Arthur Miller, a resident of nearby Roxbury who had followed Reilly's trial with consternation, entered stage right at the request of one of Reilly's supporters. Miller brought with him a cast of characters that included several other area celebrities, including author William Styron, actor Dustin Hoffman, singer Art Garfunkel, actress Candice Bergen, and actress Elizabeth Taylor—who sent a note with her contribution that told Reilly, "Hang in there, baby."

Before long, the bolstered defense committee was able to get Reilly a good appeals attorney, a dedicated private detective who would track down many crucial pieces of exculpatory evidence at great personal cost and—most important—national publicity on "60 Minutes" and elsewhere.

The hearing on a motion for retrial began on January 15, 1976. The cast was very much the same. But, as *New York Times* reporter Donald S. Connery wrote in his excellent account of the controversial case, *Guilty Until Proven Innocent*:

> A fundamental shift in awareness had taken place in the twenty-one months since the manslaughter conviction. The Reilly trial, in a sense, had never really ended. A judgment had been reached, but many questions were left unanswered. The public sense that something had gone wrong, and that the wrong man had been prosecuted for a horrible crime, was enhanced each time information not heard in the trial was revealed. Peter had become a sympathetic figure and a popular name in the news. He was on his way to becoming a symbolic victim of injustice. A classmate had published a poem about him. Someone else wrote a ballad. A book was being written.

That something else was different became readily apparent as soon as the hearing took place. Roy Daly, the polished appeals attorney, turned the tables immediately and made it clear that it was the state that was on trial, not Peter Reilly. His three-count petition noted he would attempt to prove that:

• The time sequence proffered by the prosecution was wrong and that Reilly did not have time to kill his mother and clean off the massive amount of blood the killer would have got on him before the help he had summoned arrived.

• The prosecutor had deliberately withheld exculpatory evidence from the defense.

• New evidence indicated the true killer of Reilly's mother was Reilly's boyhood friend, Michael Parmalee.

Daly scored heavily on all counts. Then the once-confident-but-now-flustered prosecutor made a fatal mistake: Thinking it would bolster his weak case, he moved to have the transcript of the original trial "be made a part and parcel of this petition for a new trial."

By doing so, he unwittingly gave Daly the opportunity to call a renowned psychiatrist and expert on police interrogations to excoriate the validity of Reilly's confession. The expert, Herbert Spiegel, gave a lucid, detailed explanation of the various phases of the interrogation. He concluded by explaining that Reilly was a person of low self-esteem, who, "in deference to the police authority . . . accepted their authority and accepted responsibility for the killing on the basis of their assertions."

Asked if Reilly was "the type of personality who would fly into a rage," Spiegel maintained that, "Because of his extreme modesty . . . and because, again, of his uncertainty about himself, not only doesn't he have the likelihood of taking on the right of an emotional outburst or rage against somebody, but I suspect strongly that it doesn't occur to him that he has the right in the first place."

Two weeks later, the judge, clearly perturbed by the failure of the prosecutor to turn over exculpatory evidence and obviously impressed by the arguments of the defense, issued an extraordinary ruling that he concluded by saying, "It is really apparent that a grave injustice has been done and that upon a new trial it is more than likely that a different result will be reached."

That was a clear warning to the prosector to drop the case. Before he could, however, the prosecutor died of a heart attack. The attorney appointed to take his place was not only dismayed at how weak the known evidence in the case against Reilly really was, but also shocked to find even more evidence that clearly showed it would have been impossible for Reilly to have committed the murder. A short time later, he dropped the charges, and Peter Reilly was a free man rather than the insecure boy who had once so easily been manipulated into confessing to the murder of his own mother.

A few months later, a superior court judge sitting as a one-man grand jury investigated the police handling of the case. The judge's report eliminated any doubts about Reilly's involvement, but failed to recommend any action against the officers who handled the case. A woman who lived with Timothy Parmalee in 1977 and a friend of Parmalee both signed affidavits stating that Parmalee had told them that he and his brother Michael had killed Barbara Gibbons and that

Michael Parmalee had also raped her. But the statements were later judged to be too unclear and lacking in substance for charges to be filed. The murder remains unsolved.[6]

As for Reilly, he "was saved from the wolves by the intervention of friends and strangers who were not content to accept the official doctrine over their own perceptions," concluded Donald Connery. "His case was the stuff of melodrama, but it was real life too, and all who were drawn to his cause were bound to ask, How many more Peter Reillys are there?"

More, you can be sure, than anyone who might know would care to confess. But enough are disclosed to make Sawyer's and Reilly's cases just the tip of a titanic iceberg.

False confessions by suspects who are, like Sawyer and Reilly, psychological putty in the hands of unprincipled police are commonplace. Some of those confessions are totally inexcusable, such as that of James Hill of Florida, a mentally retarded man whose murder conviction and death sentence were reversed in 1987 after it was determined that his mental status led him to agree with whatever police told him. Others are inexplicable, such as that of George Parker of New Jersey, who confessed to a 1980 murder committed by his girlfriend because he loved her two children and thought she was pregnant with his child. The girlfriend returned his love by, along with her sister, testifying against Parker even though he had by then recanted his confession. Over the objections of prosecutors, Parker was granted a new trial after the two women were convicted of the same murder. Charges against him were eventually dropped.[7]

Then there are cases like that of Melvin Lee Reynolds, whose childhood of illness, parental rejection, and life in a boys' home where he was often sexually abused by older residents left him a confused young man when he finally got out on his own. Despite a concerted effort to overcome the sexual disorientation his youth had left him with, false rumors about his sexual activities often made their way around St. Joseph, Missouri. One surrounded the alleged molestation of his three-year-old nephew, which Reynolds, his family, and the boy's mother all strongly denied.

But Reynolds was eventually able to settle down with a steady girlfriend, and they began making plans to marry on October 6, 1978. But those plans were destroyed when four-year-old Eric Christgen was abducted from a downtown mall that spring. His sodomized body was found in a nearby ravine after a massive search. Four days later, police were knocking on Reynolds's door because of the rumors that had always haunted him. An anonymous caller had told them Reynolds was at the mall the day the boy had disappeared. Other calls saying the boy was seen walking from the mall with a man in his mid-fifties were ignored. Police chose to focus on the 25-year-old Reynolds instead.

Reynolds denied being at the mall that day, but police remained dubious. As other leads dried up over the next months, they continued to focus their attention on him. They gave him two lie-detector tests. He passed one, and the results of the other were inconclusive. Falling into a pattern of his youth whenever he felt threatened, Reynolds tried to please his adversaries by offering to confess even though he denied killing the boy.

Reynolds's problems became worse when he agreed to being given an injection of sodium amytal, a "truth serum."

"I didn't have anything to do with it," Reynolds said when the drug first took effect. But then came a slight slip that would cause him much grief: "Before I killed—before I went to the unemployment office. . . ."

Police took that slight misstatement as an admission. They became so relentless in their questioning that Reynolds began to have doubts himself. Before long, he had signed a statement admitting to the abduction and murder. He later recanted, but was tried, convicted, and sentenced to life in prison.[8]

Almost two-and-a-half years later, however, 11-year-old Michelle Steele was abducted just two blocks from the downtown mall from which Eric Christgen had disappeared. Police arrested 54-year-old drifter Charles Hatcher, who turned out to be a serial killer with an estimated eighteen victims across the nation to his discredit. Among the murders Hatcher eventually admitted to was that of Eric Christgen, for which he was well aware Reynolds had been convicted. "You're smart enough to know," he told the FBI agent he confessed to, "that these bastards in St. Joe will do anything for a confession, even if they had to frame someone to get it." Hatcher then described the crime far more accurately and in greater detail than Reynolds had, then said he wanted to plead guilty. He eventually did on October 13, 1982, almost four years after Reynolds had been convicted. Reynolds was released the next day.[9]

Certainly one of the more mysterious of recent "confessions" is that of Bible-college student Steven Linscott, whose apparent effort to help police solve a murder ended in his conviction. Linscott's figurative nightmare started with a literal one the night before police came to the Christian halfway house for ex-convicts in the Chicago suburb of Oak Park that Linscott supervised. They told Linscott and his wife, Lois, that a 24-year-old nursing student had been murdered in her apartment in a nearby building, and that they were looking for information, no matter how nonsensical it seemed, that might give them a lead. Linscott and his wife couldn't think of anything at the time. Later, however, the 26-year-old Linscott began considering the strange nightmare that had caused him to wake up in a cold sweat about the time of the murder. The dream was about a blond man beating a person to death. All he remembered about the victim was that he or she had seemed resigned to death.

When Linscott mentioned the dream to Lois and a few classmates at Emmaus Bible College, they urged him to go to the police. Linscott began to wonder if the dream had been an "inspired experience" that was meant to help the detectives. So, even though he worried that they might think him mad, Linscott called the police. As it turned out the police did think him mad—mad enough to have committed the murder. They came to that conclusion after hearing Linscott reconstruct his vague dream. He said it took place in room with a stereo and couch. The attacker was a husky light-haired man and the nondescript victim seemed to be black. He related how the man hit the victim on the head with a blunt object that looked like a counterweight from a grandfather clock. The intrigued police asked Linscott to come into the station. They questioned him twice at great length after reading him his Miranda rights, which they explained was a mere formality he shouldn't take seriously. They then used the all-too-familiar trick of asking Linscott to speculate how he thought the murder might have occurred, after telling him the dream may have been an indication that he had psychic powers. Linscott took the bait. He was flattered that he might be able to help police solve a murder.

Was the attacker married?

"It's possible. . . . He seems real at ease, you know, with the opposite sex," Linscott replied, apparently accepting the idea that the victim was a woman.

Did he have any remorse for what he had done?

"I would hope so."

Is it still possible to catch the killer?

"I think so. . . . I know some people will do that subconsciously—leave a trace, you know."

Although Linscott wasn't concerned about the line of questioning, his wife was when he told her about it.

When the police called and asked him to come in for a second interview, Linscott asked if he was a suspect. He was assured he was not. But when the Bible student got to the station, he was interrogated by an assistant state's attorney as well as police. He was also asked to give samples of his blood, hair, and saliva—all the while being told he wasn't a suspect.

On the contrary, they told him they were doing this as a mere formality so they could officially rule him out as a suspect and then use him as a witness. But after the samples were provided, police changed their tune. They accused him of murder, although they didn't file charges.

But they didn't pursue any other leads, either, even though they still had no witnesses or physical evidence. They didn't even bother questioning a suspected rapist who lived in the neighborhood or any of the ex-cons who lived in the halfway house. Six weeks later, Linscott was finally charged with the murder based on the similarities of his dream and the actual killing. The assistant DA even admitted to the press that the evidence against Linscott was "very circumstantial," and that he left it to the jury to presume motive. The many *dissimilarities* between the murder and Linscott's dream—such as the fact that the victim had been stabbed and strangled as well as beaten, that she was white and not black, that the blunt instrument was a tire iron and not a quite-different-looking clock counterweight—were all conveniently downplayed by the prosecution. The testimony of Linscott's wife, Lois, that her husband was sleeping beside her when she got up to feed their baby at the approximate time of the murder was treated with disdain. That Linscott's physical specimens could be narrowed to only about 60 percent of the white male population and that the fingerprints found at the scene weren't his were greatly obfuscated. Yet the jury fell for the whole charade. It found the father of two guilty, leaving the once-trusting Linscott disillusioned. "Everybody trusts the system, everybody trusts the fact-finding process," he said later. "Nobody realizes that it's a slick pole, and once you start sliding on it you can't get off."[10]

It took three years for Linscott to get at least one foot back on firmer ground. That happened in 1985, when the Illinois Court of Appeals ruled the evidence against him was insufficient to sustain a conviction. But the victory was short-lived. In 1987, the state Supreme Court overruled the appeals court's ruling on the evidence, but returned it to the same forum for consideration of issues related to the fairness of the trial. The appeals court then voted to send the case back for retrial on the grounds that prosecutors, in essence, had lied to the jury during closing arguments of the original trial by their "clever, but definitely misleading" choice of words. "The American ideals of fairness in our system of justice were not just ignored, they were trampled upon," the court stated.[11]

Obviously unhappy, the prosecution also appealed this ruling to the state Supreme Court. In the interim, a report by two experts in forensic dentistry at Northwestern University had bolstered Linscott's case by concluding that subtle abrasions on the victim's body were bite marks that could not have been caused by Linscott's teeth. The report was requested by the medical examiner after he had read *Innocence,* a book about the case by Gordon Haresign, one of Linscott's growing number of supporters. The examiner, Edmund R. Donoghue, had noted subtle abrasions on the body in his 1980 autopsy report, but said he could not determine what had caused them.[12]

"Third Degree" Has Nine Lives

Police don't always resort to trickery and psychological manipulation to obtain false confessions. Some still rely on the tried-and-true "third degree" that the Miranda rule was supposed to have eliminated once and for all. Paul Reggettz III discovered the hard way that this is not always so in West Virginia. In 1979 he confessed to the murder of his wife and two children and spent eleven months in jail before being freed after a neighbor confessed to the same crime.

The sordid story started on a cold and rainy December 13, 1979, when Reggettz, whose house did not have a telephone, rushed into a restaurant a block away from his home in the Charleston-area town of St. Albans, called police, and said: "You've got to help me. My wife's dead."[13]

When police arrived, they found Venessa Reggettz, twenty-six, on the bedroom floor. She had been beaten, strangled, and stabbed repeatedly with a pair of scissors. The couple's 4-year-old daughter, Bernadette, had been strangled, and was hanging from a cord strung over a door. Seven-year-old Paul Eric was found in the bathtub. He had been choked with an electrical cord before being drowned.

After the bodies were removed, Reggettz, then a 36-year-old United Parcel Service employee, was taken to the state police headquarters for questioning—if that's what you want to call what he endured for the next twenty-one hours. According to Reggettz, he was bullied, threatened, knocked to the floor, and had a gun placed to his head before he finally confessed to the murders.

His explanation was simple: "The children were screaming and crying. My head felt like it was going to explode and I had to put a stop to the noise."

Reggettz was then taken back to his house, where he re-enacted the slaying for the police and prosecutor.

"I was put under so much pressure, tremendous pressure," Reggettz would explain later. I would have told them anything—anything —to get them to leave me alone and not put pressure on me."[14]

Reggettz was ordered held in jail without bond pending his trial. Although the charges were dropped eleven months later before he was actually tried for the crimes, Reggettz had lost his job and suffered immensely with guilt and confusion.

"Three times—and I'm not trying to get dramatic—three times I planned suicide in there. I came very near the end of my rope on three different occasions," Reggettz remembered later. "I thought dying would have to be better than living."

But ten months after the slayings, Reggettz's fortunes took a sudden turn for the better. The day after Circuit Judge John Hey refused to throw out his confession, a 17-year-old neighbor, John Moss, told police it was he, not Reggettz, who had committed the brutal slayings. When police reopened the case, they found that some of the blood at the scene didn't match that of the victims or Reggettz, but did match that of Moss. Several items stolen from the home were also linked to Moss.

The medical examiner, who originally had been influenced by Reggettz's confession and set the time of death at shortly before he would have left for work, revised the time of death to well after that.

The prosecutor finally conceded that Reggettz was at work at the time of the murders, and dropped the charges against him. Moss was tried and convicted of the gruesome murders.

Reggettz, now remarried and a born-again Christian, has much to be bitter about. But he's not. "I know a lot of people made big mistakes in my case," he said. "But the mistake would be even worse if I let it eat me alive."[15]

Bradley C. Cox has tried to keep from being bitter about the confession he was frightened into, too. But it hasn't been easy. Cox was convicted in two Ohio counties in 1980 on similar charges of rape, robbery, and burglary in each case. He was sentenced to a total of fifty-six to two-hundred years based on a confession coerced out of him by police who had warned the then-AWOL soldier that his fate would be worse if he was returned to the military.

Cox was freed two years later after a former resident of the same area in southeastern Ohio confessed to the rapes for which Cox was convicted, plus more than seventy others in eleven states under the guise of "the ski-mask rapist." Detailed confessions also led to the release of a man in Texas who had been convicted of rapes admitted to by Jon B. Simonis after he was finally nabbed in Louisiana.[16]

Cox's attorneys had said earlier that the only reason Cox had confessed was because of extreme duress. He had been interrogated for nearly eight hours, during which a polygraph exam was also administered. "There's supposed to be a difference between a polygraph test and an interrogation test," attorney Harry Reinhart said. "They're not to be done at the same time. If you took this to a professional polygraphist, they'll tell you that it's improper to use the polygraph as an interrogation tool. After he confessed, they went ahead the next day and got him to sign. They broke him one day and did the paperwork the next."

Reinhart said Cox's guilty plea on rape charges in Athens County was a "tactical" decision based on his conviction on similar charges—supposedly substantiated by Cox's confession—in adjacent Fairfield County.

Information from the Fairfield County conviction would have been admissible as evidence in the Athens trial, Reinhart said, and "nothing convicts a man quicker than getting evidence before a jury that he's been convicted before of similar crimes. The best thing for Brad was to plead guilty. It was a legal judgment. It was my decision."[17]

Did public officials learn anything from the false Cox convictions? Of course not.

"I can't recall anything like this ever happening before," said the superintendent of the prison where Cox had been kept. "Of course, if you listen to the mothers of our inmates, it happens to every prisoner," he cynically added. "The chance of an innocent man going to prison is pretty remote. You have to work pretty hard to get put in prison in this country."[18]

Confessions Come Easy

He should tell that to Robert Wilkinson, who, based on his confession, was convicted on five counts of murder in the firebombing of a home in Philadelphia. A year later, another man pleaded guilty to the crime and the mildly retarded Wilkinson was released. A *Philadelphia Inquirer* investigation then revealed that Wilkinson's confession not only had been coerced, but that at least seven other individuals were beaten, threatened, or forced by other means into making false statements against him. Several Philadelphia police officers were subsequently convicted of violating Wilkinson's civil rights in what the court said was a "brutal and unlawful" manner. Wilkinson was awarded $325,000 in damages.[19]

The shortsighted superintendent might also tell Arthur Barber how hard he must have worked to be convicted in 1967 of first-degree murder and granted a life sentence for his efforts, which included being brutally beaten by police and subjected to other abuses that a court later found part of "a pattern of lawlessness which shocks the conscience."[20] That's if you have a conscience, of course, which some cops obviously do not.

Or the superintendent might try to tell David Vasquez of Virginia how rare wrongful convictions are. Vasquez was convicted in 1985 of a murder he didn't commit, as a result of the usual mistaken identification, sloppy police work, and trickery-inspired confession. Detectives failed to read Vasquez his Miranda rights until well into the intimidating interrogation, told him they had physical evidence linking him to the crime though no such evidence existed, and subtly planted details of the crime in his mind. The confession that resulted sounded sadly familiar:

> Detective: Did she tell you to tie her hands behind her back?
> Vasquez: Ah, if she did, I did.
> Detective: Watcha use?
> Vasquez: The ropes?
> Detective: No, not the ropes. Watcha use?

Vasquez: Only my belt.

Detective: No, not your belt. . . . Remember being out in the sun room, the room that sits out to the back of the house? . . . And what did you cut down? To use?

Vasquez: That, uh, clothesline.

Detective: No, it wasn't a clothesline, it was something like a clothesline. What was it? By the window. . . . Think about the venetian blinds, David. Remember cutting the venetian blind cords?

Vasquez: Ah, it's the same thing as rope.

Detective: That's what you're talking about?

Vasquez: Um. . . .

Detective: Okay, now tell us how it went, David. . . . Tell us how you did it.

Vasquez: She told me to grab the knife and stab her, that's all.

Detective (*raising his voice*): David, no. David.

Vasquez: If it did happen, and I did it, and my fingerprints were on it. . . .

Detective (*slamming hand on table*): You hung her!

Vasquez: What?

Detective (*shouting*): You hung her!

Vasquez: Okay, I hung her.

Vasquez then began sobbing. He said once again he had not been in the Washington, D.C., suburb of Arlington, where the murder had occurred, let alone near the victim's house, but that he "had to say this because you tell me my fingerprints were there." But his denials didn't matter now. Police had enough of an admission to work on to finally get a detailed confession from the borderline-retarded suspect. And once they had that, Vasquez's attorneys later convinced him, his only way to avoid the death penalty was to plead guilty while not actually admitting he had committed the crime.

He did, and spent five years in prison before a four-times convicted murderer was linked to the crime and Vasquez was freed.[21]

How can these outrageous interrogations still go on twenty-five years after the Supreme Court's Miranda ruling?

Easy, says Patrick A. Malone. In a perceptive article in the Summer 1986 issue of *The American Scholar*, the Washington trial lawyer writes: "The creation of a suspect's right to be told his rights has not appreciably affected the confession rate. Nor has Miranda curbed the use by police interrogators of such tactics as showing the suspect fake evidence, putting the suspect to a phony lie detector test that he is guaranteed to flunk, and making fraudulent offers of sympathy and help."[22]

Despite initial misgivings by those in law enforcement, and continued attacks on the ruling by politicians, Malone notes:

> Miranda turns out to be the police officer's friend. The Miranda ruling warning has become, in the main, a benediction at the outset of every interrogation, sanctifying the very practices it was meant to end. Studies . . . have found that Miranda warnings have little or no effect on a suspect's propensity to talk. Most suspects routinely waive their rights and submit to police questions. Next to the warning label on cigarette packs, Miranda is the most widely ignored piece of official advice in our society. Even when Miranda is violated, it is rare that a confession will be ruled inadmissible or that a suspect will go free.

An even a bigger problem than the full-blown false confession, Malone writes, is a statement that is erroneous only in a few details that are often used against the suspect. Then there is the alibi statement given out of fear that, when found to be false, becomes the basis for often incorrectly concluding that the rest of the statement must also be false.

To have truly ended the practice of interrogations designed to coerce defendants to incriminate themselves, Malone concludes, the Supreme Court would have had to require that any interrogation at a police station be conducted in the presence of a defense lawyer or impartial magistrate.

"Instead," he notes, "the court allowed tactics that it found violative of the right against self-incrimination to continue as long as suspects agreed to submit to them."

Given the current status and attitude of the court, that policy is not likely to be altered judicially anytime soon.

Notes

1. "Miscarriages of Justice," *Stanford Law Review*, November 1987, pp. 114–115.

2. " 'Innocent' Convict to Go Free After 20 Years; Plans Life," *Columbus Dispatch*, February 23, 1951, p. 1.

3. Associated Press, December 26, 1984.

4. Information and all quotes used in this section were taken from "Untrue Confessions," *Mother Jones*, September 1989, p. 18; additional information supplied by "True Confession?" *Harper's Magazine*, October 1989, p. 17.

5. Unless otherwise noted, quotes regarding the Reilly case appear in Donald S. Connery, *Guilty Until Proven Innocent* (New York: G. P. Putman's Sons, 1977), pp. 288–331.

6. "Inquiry Discovers No Cause for Reilly Case Grand Jury," *New York Times*, September 26, 1979, p. B2.

7. "A Friend's Conviction Wins Man a New Trial," *New York Times*, February 9, 1986, p. 46.

8. "How Justice System Can Go Wrong," *Los Angeles Times*, p. 1, pp. 8–9.

9. Ibid., p. 9.

10. "A Vision of Murder," *People Weekly*, September 4, 1987, pp. 30–32.

11. "Court Orders New Trial for Steven Linscott," *Christianity Today*, September 4, 1987, pp. 68–69.

12. "More Good News for Linscott," *Christianity Today*, September 2, 1988, p. 47.

13. Associated Press, January 30, 1990.

14. Ibid.

15. Ibid.

16. " 'The Miracle' Happens: Cox Freed," *Columbus Dispatch*, January 23, 1982, p. 1.

17. "Confessions criticized," ibid., December 10, 1981, p. B1.

18. "Cox's case rarity, says prison chief," ibid., December 13, 1981, p. B1.

19. See generally *Philadelphia Inquirer*, December 21–24, 1976.

20. *Stanford Law Review*, p. 95.

21. "At Each Step, Justice Faltered for Virginia Man," *Washington Post*, July 16, 1989, p. 1.

22. "You Have the Right to Remain Silent," *American Scholar*, Summer 1986, pp. 367–380.

5

Bearing False Witness

It's not what we don't know that gives us trouble, it's what we know that ain't so.

—Will Rogers

In Gainesville, Georgia, two Vietnamese men are in jail awaiting trial in 1985—one for robbery, the other for murder. When it's time for the murder trial, police produce the accused thief by mistake. As the man keeps repeating, "Not me, not me," in broken English, witnesses identify him as the murderer. The defense attorney, like everyone else in the courtroom, doesn't realize the man isn't the accused murderer; he becomes fearful of a conviction and offers to plead his uncooperative client guilty to a lesser charge. The mix-up is not discovered until the last minute, when an acquaintance of both men happens into the courtroom and tells embarrassed officials they are trying the wrong man.[1]

In Galveston, Texas, Howard Mosley, who had been sentenced to life for attempted murder, is freed in 1982 after being cleared by the confession of Cornal Eugene Watts. Mosley, who had been picked out of a lineup by his alleged victim, turns out to be a full foot taller than the admitted attacker.[2]

In California, John Rexinger, twice identified by the victim of a 1957 torture-rape, is later released when the actual rapist, eight inches shorter in height, confesses in detail.[3]

In St. Louis, Maurice Williams is released after spending fifteen months in jail for a series of 1982 pharmacy robberies he was finally able to prove he had been convicted of because of mistaken identification. As Williams heads for a television studio for an interview about his plight, he is rearrested on the basis of erroneous police records.[4]

In Tennessee, the state Supreme Court rejects the appeal of mailman Douglas Forbes, pronouncing the trial that led to his conviction in two rape cases based on eyewitness testimony as having been "well nigh perfect." Five years later, he is released after a look-alike truck driver confesses to the crimes.[5]

In 1980, Jeffrey Streeter of Atlanta is asked by an attorney to replace the defendant at his table to test the accuracy of the eyewitnesses to a crime on which they are about to testify. Although the defendant is sitting nearby, three eyewitnesses identify Streeter. Before the attorney can convince the judge that Streeter is the wrong man, he is declared guilty of assaulting an elderly man and sentenced to prison. Streeter is freed on his own recognizance the next day, and his conviction is later reversed.[6]

In 1990, an elderly witness testifying in an Aurora, Colorado, murder trial identifies a reporter covering the trial for the *Rocky Mountain News* as the murderer. The witness changes her testimony after being asked to take a closer look.[7]

In downtown Seattle, 19-year-old Arthur F. Emery is standing on the street when a passing bus driver calls police and identifies him as the man who had robbed him several days earlier. After Emery has been convicted and has served nine months in prison, a man arrested in Colorado confesses to the bus robbery and tells where the stolen money is hidden.[8]

In Missouri, a Mexican-American is identified by a rape victim as her assailant even though she had originally described the rapist as "an Italian-looking man." When she is later asked to observe a second, very different-looking suspect, the woman identifies him as her assailant too. "I'm getting tired of coming down here to identify this man," she tells police.[9]

Sometimes justice is obviously too blind for its own good—and that of its innocent victims.

According to recent studies, eyewitness error is responsible for more than half of all wrongful convictions in the United States. In a third or more of such cases, the erroneous witness testimony is actually perjured. In many others, misidentification occurs in conjunction with other errors that help seal an innocent person's fate.

"Sometimes these eyewitnesses have no doubt whatsoever about the accuracy of their testimony," C. Ronald Huff writes in the Ohio State University study of wrongful convictions. "In other cases, they had either slight or lingering questions in their own minds, but nevertheless felt sufficiently confident that they were willing to testify against a defendant."

Huff adds: "Many of the cases we have identified involve errors by victims of robbery and rape, where the victim was close to the offender and was able to get a look at him—but under conditions of extreme stress. . . . Such stress can significantly affect perception and memory and should give us cause to question the reliability of such eyewitness testimony."[10]

Elizabeth Loftus, a University of Washington psychologist who has done extensive research and writing on eyewitness identification, tells of one study that found that people who watched a videotape of a violent bank robbery recalled fewer details correctly than did viewers of a less violent crime.[11]

Another reason cited for poor identification during violent crimes is what experts call "weapon focus." People remember guns in fine detail, but the face behind the gun is often recalled vaguely if at all.

But eyewitness identification is less than perfect even under less stressful conditions. Psychologist Robert Buckhout of Brooklyn College, for example, staged a test in which a photo of a man was shown on television for seven seconds. When viewers were asked to pick the man out of a lineup, only 17 percent were able to do so. "We don't have photographic memories," Buckhout said.[12]

Race also enters the picture through the "they-all-look-alike syndrome." Studies have shown, for instance, that whites are more likely to misidentify blacks than whites and that blacks are more likely to misidentify whites than blacks.

Studies are also beginning to show that distortions in memory

occur over time and often are caused by outside influences as well
as internal ones. Loftus has found, for example, that witnesses are
likely to augment their description of an accident shown to them on
film depending on what words she uses to describe it.

But we do the same type of embellishing all by ourselves, says
Steven Penrod, a long-time University of Wisconsin professor and
a prominent researcher on eyewitness testimony. "A witness tells his
story to the police, to the family, then to friends, then to the prosecutor,"
Penrod explains. Over time, he says, the story becomes more epic
legend than just a few facts. "They feel very confident about what
they now think happened and that confidence is communicated to
the jury," Penrod says. Police often aid this process by pressuring
the witness to be firmer in an identification, and initial uncertainty
has a habit of disappearing by the time of the trial.[13]

To make matters worse, witnesses also have a sympathetic audience
ready and willing to believe almost anything they have to say. In fact,
a study presented to the American Psychological Association in 1984
showed that eyewitness testimony pointing toward guilt had greater
influence with jurors than any other evidence. British researchers Ruth
Brandon and Christie Davies note in their book, *Wrongful Imprisonment*,
that the reason we give such credence to the statistically least credible
evidence is that all of us "rely continually in our everyday lives on
our ability to identify other people. By contrast, because we are not
so familiar with scientific and technical expertise, we are more inclined
to distrust it. Also psychologists have shown that we acquire our ability
to recognize and to communicate with other people very early in life,
and it is very disturbing for us to accept the fact that these basic
beliefs and skills may be fallible."[14]

But while jurors may be impressed with eyewitness testimony,
experts and judges are becoming increasingly skeptical. As Judge J.
Edward Lumbard of the Second U.S. Circuit Court wrote in his 1978
decision in *Jackson* v. *Fogg*, "Centuries of experience in the administration of criminal justice have shown that convictions based solely
on testimony that identifies a defendant previously unknown to the
witness is highly suspect. Of the various kinds of evidence, it is the

least reliable, especially where unsupported by corroborating evidence."

It is exactly for that reason that courts in Scotland have, for some time, required some form of corroboration for a case based on the identification of a single witness. Ancient Talmudic law has also long provided that a defendant could not be convicted of a capital offense unless two independent witnesses could attest to the defendant's guilt.

The U.S. Supreme Court didn't go that far, but in 1967 it did hand down three landmark cases in which it sought to establish at least some safeguards and guidelines on the admission of eyewitness identification. In *United States* v. *Wade*, the court ruled that the defendant is entitled to a lawyer during a post-indictment lineup. In this case, employees who had witnessed a bank robbery had been allowed to see the suspect in the custody of an FBI agent before they identified him in a lineup. In another decision issued the same day, *Gilbert* v. *California*, it was ruled improper that the accused was identified in a lineup conducted without notification of his attorney, who had been appointed a full sixteen days before. Finally, in *Stovall* v. *Denno*, the court ruled in the other direction. It held that a murder suspect's rights were not violated when he was identified at the bedside of the hospitalized widow of the man he was accused of slaying. But the court ruled that the identification was admissible only because of doubts about how long the witness might live, and that such identifications should be allowed only in extreme cases.

Despite these attempts to establish some identification guidelines, however, it has been business as usual in the nation's courts.

Eyewitness identification remains the backbone of the criminal-justice system, and the errors caused by the heavy reliance on such discredited evidence continue to mount.

And when it comes to misidentification, no one is sacred—not even a Roman Catholic priest. That became obvious when the Reverend Bernard Pagano was wrongly accused by witnesses in 1979 of being the gun-toting "Gentleman Bandit" who had recently robbed a string of Delaware stores.

Despite his protestations of innocence and the lack of any other evidence, Pagano was put on trial, only to be acquitted by the last-minute confession of Ronald Clouse of Brookhaven, Pennsylvania, who bore a slight resemblance to the tall, balding priest. The charges against Pagano were dropped, and the prosecutor apologized in court. Five years later, though, the priest filed an unsuccessful $5 million civil suit against several Delaware police officers because his diocese had failed to help with his expenses, which ran over $120,000, and because of the actions of the police both during his prosecution and after. Even when the charges had been dropped, the priest said, the police implied that he was still somehow involved in the crimes. "They were saying I had known Clouse, and kept coming up with a conspiracy thing," an angry Pagano said. The continued notoriety of these false claims, plus others about his personal life made at the trial, caused Pagano to be treated like a pariah by his diocese and to be denied assignment to new parish. He had become, literally, a man without a mission.[15]

Before the trial, Pagano said, the conduct of the police was even worse. "Once they had committed themselves, they were not going to look bad," he said of the four state troopers he sued. In 1981, CBS aired a TV movie, The Gentleman Bandit, that was loosely based on his story. Later, Pagano helped to establish the Hunterdon Foundation for Justice to assist innocent people who have become entangled in the judicial system.[16]

There certainly are plenty of such people around, and many don't end up nearly as lucky as Pagano, as bad as his experience might have been. In the Stanford study of the 350 people wrongfully convicted in potentially capital cases since 1900, 193 convictions were the result, at least in part, of erroneous witness testimony—some inadvertent, some quite deliberate.

Of those 193, several paid the ultimate price for the witnesses' mistake. One of the latest was James Adams of Florida, which is a leading state in both executions and wrongful convictions. In 1974, Adams was convicted of first-degree murder and sentenced to death. He was executed in 1984. Witnesses placed Adams's car at the home of the victim at the time of the crime. Some of the victim's jewelry was found in Adams's car trunk, yet Adams maintained his innocence, claiming he had lent the car to his girlfriend. Although a witness said he saw Adams driving away from the victim's home shortly after the crime, the witness had been driving a large truck in the opposite direction, and probably could not have had a good view. It was also discovered later that this witness was angry at Adams for allegedly dating his wife. A second witness heard a voice in the victim's home at the time of the murder and saw someone who appeared to be female fleeing. He identified the voice as a woman's, not a man's. And the day after the crime he stated that the person he saw fleeing was definitely not Adams. Even more important, a hair sample found in the victim's hand, which was likely that of his killer, did not match Adams's hair. Unfortunately, much of this information was developed by a skilled investigator *a month after* Adams's execution.[17] A request for even a short stay was denied by Governor Bob Graham, who based much of his voter appeal on his hard-nosed support of quick executions. He was later rewarded for his popular stance by being elected to the U.S. Senate. (His successor, unfortunately, proved to be just as trigger-happy.)

Christian Amado of Massachusetts was luckier than Adams. Amado was convicted of first-degree murder and sentenced to life in prison in 1980. His conviction was overruled on appeal, however, and the trial court was ordered to enter a judgment of acquittal for one very good reason: The evidence linking Amado to the crime was that of an eyewitness who had at first told police that a photo of Amado resembled the killer but testified at the trial that Amado was *not* the killer. Amado was released in 1982 after serving two years.[18]

Another Florida folly was the 1979 conviction of Brett Bachelor. Bachelor was convicted of second-degree murder and sentenced to fifteen years. But at the subsequent trial of a co-defendant, evidence was produced to show that a key witness had erroneously identified Bachelor, and he was ordered released from prison. His co-defendant was acquitted.[19]

There is a great deal of selectivity regarding which witnesses will be listened to by the courts and which won't. In an amazing example of this, Robert Ballard Bailey was convicted of first-degree murder and sentenced to death in 1950 despite the testimony of officers of the Charleston, West Virginia, police department, who said they were in the process of unsuccessfully pursuing his speeding, weaving car at the exact time of the murder. Even though the police knew Bailey by sight, they made sure they would be able to prove he was the drunken driver by perforating the car's back end with bullets. As Bailey managed to escape through the hills on back roads, he was observed driving by several people who knew him well. The two witnesses who identified Bailey as the murderer, on the other hand, did not know Bailey and said the murderer had been stone sober.

Only two days before his scheduled execution, his doubtful prison warden called in author Erle Stanley Gardner and his then-famous Court of Last Resort, a panel of experts sponsored for a number of years by *Argosy* magazine in their efforts to exonerate innocent convicts. When Gardner and two associates arrived and assessed the case, they decided to give Bailey several lie-detector tests, all of which indicated his innocence. Gardner then got through to a skeptical Governor Okey Leonidas Patteson early on a Saturday afternoon. The governor met with them an hour later, and agreed to delay the execution while the investigation continued. The Court of Last Resort then began its investigation in earnest.

Gardner later wrote:

> At the end, we became convinced that the evidence in the case presented a cockeyed picture. It didn't establish Bailey's guilt beyond a reasonable doubt. We picked up the prosecutor in the case and went to Governor Patteson to make a report showing exactly what we had uncovered.
>
> Governor Patteson heard the report and promptly commuted the sentence . . . to life imprisonment, stating that in the present condition of the evidence he was far from satisfied with the verdict and there was a reasonable doubt to say the least as to Bailey's guilt, and he called on the state police to institute a new investigation of the murder right from the beginning.[20]

That investigation eventually led to Bailey's release under a conditional pardon, which became unconditional in 1966.[21]

When it comes to persistence at overcoming a conviction based on mistaken identity, Tony Cooks deserves special mention. It took five trials and seven years for Cooks to prove his innocence, but he finally did so in 1986, when a California jury exonerated him of a murder charge he had contended all along was based on his resemblance to a neighbor. The Cooks case was the subject of a 1983 *Los Angeles Times* article that raised questions about his guilt. His first and third trials ended in hung juries, the second in a mistrial and the fourth in conviction. But the judge in that trial, normally known for his toughness with defendants, threw out the conviction. The prosecution appealed, however, the verdict was reinstated, and the judge was forced to pronounce sentence. When he did, the judge called the defense attorney "totally incompetent" and the police investigation "the worst job of investigation I have ever seen." He then ordered Cooks to prison for sixteen years to life, but freed him on $5,000 bail pending appeal. At that point the *Times* revealed that the case was based on mistaken eyewitness identification and perjury by a self-confessed participant in the slaying. On appeal, Cooks won the right to a fifth trial, at which previously undiscovered evidence was introduced showing that the eyewitness had told his since-deceased probation officer that his testimony was "a lie" made up to satisfy a persistent detective who wouldn't take no for an answer. After the jury voted to acquit Cooks and end his long struggle, jury foreman Valerie Wester said, "We felt the wrong identification was made," and urged that Cooks's look-alike be investigated.

While members of Cooks's family, who had been forced to sell their home to pay defense fees, celebrated and prayed in the courthouse hallway, Cooks expressed disappointment that prosecutor Thomas Gray, who had pursued him so relentlessly for almost eight years, didn't show up to hear the verdict. "Mr. Gray should have known a long time ago that I didn't do this," Cooks said.[22]

Edmond D. Jackson could certainly empathize with Cooks's plight. In 1971, Jackson was convicted of murder and felony murder and given two concurrent sentences of twenty years to life in prison. In 1978, however, Jackson's petition for habeas corpus (a practice Chief

Justice Rehnquist wants to limit) prompted a federal court to throw out his conviction because it was based on unreliable eyewitness testimony by four people and because "not a scintilla of [other] evidence was offered at the trial to connect [the] petitioner to the crime." In ordering Jackson's release, the judge said, "I shudder to think what the situation would have been in this case if there had been a mandatory death penalty."

Judge J. Edward Lumbard lectured,

> The dangers of convicting on identification testimony alone are well known to those whose duty it is to prosecute crime. Yet here, the prosecutor and police were content to consider the case solved in reliance on questionable identification procedures and despite the fact that other suspects had been called to their attention. It is difficult to understand why the district attorney of Queens County would have proceeded with the trial of the charges against Jackson on such highly dubious evidence and negligent investigation conducted by the detectives.
>
> Neither the press of business [nor] the urgency to solve so serious a crime as that committed by the gunman can justify the negligent use of unreliable procedures in place of thorough and careful investigation.[23]

The investigation of the holdup had been headed in an entirely different direction at first. After looking at mug shots, two of the four witnesses named the same man as the gunman. But then one of the other witnesses pointed to Jackson, who happened to be in the police station on another matter. A lineup was quickly arranged, and all four suddenly were in agreement that Jackson was the robber. But three of the four had possibly been influenced by the fact that they had seen Jackson sitting at a bench shortly before the lineup. Judge Lumbard pointed out that the witnesses had had little opportunity to see the gunman at the shooting, had never seen the gunman before, and had varying degrees of certainty about the identification when they saw Jackson a month after the shooting.

The name Jackson was doubly significant in a highly publicized mistaken-identity case in Ohio in 1982. The case started inauspiciously enough when Columbus police received a call that a man was loitering around a townhouse on the city's north side. But what seemed like a routine case soon transformed into the bizarre. When police arrived at the scene, they found that the loiterer had become an intruder. The man they found inside the house was wearing a ski mask and carrying a wide array of burglary tools. That wasn't all that unusual. What was unusual was the identity of the suspect: Dr. Edward F. Jackson, perhaps the city's most prominent black internist. The case became even more curious when officers searched Jackson's Mercedes-Benz. Inside, they found a sheet of paper containing a lengthy list of rape victims in Jackson's handwriting. Most of the women on the list had been classified as being among the more than one-hundred victims of the elusive "Grandview rapist," who had made the suburb of Grandview Heights and the surrounding Columbus neighborhood his personal stalking ground with seeming impunity. The improbable fact that the rapist was a doctor actually made quite a bit of sense when investigators began to review the files. A number of the "Grandview rapist's" victims had noted that he wore rubber gloves and took their pulse after the assault.

Then the curious got curiouser and curiouser. As police checked off the names on Jackson's precise victims list, investigators realized they had mistakenly arrested and successfully aided in the conviction of another Jackson—William Bernard Jackson—for two of the rapes on the doctor's list. It didn't take long to see why when photos of the two Jacksons, who weren't related, were compared. The resemblance between them was striking. Both were tall and thin. Both had short Afros, scraggly beards, and mustaches. Their other facial features were remarkably alike as well. It is easy to see how the victims could have been so certain when they identified William Bernard Jackson as their assailant. In fact, the detective who gathered the evidence, the prosecutor who handled the case, the judge who presided at the trial, and the jurors who convicted William Bernard Jackson all later said they would do the same thing again if they were faced with the same evidence. What happened was a tragedy, they said, but the kind of tragedy that sometimes just can't be prevented.

The prosecutor admitted that "eyewitness identification is unreliable. But that's what the jury is there for. They have to decide if it's reliable or not." Anyone who has listened to the experts on eyewitness identification, of course, would know that it's not. Unfortunately, such experts are often disqualified from testifying by skeptical judges in states where such testimony is permissible; in other states, their testimony is prohibited altogether. But if eyewitness identification were treated with more skepticism in the investigation of the case, of course, other factors might be uncovered to alter the outcome. As it was, the case against William Bernard Jackson came down to a choice between the word of the victims, who positively identified him as their assailant, and Jackson's family members and friends, who said he was with them on the nights of the crimes. In such cases, the victims' testimony almost always wins—as it did in this instance.

To their credit, Columbus police didn't dally about admitting their mistake and correcting it. Just seven-and-a-half hours after Dr. Edward Jackson was indicted on ninety-four counts, including thirty-six rapes and forty-six burglaries, the "wrong Jackson," as he had become known, was released from prison after serving nearly five years for rapes he did not commit. When he arrived in Columbus, William "Billy Jack" Jackson didn't try to hide his bitterness. "They took away part of my life, part of my youth," he told reporters. "I spent five years down there and all they said was, 'We're sorry.' I didn't get no compensation for the time I did, no money [he later received $717,500 from the state], no job, nothing. And they can never make up those five years."

Jackson said he always knew he would eventually be released, that it was only a matter of time. "This is exactly how I thought it would end," he said. "I figured one day they'd find a guy committing crimes and say, 'We got a guy in the pen for this.' "[24]

He said he held no grudge against the women who identified him as a rapist. Instead, he said the police should "take the blame for everything. They knew from jump street [the start] that I didn't do it. They told me, 'You can go out there and try to better your life and don't let it destroy you.' I said, 'Man, what are you talking about? You already destroyed my life.' "

As if to prove his point, William Jackson was in and out of

minor trouble with the law on several occasions in the first few years after his release. In an interview after his first year of freedom, he said that his conviction still followed him like a cloud he could not escape. "If I could at least get a job, I wouldn't have to be standing around," he said. "But nobody's going to hire no jailbird. I'd show them the newspaper clippings that say I was innocent, but they don't want you. No way."

William Jackson's complaint is a common one made by the wrongfully convicted. One who had a better chance than most ever get to express those feelings was Leslie A. Vass, who spent almost ten years in Maryland prisons after he was convicted of armed robbery when he was seventeen. Vass was released in 1984, when an investigator for the state public defender's office, acting on a hunch, went back to Vass's alleged victim, who looked at the photo and realized he had identified the wrong man. After the state Board of Public Works voted in 1987 to pay Vass $250,000 as compensation for the mistake, Vass asked to testify before the board on why that amount couldn't begin to make up for the damage done to him—and that, indeed, perhaps no amount of money could.

As the nervous, bespectacled Vass spoke, he tucked his hands inside the pockets of a gray double-breasted suitcoat. He had been waiting for this chance since 1975, after a holdup victim had pointed out the high-school junior, who had a clean record and was a member of the school basketball team. Vass told the panel that since his release three years earlier, he had found it hard to find a job even though he had earned his high-school diploma while in prison. To get by, Vass said, he had painted houses, mowed lawns, and repaired friends' cars.

"This is something I've been really working on," Vass told the board of his prepared testimony. "But to stand here and tell you what I went through, I can't do. It's deep inside of me. It hurts." Nonetheless, Vass said, he was trying to make the best of his life. He said he wanted to work with teenagers to help keep them out of trouble, and would soon be starting college. "The only thing I wanted to do was come here and explain to the board how I felt, what I had been through," Vass said. "I was heard. Now I just want to walk away from here and get on with my life."

Another young man facing the same challenge in 1990 after enduring a similar ordeal was Randall Lynn Ayers of Cincinnati, who was convicted in 1982 of a brutal crime to which another man finally had confessed. After an emotional reunion with his family outside the Hamilton County Justice Center on July 20, 1990, Ayers, who had spent a third of his life in prison while serving his fourteen-to-fifty-year sentence, told the press he was "surprised" at the turn of events. "It was a long wait. I didn't believe this would happen. I had given up," he said.

Ayers said his first act would be to visit his grandmother. That hardly sounds like the kind of person who could have raped, robbed, and shot a 15-year-old girl, but that is what Ayers was accused of doing back in 1981.

Ayers was a 17-year-old high-school senior who planned to join the Marines after graduation when he was arrested and charged with the ruthless attack after the victim happened to see him standing among a group of students at his school. Ayers pleaded not guilty at his trial, and friends testified he had been drinking beer and smoking marijuana with them in an abandoned car at the time of the assault.[25]

That may not be a serious felony in the law books, but it became so in the real world. Jurors later said the witnesses' admission of such activities had had a bad effect. "The boy himself made a terrible impression," one juror added. "His friends did the same thing."

The victim did just the opposite. "Her testimony was powerful," said Judge Thomas A. Crush, who presided at Ayers's trial. "She remembered the face. It just happened that somebody else had the same face." Crush admitted he had always had some misgivings about the case because there was no other evidence linking Ayers to the crime. He could have dismissed the charges if the witness had shown any uncertainty, but that just wasn't the case. "When the victim gets on the stand and says, 'That's him!' that's the specific factual question Ayers did not want me to decide [because the law requires judges to accept such testimony as truthful if the witness shows no uncertainty]. He wanted the jury to decide it."

And the jury did. After thirteen hours of fractious discussion, its members voted to convict Ayers of all charges. The jurors' comments after Ayers's release revealed some interesting details of how juries come to the wrong conclusions in court in general and in eyewitness-identification cases in particular.

One juror who held out the longest for acquittal said he wasn't convinced of Ayers's guilt because of an apparent discrepancy between the boy's height and the victim's description. During the trial, the girl said her attacker was one or two inches taller than she was. But Ayers was an inch shorter. That had caused some doubts, he said, because "girls always notice if they're taller than you."

But the juror said he had come under increasing pressure from the others to vote for conviction. "I was kind of badgered by the rest of the people in there," he recalled. The women jurors kept telling him women never forget the face of an attacker, he said, and "everybody seemed to be on my case."

As the stalemate continued, the jury foreman decided to inform Judge Crush that they were deadlocked. But Crush gave them the answer all judges do at first: Go back and try again. As it turned out, he thought the jury was leaning in quite a different direction. "All of us thought one or two were holding out for guilt," Crush said after Ayers's release. "It was a surprise that they came back with a guilty verdict."

To many jurors, the deciding factor came when, during the trial, Ayers was placed next to the victim to show their differing heights. "She almost fainted when he stood next to her," a juror said. "That had an emotional impact on us."

Despite the victim's strong role in gaining Ayers's conviction, though, he didn't seem to hold it against her. "I don't feel animosity," he said. "I think at the time she believed it was me. She was doing what she had to do."

But Ayers did what he had to do as well. When he went before the parole board in 1985 and in early 1990, board members voted not to release him, Ayers believed, "because I wouldn't admit to it."

The most unfortunate thing of all about this case, however, was when the presiding judge said Ayers's release wouldn't cause him to change how he handles eyewitness testimony. "I guess you could pass a law saying eyewitness testimony is not admissible," Judge Crush said. "But that would set a lot of obviously guilty people free."

So much for William Blackstone's much-quoted but little-followed declaration that "it is better that ten guilty persons escape than one innocent suffer." Neither has to be the case anyway, of course, if the proper procedures are established and adhered to. But most people would rather simply look the other way—even if the evidence is overwhelming that the justice system they think they see is more myth than fact. Until Americans realize that, we will continue to see tragedies like that of:

• Aaron Lee Owens, who was convicted in 1973 on two counts of first-degree murder on the basis of erroneous eyewitness identification and sentenced to life in prison. Owens's case was reopened in 1979 after the man convicted of the murders along with him admitted that Owens had had no role in the killings but refused to say who had. After an extensive reinvestigation by the Alameda County, California, prosecutor's office, it was determined that a man who resembled Owens had committed the crime. After Owens became a free man in 1981, he said: "I'm not mad at any particular people. I'm disappointed in the system. This never would have happened if [the prosecutors] had done their jobs properly in the first place."[26]

• Gordon Morris, who had a jury selected and was tried, convicted of murder, and sentenced to death all in one day of Texas-style justice in 1955. An investigation conducted by the victim's doubtful brother later demonstrated, however, that Morris was physically incapable of committing the murder and that the conviction had been based on mistaken identification. Three days before Morris's scheduled execution, his sentence was commuted to life. When the jury foreman heard of the new evidence, he reinvestigated the case himself, tracked down the other members of the jury, and got them as a group to urge that Morris be pardoned. He was, finally, in 1976.[27]

• Bobby Joe Leaster of Massachusetts, who was convicted of first-degree murder in 1971 and sentenced to life. Leaster was arrested ninety minutes after a store owner was fatally shot during a robbery in September 1970, because his clothes matched those of the assailant. Leaster was then positively identified by the victim's wife and a customer. He was released in December 1986 after new evidence surfaced and the district attorney declined to seek a retrial. The evidence, a .22-caliber gun that proved to be the weapon used to kill the shopkeeper, was discovered in the evidence room of the Boston Police Department. Records showed that the gun had been discarded by a man being pursued by police who had responded to an armed robbery report sixteen days after the one Leaster had been accused of. The investigation that eventually led to the gun started in 1977, when two attorneys became convinced of Leaster's innocence and volunteered to work on the case at an eventual cost to themselves of $400,000 in time and expenses. In 1986, a Boston teacher who read about their effort reported he had seen two men he knew by name running down a street in the same area as the crime that day, and that neither of them was Leaster. He said he was only thirteen years old at the time, and didn't connect the two to the robbery-murder until he read about Leaster's case.

The teacher gave police the one name he still recalled. That prompted the probe that turned up the gun. Police then admitted that they may have originally overlooked a prime suspect who was believed to have committed a number of armed robberies in the area at the time.[28]

• Calvin Lyons of Akron, Pennsylvania, who was released in 1984 after spending four years of a ten-year sentence in prison for an armed robbery to which another man confessed after he "found God." According to the district attorney, the two men shared many physical similarities. "They both had the same weight and build," he said. "They both had deep-set eyes and curly, light-colored hair."[29]

• Gordon Hall of California, who was convicted of first-degree murder in 1978 based on the identification of two eyewitnesses who later admitted they had been mistaken. On retrial, Hall's alibi was confirmed by several witnesses whom Hall's first attorney had not bothered to call. All charges were dropped in 1982.[30]

• Everett Malloy of Texas, who was convicted of murder and sentenced to fifteen years in prison in 1984 based on the eyewitness identification of four people. He was set free just two months later, however, when an anonymous tip led police to a woman who had witnessed the murder but had been afraid to come forward. Her information led to the filing of charges against the true killer.[31]

• Marion Coakley of New York, who was freed in December 1987 after serving twenty-six months for a rape he was convicted of committing after being picked out of a police lineup. The judge who ordered Coakley's release said the "miscarriage of justice" could have been avoided if a test had been conducted to compare his blood type with that of semen found on the victim's underwear. Tests had been requested before Coakley's trial, but were never completed. A new team of defense attorneys had the tests conducted, and they showed that Coakley had type A blood and the rapist type B.[32]

• Bradford Brown of Washington, D.C., who was convicted in 1975 after an eyewitness identified him as the man who murdered Rodney Frazier during a robbery attempt. The witness had originally hesitated when shown a picture of Brown, but by the time of the trial seemed as certain as one can be. Brown claimed he had spent the night of the crime, November 2, 1974, at a birthday party for his 6-year-old niece. The child and several relatives corroborated his account. But Brown was convicted and sentenced to eighteen years to life. His family raised $3,000 for an appeal, but the conviction was upheld. In 1979, however, a Washington detective was told by an informant that Brown wasn't Frazier's killer. He said it was Richard Harris, who had several robbery convictions on his record. The killer was known to have stopped by Frazier's apartment earlier the night of the murder and had scribbled a telephone number in a message to Frazier's father. The number had never be linked to Brown and had been filed away. But Detective Robert Kanjian was quickly able to link it to Harris, who eventually pleaded guilty to manslaughter in the case.[33]

• Steven Titus, a middle-class Seattle resident with no criminal record who was identified as a rapist by his alleged victim. The conviction was overturned when the *Seattle Times* proved that another man was responsible. Titus later died of a heart attack that his family and friends attributed to the stress of his ordeal.

• Robert Watson of Florida, a hard-working, devoted family man who was convicted of robbing a Kwik Serv grocery store in Mulberry, Florida, about a hundred miles south of his home in Sanford. Watson had been identified from his photo by the two victims, who later unhesitatingly picked him out of a police lineup. When *Tampa Tribune* reporter John Frasca noticed that an identical crime was committed in Mulberry after Watson had been incarcerated, he investigated and revealed in a Pulitzer Prize–winning series of articles that both crimes had been committed by a look-alike who was working in tandem with a Mulberry police officer.[34]

• Malcolm Emory, who was convicted of assault and battery on a police officer based on the eyewitness testimony of the officer who arrested him during a campus protest at Northeastern University on the night of January 29, 1970. Boston police officer Vincent Logan told the court that he saw Emory holding and then hurtling objects that looked like "a rock," "half of a red sidewalk brick," and "a piece of concrete." Emory claimed he was merely leaving the library at the time with an armful of books when he got caught up in the melee, but he was convicted and received a six-month suspended sentence. As a result, Emory lost his job with the U.S. Naval Sound Laboratory, his security clearance, and a scholarship, which forced him to drop out of school. He also forfeited his driver's license for six months and was denied the right to vote in the 1972 elections.

In 1985, during a return visit to Boston, Emory decided to stop by the library to review newspaper coverage of the demonstration at which he was arrested. When he discovered his face in the crowd of one of the photos published in the *Boston Globe,* he and an attorney received permission from the *Globe* to review other photos taken that night that weren't published. Sure enough, they discovered a photo of Emory clutching his books—not rocks, bricks, or concrete—as police dragged him away. When they filed a motion for a retrial, the prosecutor dropped the charges. Northeastern then granted Emory a scholarship to complete the physics program he had been forced to drop out of.

• Nathaniel Walker of New Jersey, who served eight years of a life-plus-fifty-years sentence for a kidnapping and rape in what he insisted all along was a case of misidentification by the victim. Walker was freed in 1986 through the efforts of James McCloskey, the minister who was also instrumental in clearing Joyce Ann Brown in Dallas. In this case, McCloskey developed enough exculpatory evidence to convince an attorney to volunteer his assistance. The attorney eventually located a sample of semen taken from the victim that for some reason had never been tested for blood type. When it was, it showed evidence of both A and B blood types. Walker was found to be type A. When the victim was found in Florida and tested, she also was found to be type A. The conclusion was obvious: The rapist was type B, which meant Walker wasn't the rapist. Five days after the results were in, on November 5, 1986, Walker was a free man.

• Steve Fossum, a Texas oil-well roustabout who was convicted of rape based on his identification by his two alleged victims in early 1985 and sentenced to twelve years in prison. Fossum was freed a year-and-a-half later after two journalists from his home state of Minnesota who had been urged to look into his case by friends produced a documentary that exposed sloppiness and laziness on the part of both police and Fossum's attorney, and revealed crucial physical evidence that cleared him.[35]

• Enrique Davila Suarez of Hialeah, Florida, who answered a knock at his door one night in 1985 and soon found himself under arrest for a murder in Brooklyn, New York. Davila not only had never been arrested before, he had never been anywhere near Brooklyn before. Some eighteen months later, Davila was released from jail after it was determined he was the victim of mistaken identity. Despite alibis from his family, employer, and fellow employees that placed him at work and at home around the time of the murder in New York, Davila was extradited from Florida and held in jail awaiting trial until detectives confirmed his alibis several months later. Davila had become a suspect because the murderer was believed to be a member of a Cuban organized-crime group. When authorities in Florida were notified, they sent to New York several photos of persons matching the description, and Davila's was picked out by witnesses. Because he had no record, police could not explain how his picture came to be included among those sent to New York, or whether it actually was a photo of Davila. All the chief of the homicide bureau in the Brooklyn district attorney's office would say was, "Our job is to do justice, and we worked hard to uncover the truth." Some justice: a year-and-a-half of Davila's life to clear up something that should have only taken hours. Some truth: a total lack of explanation about how the misidentification ever occurred.[36]

The Frame-Up Artists

But as bad as arrests and convictions made on erroneous testimony by witnesses may be, the far-too-frequent patently false testimony of witnesses is much worse. These individuals aren't honestly mistaken. They are pernicious perjurers. And the damage these false witnesses do is often devastating to individuals and families alike.

Take the case of Mary Hampton of Louisiana. In 1961, Hampton, then nineteen, was convicted on two counts of first-degree murder and sentenced to life in prison. She was convicted on the basis of the false testimony of her self-confessed "accomplice," a former boyfriend who was facing the death sentence in Florida for a murder conviction obtained primarily through Hampton's testimony, which she had given despite his threat of revenge. And revenge he got—by implicating her in the Louisiana murders, to which Hampton confessed after authorities threatened her with the death sentence if she didn't. Her plea was accepted even though authorities knew her ex-boyfriend's testimony was faulty and that she had believable alibi witnesses.

Fortunately for Hampton, *Miami Herald* reporter Gene Miller became interested in her case in 1963 and documented both the reliability of her alibi and the unreliability of the inculpatory testimony. After a special hearing in 1966, Hampton's sentence was commuted to time served and the parole board ordered her release.

Another person framed in revenge for his cooperation with police was Harry Dale Bundy of Zanesville, Ohio. In 1957, after Bundy provided police with information on two murders that co-worker Russell McCoy had told him he had committed, McCoy returned from Amarillo, Texas, where he had been in hiding, and turned himself in. Then he turned the tables on Bundy by implicating him in two other murders. Based on McCoy's testimony and the later-discredited identification of a young girl, Bundy was convicted of the first-degree murder of a Uniontown market manager, Reynold Amodio, during an armed robbery that had left Amodio and a clerk dead. Bundy claimed he had been drinking with friends in his hometown of Canton, where McCoy had dropped him off earlier that day, at the time of the crime. Several witnesses confirmed his alibi, but to no avail. He was sentenced to die in the electric chair.

A few days before Bundy's scheduled execution on November 8, 1957, Norma Brajnovic, owner of an Amarillo liquor store across from the bus station where McCoy had left the murder weapons, picked up a copy of *Inside Detective* magazine someone had left on the counter. As she thumbed through the pages, Brajnovic was stopped by a photo of McCoy that appeared in a story by Bundy's wife.

"My husband is innocent," Mary Bundy pleaded in the article. "Maybe you know something that will help. Please! Don't let them kill my husband." Mrs. Bundy went on to relate details of the case and how many people, "including the widow of the man he is accused of murdering," believed Bundy had been framed by McCoy. She said the market manager's widow, Grace Amodio, had contributed $10 to the fund set up by friends to finance an effort to obtain a new trial for her husband. "If you saw McCoy (alone) in Uniontown on the night of last November 23, or if you saw Dale Bundy in Canton that night, please come forward," Mrs. Bundy pleaded.

Brajnovic, of course, had seen neither in faraway Ohio that night. But she did recognize McCoy as the man whose strange comments to her several months earlier had bothered her ever since. McCoy had bought a bottle of vodka, then started up a conversation.

When Brajnovic asked him if he was visiting friends in the area, McCoy replied, "No, I don't have a friend anymore. I did have one friend, but he turned against me." When she suggested McCoy could make new friends, he said, "It's too late for that. I already killed four people and I'm going to kill another one, but this one will be legal." When Brajnovic said there was no such thing as a legal murder, McCoy grinned and responded, "There will be. I'm going to have the law do it for me."

Suddenly, Brajnovic understood what McCoy had meant. She quickly contacted Mrs. Bundy, and the appeals court stayed Bundy's execution pending hearing for a new trial based on the new evidence. At the second trial, several more witnesses testified that Bundy had been in Canton when the murders occurred, and Brajnovic related her conversation with McCoy. The jury took only one ballot to acquit Bundy, all thanks to a chance reading of a magazine story about his case by a woman several hundred miles away.[37]

Perhaps the most-publicized recent case of false testimony leading to a conviction was that of Gary Dotson of Chicago. In 1985, Dotson was just another obscure inmate serving time for a 1977 rape he had always maintained he hadn't committed, when his remorseful accuser, Cathleen Crowell Webb, made national headlines by publicly declaring not only that Dotson was innocent, but that no rape had even occurred. Webb said she had made up the whole story out of fear that she might be pregnant by her boyfriend, which she knew would infuriate her strict foster parents. She said that when police arrested Dotson, who by chance resembled the fictional assailant she had described, she didn't have the courage to change her story.

A born-again Baptist and the mother of three children, Webb said "obedience to God" prompted her to come forward and recant her accusation. Instead of being praised for her courage, Webb's recantation was met with ridicule in the media and in legal circles. One of the few exceptions was a lengthy interview with Charles P. McDowell, chief of the U.S. Air Force's Special Studies Division of the Directorate of Investigative Analysis in the Office of Special Investigations. In the interview, which was published in the respected *Chicago Lawyer*,

McDowell said a comparison of details of Webb's 1979 testimony with a model he had developed to help investigators recognize false allegations indicated that Webb was now telling the truth. The single most important indication that Webb had originally given false testimony, McDowell said, was the existence of scratches on her abdomen that seemed to form letters or words. He said such markings were seen in several of the 212 *false* rape accusations the Air Force had studied, but in *none* of the 460 proven cases of rape examined. McDowell also said the reason Webb had given for making the accusation was one of the two most common uncovered by the research—a way to explain a problem, such as pregnancy, venereal disease, or evidence of promiscuity. The other most common motive was revenge.

The best Dotson could get from Webb's dramatic and unexpected admission, however, was a commutation of the rest of his sentence by a dubious Governor James R. Thompson. The grandstanding governor was hardly doing Dotson that big a favor, though. A spokesperson for the Illinois Department of Corrections said that among the 124 convicted Cook County rapists released in 1983, the average time served was four-and-a-half years. Dotson had already served six years.

The next four years were tough ones for Dotson, who was ill-prepared to handle his sudden fame and freedom, as well as the fact that in the eyes of the law he was still presumed guilty. Dotson battled an alcohol problem; he married, fathered a child, and was quickly separated from his wife; and he was arrested several times for traffic violations and once after a domestic disturbance. Thompson gave him a "last chance" release in 1987, but Dotson soon landed back in jail for violating parole. "I was living a nightmare I couldn't escape," he explained later. "I got sick and tired of trying to prove I was innocent, so I crawled into a shell, and then I didn't know how to get out of it."

Dotson was finally given a chance to break through that shell in August 1989, when he heard Cook County Judge Thomas R. Fitzgerald announce at a hearing on the rape charge: "You, sir, are discharged." Dotson had finally been cleared after attorney Thomas Breen, convinced Dotson was being abused by the system, petitioned the court to release Webb's semen-stained underwear for DNA analysis, which had not been perfected by the time of the original investigation. The test results eliminated Dotson and found the semen to be compatible with that of Webb's old boyfriend. But Governor Thompson, who had made his original claim to fame as a law-and-order U.S. attorney, still stubbornly refused to clear Dotson with a pardon. Breen then went back to court, and Judge Fitzgerald ruled the DNA test admissible and overturned Dotson's conviction. As Dotson's brother and sisters hugged him and jokingly pinched his arm to convince him he wasn't dreaming, an obviously relieved Dotson sighed, "It's over. It's really over."

In Harrisville, New Hampshire, Webb also expressed relief. "It came twelve years too late and not a moment too soon," she said. "Every time I looked at my [now four] children, I thought of the suffering I caused the Dotson family."

As for Dotson, he announced that he hoped to build on his bitter experience. He said he planned to attend college and pursue a career in counseling. "I've been thorough enough to relate to a lot of problems," he said.[38]

Counseling victims of false rape accusations could be a full-time job in itself. According to the comprehensive Air Force study conducted by McDowell, a minimum of 20 percent of rape accusations are false. The Dotson case, in fact, inspired several other women to recant their accusations in 1985.

One of them, a Maryland woman who recanted a rape accusation against a former boyfriend in a case that sent him to prison for thirteen-and-a-half months, was fined $150 and ordered to help rape victims for one thousand hours. "I want you exposed to the real trauma of someone who has been exposed to a rape experience," said Judge Robert H. Heller Jr. of Anne Arundel County Circuit Court. Kathryn Hargis Tucci had been seventeen when she exacted revenge against her former boyfriend, Mark F. Bowles, for ending their relationship. When informed of Tucci's sentence, the since-released Bowles said: "That's pretty wild. I've chalked it up to experience. It has been a lesson to me to pick my friends wisely."

A Nebraska judge came up with a novel sentence for phony rape accusations when he sentenced a woman in 1990 to apologize in radio and newspaper ads to a man she had falsely accused of rape. Dawson County Judge John Murphy not only sentenced Elizabeth Irene Richardson to 180 days in jail and placed her on two years' probation for perjury, he also ordered Richardson to apologize to Garry Nitch in half-page ads in every newspaper and in a prime-time spot on each radio station in the central Nebraska county of twenty-two thousand people. The estimated cost of the order was $1,000. Richardson had accused Nitch of raping her in September 1988, and he was arrested and charged with sexual assault. After the case was later dropped because of lack of evidence, Richardson told friends the rape charge was a hoax designed to get the attention of her husband, a truck driver who was often away from home. She originally appealed her perjury conviction, but later withdrew the appeal when she decided the state supreme court might give her a longer jail sentence if it ruled in favor of her objection to the paid apologies.

But Nitch said it would take more than the ads to right the wrong done to him. "You can't change a wrong to a right, and I think the sentence could have been stiffer," he said. "I lost a job. I had to get a lawyer. The kids at school were saying to my kids, 'Your dad's a rapist.' "

Michael Chandler of Houston could certainly empathize with Nitch. He was released from jail in 1986 after serving ten months of an eight-year sentence for an alleged rape of a 10-year-old girl who admitted she had lied to distract her mother from her report card, of all things. Chandler, the mother's boyfriend, said he remembered watching a television program about sexual abuse of children with the girl, and believed it might have given her the idea to accuse him.

Chandler was the victim not just of a false accusation, but of a wave of child-abuse hysteria that swept the nation in the mid-1980s, largely in response to the sensational but later greatly discredited allegations made in two cases: the California McMartin Preschool case, in which seven teachers were charged with molesting forty-one children, and a Jordan, Minnesota, witch hunt in which twenty-four adult members of an alleged "sex ring" in the tiny town were charged with molesting forty children.

Not one conviction came out of any of the two cases' charges by the time the lengthy litigation had ended in 1990. Yet the original accusations, which were greatly magnified by frenzied press coverage, prompted a huge upsurge of similar accusations across the country. No one was immune: Doctors, lawyers, priests, ministers, rabbis, police officers, fathers, mothers, brothers, sisters, close and distant relatives, neighbors, and a host of others found themselves suddenly being accused of sexual abuse, and the burden was on them to prove their innocence rather than for the state to prove their guilt. But that was okay with Cynthia C. Tower, a professor of behavioral sciences at Fitchburg State College in Massachusetts, who wrote a book on child abuse for the National Education Association. "I'd rather be apologizing to the falsely accused and helping him get a fair hearing than to ignore one child in need of help," she said in 1984. If she kept her word, though, she'd be doing a lot of apologizing. Because the number of child-sexual-abuse accusations tripled between 1980 and 1984, then soared even higher from there. Child-protection authorities labeled 80 percent of those reports "unfounded," which was double the rate five years earlier.

Among the 1.3 million reported sex-abuse cases in 1984 were cases involving a single kiss on the lips, changing a diaper, repairing teeth, a doctor doing a physical examination, and another doctor who took a verbal sexual history on a 12-year-old girl with acute abdominal pain.[39]

What this all adds up to is a lot of false accusations—and false convictions. Unfortunately, such tragedies are rarely exposed unless the accuser recants, as an 18-year-old Washington, Pennsylvania, woman did in 1985. The contrite teenager testified that she had lied when she accused her mother's common-law husband of sexual abuse in 1981, when she was thirteen. Based on her testimony, William Davis had been convicted and imprisoned. During a court hearing on a motion for a new trial in 1985, however, Ronda Baker recanted her accusation.

"He hit on my mother. I fabricated the story because I wanted him to stop," Baker said.

Davis's attorney said Baker had "wanted to get him out of the house. . . . She didn't want him to go to jail," and didn't know what to do when he did.[40]

Regardless of whether such false sex-abuse accusations are treated in criminal or civil court, and regardless of whether they are proved or disproved, the results are devastating. As Ralph Underwager and Hollida Wakefield of the Institute of Psychological Therapies in Minnesota wrote in *Playboy* at the time the hysteria was at its height:

> We have spent years dealing with sexual abuse and are aware that abuse can and does occur—far too often. But any American can be accused by anyone of sexually abusing a child. The accusation is believed because "children never lie about sexual abuse." Until recently, we were the only ones in our area willing to say that it is not true that children never lie. Whatever the situation, the person falsely accused is destroyed.
>
> Children can be put in foster homes; parents can have their visitation rights stopped or criminal charges filed against them. If you're accused, friends and neighbors believe you're guilty. You may lose your job. You may not see your children for months or even years. You may bankrupt yourself with legal fees. You can be sentenced to a long prison term. Even if you are finally acquitted of criminal charges, you may still have to fight in family court to see your children.
>
> Fathers in custody suits involving young children are particularly vulnerable. If your wife accuses you of sexually abusing your child, she may immediately get custody. You may be prevented from seeing your children until the matter is "resolved" in family court. In the meantime, you continue to pay child support whether or not you have contact with your children. Even if you are cleared, your relationship with your child is permanently damaged.
>
> The exploding number of allegations and the procedures followed by child-protection teams, police, and prosecutors match the Salem witch hunts and the McCarthy anti-Communist hearings. It is becoming clear that questionable tactics by mental-health professionals, police, and prosecutors are common. Victims of this modern-day witch hunt can be subjected to an inadequate or nonexistent investigation, brainwashing of their children by investigators and therapists, cover-ups and conspiracies by law-enforcement officials, and family courts that destroy families rather than protect them.

The case of a well-regarded, hard-working pediatrician who committed suicide in 1984 shows just how devastating such false accusations can be. The doctor had examined a 13-year-old girl for unexplained numbness in the genital area. No nurse or other adult was present. The girl charged that the exam was sex abuse. Three police officers then showed up in the doctor's crowded office with a search warrant to go through his files. He and his employees were questioned and requestioned. The embarrassed doctor could not bring himself to tell his family. He left a message that he was leaving town on an emergency, and was found dead of an overdose in a motel the next day. The resulting media coverage was so sensational that one newspaper later apologized for its treatment of the story.

In a similar case, a young family doctor in California was indicted for the sexual abuse of seventeen girls because he routinely listened to the chest and checked for inguinal hernia in all the girls during sports physicals. His wife, a nurse, was present during the exams, but he was charged anyway. The girls later admitted they had lied to gain attention.[41]

Religious professionals have become highly vulnerable to false accusations, partly as a result of a number of well-publicized cases of verified abuse. Rabbi Melvin Teitelbaum of the Ahavath Israel Congregation in Hollywood, California, for instance, became one of them when he was charged in 1984 with abusing a 13-year-old boy with a history of emotional illness. The charges were later dismissed at the request of the district attorney when the boy greatly altered his story after being confronted with proof that the rabbi was elsewhere at the time of the alleged incident.

The prosecutor said the change in the boy's story was "devastating" to his credibility.[42]

Day-care workers also became fair game, of course, after the McMartin case generated so much publicity. One such victim was Robert Reeder Jr. of London, Ohio, who was charged with four counts of gross sexual imposition involving children at a day-care center where he worked part-time. Shortly after the investigation of Reeder began, children's services workers appeared at his home demanding to question

Reeder's own children privately. When he and his wife refused them entrance, they returned with a court order and removed the children from the home.

Reeder was eventually acquitted of all the charges against him, and the judge who heard the case issued a scathing critique of the way the investigation had been conducted—especially the way the alleged victims were asked leading questions. Yet it took the Reeders another *ten months* to get their children back from the children's services agency, even though it was never even alleged that the children had been abused.

The most common source of false child-abuse accusations is one parent, usually the mother, making them against the other. The reasons are obvious: It is what Phoenix attorney Robert Hirschfield, who specializes in family law, calls "the nuclear weapon of domestic relations. When all else fails, drop the bomb."

And drop it they do. One of its victims was Ernest Coates, a freelance writer and former Associated Press foreign correspondent who was acquitted of aggravated sexual assault on his two children in a case that had been brought by his ex-wife. Despite the acquittal, Coates was introduced at the 1986 convention of the National Congress for Men as a man who "sees his children only in his dreams." In his highly emotional speech, the Australian-born Coates claimed he was still being kept from his children by a coalition of state-paid psychologists, young lawyers on the make, and a troubled wife. It was a tale with which many in the audience said they could identify. And few were optimistic that the problem would change anytime soon because, as one of them put it, "men always come off on the short end of sympathy."[43]

Nathaniel Carter of New York City discovered that to be the case even in murder trials. Carter was convicted of murder on the strength of the testimony of his ex-wife, who told how she had been forced to watch helplessly as Carter attacked and killed her foster mother with a knife on September 15, 1981. Two years later, when police told the woman they were reopening the case because of new evidence favorable to Carter, she mistakenly thought they correctly suspected her of the crime and, to their surprise, confessed. Despite her admission, which led to the freeing of Carter, Delissa Durham was not charged with the crime because authorities had promised her immunity from prosecution for the murder when she originally testified before the grand jury. She was also granted immunity from perjury charges in exchange for her testimony clearing Carter. The only thing she got from the state for her crimes was a $20 bus fare home to Connecticut.[44]

Frame-up artists come in all ages, too. On one extreme is the 1979 conviction of Charles Daniels for sexually assaulting and attempting to kill a 2-year-old boy in Queens, New York. Daniels's chief accuser was a 10-year-old boy who identified Daniels as the person who allegedly assaulted the toddler and threw him off a rooftop on September 27, 1978. In 1985, the Legal Aid Society discovered new evidence indicating that it was the 10-year-old boy, not Daniels, who had committed the crime. After Daniels's release, New York City agreed to pay him $600,000 because of the harassment, beatings, burns, death threats, and so much other mistreatment he received in prison because he was an alleged child molester; things were so bad for him in jail that he was sometimes kept in solitary confinement for his own protection. "Going through what I did is almost as bad as being executed for a crime you didn't commit," Daniels said.[45]

At the other extreme was wheezing, toothless, William "Pop" Campbell, who admitted before he died of natural causes in 1983 that he had framed fellow Georgia inmate Henry Drake for a 1975 murder Campbell had actually committed because he thought Drake had turned him in for another crime.[46]

Just how easy it is to frame someone for a crime they didn't commit, regardless of age or location, became readily apparent in 1989, when jailhouse informer Leslie White showed Los Angeles County prosecutors how—by using a jail telephone and pretending to be a bail bondsman, prosecutor, or police detective—he could gather enough information about a murder case to convince authorities that a defendant he had never even met had confessed to him while in prison. White also admitted he had committed perjury in more than one case and hinted that some men may be on death row because of informers' testimony. In return for such testimony, White said, informers receive prison furloughs, parole recommendations, reductions in bail, payments from a witness fund, and other questionable forms of compensation.

In reaction to White's disclosures, the California Attorneys for Criminal Justice demanded appointment of a special prosecutor to investigate the use of payments to jailhouse informers as possible malfeasance. "They shouldn't be using these people, because they know they're lying," said Leslie Abramson, the group's president. "The real tragedy is that they only use these guys in cases where the evidence is weak. So they are increasing the risk of convicting the innocent."[47]

But, as we shall see, prosecutors are not beyond doing almost anything to obtain a conviction. And the same can be said for police officers. "What would surprise and even shock most jury members is the extent to which police officers lie on the stand to reinforce the prosecution and not jeopardize their own standing within their own particular law-enforcement community," says the Reverend James McCloskey. "The words of one twenty-five-year veteran senior officer on a northern New Jersey police force still ring in my ears: 'They [the defense] lie, so we [police officers] lie. I don't know one of my fellow officers who hasn't lied under oath.' "[48]

Inexpert Experts

The latest entrants in the courts' witness parade are "expert witnesses," who used to be a rarity but now are a near-necessity. A 1923 federal court decision, *Frye* v. *United States*, helped to limit the number of experts who testify by banning those who are "not generally accepted by the scientific community." But that was before anyone who wanted to call themselves a scientist could get away with it. Now we have self-described experts for everything under the sun, and they are all willing to testify—for a handsome fee, of course. And they have become such an important part of the legal process that a lawyer can be sued for not calling one.

Prosecutors have a distinct advantage in the expert game, however, because they have a stable full of government experts they can call upon and a generous budget to pay those on the outside as needed to present their case. Defense attorneys have no such luxury. Unless their client has considerable resources, their use of experts is limited, if it exists at all.

But the demand is big enough that ads for "litigation support" by professional experts are now an important part of most legal journals. And for the attorney who doesn't have time to find the right expert personally, there are expert-witness clearinghouses, one of which claims to have pool of 15,000 experts in 4,500 specialties.

As the "litigation support" business grows and becomes more competitive, it no longer means government experts are necessarily the best, even though they are usually given credibility by juries because they are not viewed as "hired guns" even when they are. Yet, in the case of police-lab technicians and other government employees, as we have seen, they quite often are no more credible and no more competent. And some politically connected outside experts are called upon so often to take the government's side that their credibility soon becomes highly questionable.

That certainly has been the case with James P. "Dr. Death" Grigson, the psychiatrist who played such a crucial and controversial role in obtaining the death sentence for Randall Dale Adams and a number of other Texas defendants. Grigson's role in death-sentence cases has not only led to the questioning of his professional ethics by the American Psychiatric Association but also to three adverse decisions by the U.S. Supreme Court.

In 1981, the court ruled unanimously in Estelle v. Smith that a psychiatrist like Grigson must tell a defendant in a capital case that the outcome of an examination can be used against him or her. Two years later, in Barefoot v. Estelle, the court ruled that Grigson's dubious assertion that he could predict the behavior of a patient without talking with the patient was admissible at trial. And in 1988, in Satterwhite v. Texas, the court expanded on the Smith ruling by saying that Grigson's testimony, based on an examination that took place without the knowledge of the defendant's attorney, nullified any subsequent death sentence.

Grigson's insistence that he can predict criminal behavior is what garners him the most criticism. Among his most vocal opponents is Henry Schwarzschild, director of the American Civil Liberties Union's Capital Punishment Project. "It is universally agreed among reasonably enlightened people that he really is a menace and ought to be censured," Schwarzschild said.

The American Psychiatric Association has also stated on several occasions that as far as empirical evidence is concerned, psychiatrists have not shown the ability to predict violent behavior over the long term. "Studies show that in prediction studies, only a minority of people predicted to be dangerous turn out to commit violent acts," said Paul S. Appelbaum, chairman of the association's Judicial Action Committee.[49]

Yet Grigson remains popular with Texas prosecutors because he gets results. "Bottom line," one district attorney said, "he's good at what he does."[50] Whether he's accurate doesn't seem to matter.

The same goes for Louise Robbins, a professor of anthropology at the University of North Carolina/Greensboro, who became a highly popular expert on footprints. Robbins became a favorite of the nation's prosecutors in the early 1980s despite her $1,000-a-day charge for testimony. Newspapers began to describe Robbins as a female "Quincy" when she helped to win the convictions of more than twenty people with her impressive, authoritative testimony, before illness took her off the courtroom syndicate.

The only problem was that Robbins's testimony hardly enjoyed the respect of her peers. In early 1987, a national panel of 135 anthropologists and attorneys concluded that Robbins's vaunted shoeprint-identification analysis simply "doesn't work" because of its impreciseness. William Bodziak of the FBI Crime Lab was even more direct. He called it "totally ridiculous." And Melvin B. Lewis, professor of law at the John Marshall Law School in Cleveland, described it as "snake oil."[51] One can only guess what those convicted on the basis of her testimony now call it.

Although most expert witnesses are both qualified and honest, many are willing to jump through any logical hoops necessary to please their employer.

In his book *Inside the Crime Lab,* Jay Cameron Hall contends that some experts stray into territory "so unfamiliar that his testimony becomes sheer malpractice." He continues:

> Few criminalists would consider testifying that a single hair can be so personalized that it positively identifies a particular individual. Yet for years, one notorious individual testified as the moon struck him, sending possibly innocent people to jail on such incredible evidence as a single human hair. . . . Until his recent death this man testified, often completely on the wrong side of the facts, for over three decades. Surely he should have been disqualified, even jailed for perjury, yet one of his last acts in a long and dishonorable career was to identify the alleged handwriting of Howard Hughes in the power struggle over control of the elusive billionaire's enormous Nevada holdings.[52]

Overeagerness also seems to have been involved in the case of Gary Dotson, too. As it turned out, the police expert who testified that the stains on Cathleen Crowell Webb's panties matched Dotson's blood type told only half the story. What he did not say—and what turned out to be the case—was that Webb's own vaginal discharges could have caused the stains that implicated Dotson, because she and Dotson had the same blood type. When the expert was asked about why he hadn't pointed that out during his testimony, he replied: "I guess I wasn't asked."

Sorry, Gary.

Notes

1. "Race and Blind Justice Behind Mixup in Court," *New York Times,* November 3, 1985, p. 26.

2. Associated Press, September 3, 1982.

3. "Convicting the Innocent," by D. E. J. McNamara, *Crime & Delinquency,* vol. 15, 1969, p. 60.

4. *U.S. News & World Report*, p. 46.

5. Ibid., p. 45.

6. *Guilty Until Proved Innocent: Wrongful Conviction and Public Policy*, p. 14.

7. "Witness Identifies Reporter as Killer, Then Recants," *Editor & Publisher*, August 11, 1990, p. 11.

8. *The Innocents*, p. 101.

9. *U.S. News & World Report*, p. 46.

10. *Guilty Until Proved Innocent: Wrongful Conviction and Public Policy*, pp. 9–10.

11. E. F. Loftus, *Eyewitness Testimony* (Cambridge, Mass.: Harvard University Press, 1979), p. 83.

12. *U.S. News & World Report*, p. 46.

13. "Never Forget a Face?" *Hippocrates*, November/December 1988.

14. Ruth Brandon and Christie Davies, *Wrongful Imprisonment* (London: Archon Books, 1973), p. 43.

15. "Priest Sues to Clear Name, Battle Injustice," *USA Today*, March 12, 1984, p. 2.

16. Associated Press, July 8, 1985.

17. *Stanford Law Review*, p. 91.

18. Ibid.

19. Ibid., p. 93.

20. Erle Stanley Gardner, *The Court of Last Resort* (New York: William Sloane Associates, 1952), pp. 232–245.

21. *Stanford Law Review*, p. 93.

22. "Man Acquitted of Murder—After 5 Trials and 7 Years," *Los Angeles Times*, November 11, 1986, p. 3.

23. "1970 Murder Conviction Voided; Judges Criticize Queens Officials," *New York Times*, December 23, 1978, p. 1.

24. In general, see *Columbus Dispatch*, September 22, 1982, p. 1; September 23, 1982, pp. 1 and B6; and September 24, 1982, p. B4.

25. *Cincinnati Post*, July 20, 1990, p. 1. Also, Associated Press, August 5, 1990.

26. "Man Wrongly Convicted of Murder Wins Freedom," *Jet*, March 26, 1981, p. 30.

27. *Stanford Law Review*, p. 149.

28. "Leaster Wins Freedom As Retrial Bid Is Dropped," *Boston Globe*, December 27, 1986, p. 1.

29. Associated Press, March 29, 1984.

30. *Stanford Law Review*, p. 122.

31. Ibid., p. 143.

32. "26 Months In a Prison, Wrongly," *New York Times*, December 16, 1987, p. B1.

33. "Tip Leads to Actual Killer, Freedom for Innocent Man," *Washington Post*, August 31, 1979, p. C2.

34. John Frasca, *The Mulberry Tree* (Englewood Cliffs, N.J.: Prentice-Hall, 1968).

35. "Two Reporters Convince the Governor that Texas Jailed An Innocent Man," *People Weekly*, September 8, 1986, pp. 53–54.

36. "After 18 Months of Mistaken Identity, Suspect Is Freed," *New York Times*, September 12, 1986, p. B1.

37. *The Innocents*, pp. 130–136. Also, *Columbus Dispatch*, October 6, 1957, p. 20A, and June 20, 1958, p. 16A.

38. See generally, Cathleen Crowell Webb and Marie Chapian, *Forgive Me* (Old Tappan, N.J.: Fleming H. Revell Co., 1985). Also, "Jailed For A Rape That Never Happened, Gary Dotson Has His Name Cleared At Last," *People Weekly*, August 28, 1989, p. 80.

39. "When Sex Abuse Is Falsely Charged," *Medical Aspects of Human Sexuality*, July, 1985, pp. 116–124.

40. Associated Press, April 26, 1985.

41. Ibid.

42. "Rabbi Sues Over False Charges of Molestation," *Los Angeles Times*, May 24, 1985, p. 27 I.

43. "Men Have Rights Too," *Time*, November 24, 1986, p. 87.

44. See generally, *New York Times*, March 26, 1984, p. B2; March 16, 1984, p. B1; and March 15, 1984, p. B1.

45. Associated Press, January 18, 1985.

46. "Phony Story Put Man on Death Row for 9 Years," *Los Angeles Times* (wire service version), December 23, 1988.

47. "Use of Jailhouse Informers Reviewed in Los Angeles," *New York Times*, January 3, 1989, p. A14.

48. "Convicting the Innocent," *Voice for the Defense*, December 1989, p. 21.

49. "Expert Witness Is Unfazed by 'Dr. Death' Label," *New York Times*, June 10, 1988, p. B9.

50. Ibid.

51. "From the People Who Brought You the Twinkie Defense," *Washington Monthly*, June 1987, pp. 33–34.

52. *Inside the Crime Lab*, pp. 245–246.

6

The Prosecutor as Persecutor

The prosecutor has more control over life, liberty and reputation than any other person in America.
　　　　—Former U.S. Attorney General Robert H. Jackson

"Free at last, free at last. Thank God almighty, I'm free at last!" James Richardson tearfully shouted words borrowed from Martin Luther King Jr. on April 26, 1989, as he joined ten other people in Florida alone who were released in the previous decade because of their innocence or serious trial errors after being convicted and sentenced to die in the electric chair. In Richardson's case, freedom came after he suffered through twenty-one brutal years behind bars for the poisoning deaths of his seven children.[1]

On the previous day, a judge had ruled what Richardson and his attorneys had contended all along: that the poor, black, former orange-picker's 1968 trial on a charge of murder had been tainted by misconduct by the prosecutor and by perjured testimony.

"Tainted" was really too nice of a word to describe what prosecutors in the small southwestern Florida town of Arcadia had done to obtain Richardson's conviction and death sentence, which at one point brought him so close to execution that his body was shaved and his coffin built before his sentence was commuted to life. Besmirched, contaminated, *poisoned*—yes, that is the right the word: The prosecutors had poisoned the legal process to prove he had poisoned his own children, even though ample evidence existed that the real murderer was the disturbed baby sitter who had actually fed them the contaminated food that tragic day. But prosecutors chose to ignore that evidence, apparently because of the woman's close friendship with DeSoto County Sheriff Frank Cline. They convicted Richardson in a strange case where none of the three key witnesses were called out of fear of what they would say, and perjured testimony by others was offered in their stead.

The prosecution's carefully contrived ploy finally collapsed, however, when crusading attorney and author Mark Lane, whose 1971 book *Arcadia* had claimed Richardson was framed, obtained from an unidentified source a file full of evidence that had been suppressed during the trial. Lane said documents in the file showed "absolute proof of criminal conduct" by the prosecutors and Sheriff Cline, and refuted claims that Richardson had killed the children to collect on an insurance policy, because no such policy existed. The file also showed that Richardson had *not* confessed to a fellow inmate who had later testified that he had. Finally, Lane said, the file showed that the murderer was indeed the baby-sitter, and that she had actually confessed to the crime on several occasions in conversations with acquaintances, but that prosecutors chose to suppress the evidence because they had already committed themselves too heavily and too publicly at that point to close the case against Richardson.

At 8:26 P.M. on June 17, 1986, about a hundred miles south of where Richardson languished in prison, 18-year-old Todd Neely, his mother, Edith, and her husband-to-be, Lewis Crosley—an engaging man whose family had once owned the Cincinnati Reds—ordered before-dinner drinks at a Jensen Beach, Florida, restaurant.[2] According to all three, they had a friendly dinner together and left, as verified by the time-stamped receipt, at 9:30 for the 11.3-mile drive home.

In the middle of their dinner, at 9:12 P.M., a woman from their Port Salerno apartment complex called 911 to report that a teenage boy had forced his way into her home about five minutes earlier, threatened to rape her, and stabbed her during a struggle. The youth then fled. The woman later described her assailant as a boy with braces whose age was "sixteen, max."

As police canvassed the neighborhood asking if anyone knew of a teenager with braces, one woman said she knew of only one teen, and pointed to his red Volkswagen in the apartment complex's parking lot. A license check identified the car as that of Todd Neely. Thus began the nightmare of a young man with a seemingly perfect alibi who had no braces and had never been in serious trouble.

The victim later identified Neely as her assailant after looking at a photo of him taken from a three-year-old high-school yearbook. It seemed immaterial that Neely had a time-stamped receipt to show he was at a restaurant 11.3 miles away at the time of the crime and that he didn't wear braces. Police and the young assistant prosecutor handling the case were sure they had their man. When other neighbors provided information about another, younger boy in the neighborhood who wore braces and had a criminal record, the reports were ignored and kept from the defense.

On January 15, 1987, the trial judge said the case was so interesting that " '60 Minutes' could do a thing on it." Then, because of the victim's positive identification, the judge found a shocked Neely guilty of attempted murder and sentenced him to fifteen years in prison in a case conservative syndicated columnist James J. Kilpatrick would later call "a wretched story of bungled police work, suppressed evidence, and overzealous prosecutors."

The day after the conviction, the Neelys and Crosley began receiving calls from outraged neighbors who said they had told police about another boy who lived in the neighborhood who not only wore braces but closely resembled the composite drawing they had been shown by police. They later were told the youth had even bragged about committing the crime for which Todd Neely spent ninety-two days in jail before he was released pending disposition of his appeal.

It was not until June 27, 1990, that the appeals court threw out Neely's "seriously flawed" conviction and ordered a new trial. In doing so, the three-judge panel sided with a retired judge who had ruled in 1989 in a special hearing that prosecutors withheld crucial evidence leading to the other suspect in the attack.

"Had the newly discovered evidence been presented to the court in the original trial," the judge wrote, "such evidence would have conclusively prevented the entry of a judgment of guilt." After the appeals court's stinging ruling, however, the county prosecutor at first still insisted that Neely was guilty and that he would prove it in a new trial. Several days later, however, he mysteriously changed his tune. He announced that he had become convinced that Neely was innocent and said the charges against him would be dropped. So ended an ordeal that had cost young Neely four years of his life and his parents more than $281,000 in legal expenses. "I can't forgive the prosecutors for what they did and how they did it, but I'm thankful they at least have admitted that a mistake was made," a relieved Edith Crosley told me in a telephone interview after the good news had sunk in. But she added that she remained appalled at just how far a misguided prosecutor could and would go just to win a case. She really shouldn't have been, though.

Politics, Power, and the Prosecutor

Whether they are called prosecutors, district attorneys, or state's attorneys, prosecuting attorneys are what make the American system of justice work—or not work. According to a study by the Illinois Association for Criminal Justice, prosecutors are 70 percent responsible for enforcing the law, the police 20 percent, and the judges 10 percent.

Legal scholar Raymond Moley's *Politics and Criminal Prosecution,* first published in 1929, explains the reason for such figures: "The potentialities of the office are limited by scarcely anything except the skill, the intelligence, and the legal and political capacity of the incumbent."

Protection from civil liability for their official acts, Moley says, encourages prosecutors to partake of the kinds of abuses seen repeatedly across the nation. He writes:

> A noteworthy study of the prosecuting attorney in action could be made from an examination of the criminal appeals of almost any of the states. Here in the allegations of the defeated counsel is set forth as illuminating an account of legal malpractice as has ever been pictured.

It is true that from such a source one is not likely to find the shades of meaning and the surrounding circumstances which temper the severity of the picture. But when every factor favorable to the prosecuting attorney is considered, the record is a sorry one. Every state has its share of examples of sharp practices, of disobedience of the court, extravagant and abusive language, the use of forged testimony, almost unbelievable ignorance of the law, and the demagogic appeals to the mob spirit.[3]

There are two major causes for such abuses. One is the adversary system of American courts. It turns the trial into a competitive game that must be won at all costs, rather than a sincere search for truth. As a result, prosecutors get so caught up in outmaneuvering the opponent that they frequently cross the line into withholding or fabricating evidence, allowing perjured testimony, and making exaggerated attacks on the defendant. The second cause is the generally elective nature of the office. To get re-elected, or elected to a higher office, prosecutors feel compelled to maintain a high ratio of convictions to indictments.

This is particularly true because, as Moley sadly notes, "It is well known that except in unusual instances the grand jury is a rubber stamp for the prosecuting attorney." Because everyone knows the case is the prosecutor's from the beginning, the prosecutor feels greater pressure to obtain a conviction.

The belief in obtaining convictions at all costs is rather ironic when you consider that one of the most famous prosecutors of the century based much of his celebrity on cases he "lost" rather than "won." The reputation of Homer Cummings, who would later serve as U.S. attorney general from 1933 to 1939, had its origin in a case he handled in 1924 as a prosecuting attorney in Bridgeport, Connecticut. Cummings was presented by police with the murder of a Roman Catholic priest; the case had outraged the community, and the evidence against defendant Harold Israel had seemed overwhelming. Israel already had confessed to the murder and a ballistics expert would testify at the trial that Israel's gun was the murder weapon. But the more Cummings dug into the case, the less he liked it. By the day of the trial, in fact,

Cummings was convinced that Israel's confession had been coerced and that the witnesses against him were either mistaken or lying—all of which he demonstrated during the trial. "Without question," one analyst observed later, "Israel would have been hanged if it had not been for the conscientiousness of the Connecticut prosecutor."

Rather than hurt his reputation, Cummings's belief that a prosecutor's job is to protect the innocent as well as convict the guilty made him nationally famous and undoubtedly helped lead to his appointment as attorney general. Even in that position, Cummings continued to live up to his reputation. When he received information that one of his assistants had wrongfully convicted two Washington college students of setting fire to a fraternity house, Cummings personally appeared in court to accept responsibility for the error and ask that the convictions be set aside. Aided by the new evidence that had caused Cummings to admit the mistake, the two defendants were acquitted at their second trial.[4]

But, despite his success, Cummings would probably be even more of an oddity today than he was then.

Brian Forst, former director of research at the private Institute for Law and Social Research and at the Police Foundation, contended in an article in the *Washington Post* in August 1990 that prosecutors have more opportunities built into the system to encourage abusive practices than ever before, and that many don't hesitate to take advantage of them. Arguing for stricter guidelines on how cases are handled, Forst wrote:

> Prosecutors are sworn to bring to justice those who violate the law. Where the law is less than explicit, prosecutors are left to exercise discretion to ensure that cases are processed justly and effectively. The less explicit the law, the greater the discretion; the greater the discretion, the greater the opportunity for uneven treatment of cases—that is, for disposition in a manner driven by the individual prosecutor. Inevitably, then, the attorneys in some 8,000 state and local prosecution agencies and 93 federal offices weigh not only legal considerations, but practical and political ones as well, in deciding the fate of more than 12 million persons arrested each year.

A mob mills around the body of Leo Frank. In 1913 Frank had been wrongfully convicted of murdering a 13-year-old girl. When the governor, who doubted Frank's guilt, commuted his death sentence, anti-Semitic citizens abducted Frank from prison and lynched him. In 1986 the Georgia Board of Pardons finally granted Frank a "posthumous pardon." *(Photo courtesy of the American Jewish Archives.)*

Photo from the set of the film *The Thin Blue Line*, directed by Errol Morris. This award-winning documentary chronicled the staggeringly inept investigation that led to the wrongful conviction of Randall Dale Adams for the murder of a Texas police officer. Pressure generated by public response to the film forced Dallas prosecutors to re-open the case. Adams was later cleared of charges—after spending twelve years in prison and some time on death row. *(Photo by Mark Lipson.)*

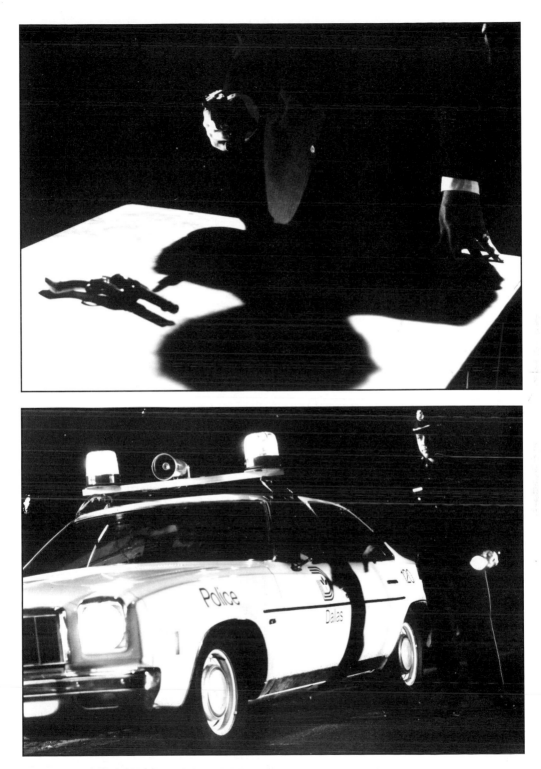

Stills from *The Thin Blue Line*. Randall Adams claims that Detective Gus Rose aimed his revolver at him during interrogation. Gus Rose states that he had a "friendly conversation" with the accused. *(Photos by Mark Lipson.)*

David Harris *(above)* bragged to friends that he killed a cop in Dallas. He later changed his story, accusing Randall Adams, a hitchhiker he had picked up earlier that day. *(Photo by David Hohmann.)* Randall Dale Adams *(below)* is greeted by his mother, Mildred, in Columbus, Ohio, after his release from prison. *(Photo courtesy of the* Columbus Dispatch.*)*

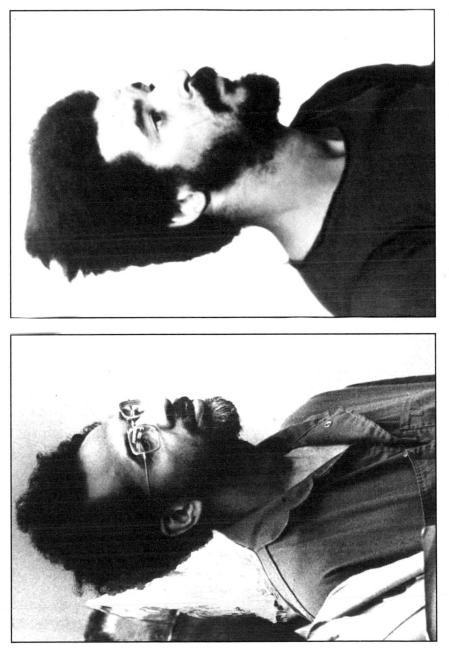

A case of mistaken identification. William Bernard Jackscn (*right*) spent five years in prison after being convicted, on the basis of eyewitness testimony, of raping two women who were in fact raped by Dr. Edward F. Jackson (*left*). In an interview after his first year of freedom, Wiliam Bernard Jackson said his conviction followed him around like a cloud. "Nobody's going to hire a jailbird," he said.

Lenell Geter walks out of court after being granted a new trial. Geter's "suspicious" habit of spending his lunch hour reading books and feeding the ducks at a local park got him into a lot of trouble in the mostly white town of Greenville, Texas. *(Photo by Bill Haber/Associated Press.)*

Malcolm Emory was convicted of assault and battery of a police officer based on the testimony of the officer who arrested him during a campus protest at Northeastern University in January 1970. Fifteen years later, Emory and his attorneys received permission from the *Boston Globe* to review photos of the demonstration. The above photo, which shows Emory clutching his books (not bricks or concrete), eventually cleared Emory. Northeastern then reinstated Emory's full scholarship to study physics, the program he was forced to drop out of after his conviction. *(Photo courtesy of the* Boston Globe.*)*

Todd Neely is led out of court in tears after being convicted of stabbing a Florida woman. His attorneys argued that Neely was eating dinner with his family at a restaurant at the time of the stabbing: A computerized receipt showed that the family was there, and their waitress remembered them. But detectives claimed Neely left the restaurant, drove twelve miles to the scene of the crime, attacked the woman, then sped back to the restaurant. Circuit Judge C. Pfeiffer Trowbridge said at the trial's end that the case was "bizarre enough that '60 Minutes' could do something on it"—then found Neely guilty and sentenced him to fifteen years in prison. *(Photo courtesy of David Lane and the* Stuart News.*)*

The opportunities for uneven action run through the entire process and provide a potential playground for politically motivated prosecutors. It is prosecutors who decide which arrests and police charges to file in court and which to reject, how much attention to give each case, whether to induce and accept a plea and reduce charges, how much to reduce charges, whether to induce one defendant to plead guilty to reduced charges in return for evidence against another defendant, and what sentence to recommend to the judge.

Unfortunately, those "opportunities for uneven action" have been used to bring about some of the most infamous miscarriages of justice in American history, either because of the magnitude of the misconduct, the notoriety of the case, or both.

Famous Victims

One of the earliest and most notorious examples of prosecutorial misconduct was the framing of two controversial radical labor leaders —Thomas J. Mooney and Warren K. Billings—for the 1916 Preparedness Day bombing in San Francisco, in which ten people were killed and forty injured. Amid hysteria deliberately fanned by the district attorney, the two were tried and convicted of the crime. Mooney was sentenced to death, Billings to life in prison. It was only through the intervention of President Woodrow Wilson, who had serious misgivings about the convictions, that Mooney was not executed. In 1932, one of a series of reports by President Herbert Hoover's National Commission on Law Observance and Enforcement, better known as the Wickersham Commission for its senior member, George W. Wickersham, reached the following conclusions after thoroughly investigating the case:

• There was never any scientific attempt made by either the police or the prosecution to discover the perpetrators of the crime. The investigation was in reality turned over to a private detective [who worked for the company Billings and Mooney were in the process of trying to unionize at the time of the bombing], who used his position to cause the arrests of the defendants. The police investigation was reduced to a hunt for evidence to convict the arrested defendants.

• There were flagrant violations of the statutory law of California by both the police and the prosecution in the manner in which the defendants were arrested and held incommunicado, and in the subsequent searches of their homes to procure evidence against them.

• After the arrest of the defendants, witnesses were brought to the jails to "identify" them, and their "identifications" were accepted by the police and the prosecution, despite the fact that these witnesses were never required to pick the defendants out of a lineup, or to demonstrate their accuracy by any other test.

• Immediately after the arrest of the defendants there commenced a deliberate attempt to arouse public prejudice against them, by a series of almost daily interviews given to the press by prosecuting officials.

• Witnesses were produced at the trials with information in the hands of the prosecution that seriously challenged the credibility of the witnesses, but this information was deliberately concealed.

• Witnesses were permitted to testify at the trials, despite such knowledge in the possession of the prosecution of prior contradictory stories told by these witnesses, so as to make their mere production a vouchering for perjured testimony.

• Witnesses were coached in their testimony to a degree that approximated subornation of perjury.

• The prejudice against the defendants, stimulated by newspaper publicity, was further appealed to at the trials by unfair and intemperate arguments to the jury in opening and closing statements of the prosecuting attorneys.

• After the trials, the disclosures casting doubt on the justice of the convictions were minimized, and every attempt made to defeat the liberation of the defendants, by a campaign of misrepresentation and propaganda carried on by the officials who prosecuted them.[5]

Despite the overwhelming evidence pointing to the two men's innocence, it was 1939—seven years after that scathing report—before Governor Culbert L. Olson pardoned Mooney and commuted Billings's sentence to time served. "I am convinced that Mooney is innocent, that he was convicted on perjured testimony, and is entitled to a pardon," Olson said. Billings was finally given a complete pardon by Governor Edmund G. Brown in 1961.

As infamous as it was, the Billings-Mooney case merely set the stage for Nicola Sacco and Bartolomeo Vanzetti, whose 1921 trial in Massachusetts was called by the *Stanford Law Review* "probably the most controversial death penalty case in this century."

Sacco and Vanzetti were immigrant radical anarchists who happened to be armed when they were snared in a round-up of suspects for a murder committed in the course of a gang's armed robbery of an armored truck at the height of the "Red Scare" of the early 1920s. Prejudice was so great against them that the judge described the two defendants as "anarchist bastards" in an off-the-bench comment during the trial. But it was the prosecutor who made up the case against them by a highly selective use of evidence that played on prejudice more than reason; he then made it stick with a well-primed jury. In essence, Sacco and Vanzetti were tried not for armed robbery and murder, but for their strangeness and anarchist beliefs.

A 1977 report prepared by Governor Michael Dukakis's chief legal counsel concluded that

> Many of the questions asked, and many of the responses elicited, seem to have been devoted to making it ring in the jurors' minds that the defendants were radicals—which is, of course, precisely what they claimed—rather than to establishing that their justification for their actions upon arrest was trumped up, which was the point the prosecution ostensibly wished to prove. . . . There is a substantial possibility that some prejudicial influence was imparted to the trial, and an even greater probability that the judge's hostility to the defendants influenced the exercise of his discretion, particularly in such critical matters as deciding the motions for a new trial.

During his cross-examination of Sacco, the report added, the prosecutor

> dwelt upon Sacco's trip to Mexico to escape the draft, even though the trip bore no relationship to the crime. He ridiculed and unfairly distorted the political beliefs of Sacco in a manner that appeared calculated to rouse anti-foreign animosity the jury may have had toward the defendant. . . . The prosecutor's appeal to the jury's post-World

War I prejudice against draft dodgers and alien anarchists was intensified by Judge Thayer's opening remarks to the jury and the first words
of his charge. . . . "Gentlemen, I call upon you to render this service
here that you have been summoned to perform with the same spirit
and patriotism, courage and devotion to duty as was exhibited by our
soldier boys across the seas."

The reason for the appeal to passion, of course, was the frailty
of the evidence against the defendants. The prosecution's witnesses
often contradicted one another, while the defense produced several
seemingly certain alibi witnesses. No explanation was even given as
to who the five other robbers might have been or what happened
to the money taken, since none of it was found in the possession
of the two defendants. Ballistics experts now dispute the validity of
the only physical evidence offered against Vanzetti—that one of the
bullets found in the victim's body was fired from his gun. And the
attempt to link a hat allegedly found at the scene with Sacco has
since been discredited because of the admission that it was tampered
with in a way to make it seem like one Sacco wore.

Nonetheless, the two confused, poorly educated men were convicted and sentenced to death. They spent six years on death row
trying to prove their innocence. In 1925, another Massachusetts inmate already facing the death sentence confessed to the crime and
said Sacco and Vanzetti had not been involved. Subsequent investigation convinced most objective observers that he was telling the truth.
But the prosecutor was not an objective observer, and he pushed
for the executions in 1927 after all appeals had been exhausted. Both
men insisted on their innocence to the very end. In 1977, the fiftieth
anniversary of the executions, Governor Dukakis signed a cautiously
worded proclamation setting aside August 23 as a memorial day for
the two men and declaring that "any stigma and disgrace should be
forever removed from the names of Nicola Sacco and Bartolomeo
Vanzetti." Dukakis further called upon the people of Massachusetts
to "pause in their daily endeavors to reflect upon these tragic events,
and draw from their historic lessons the resolve to prevent the forces

of intolerance, fear, and hatred from ever again uniting to overcome the rationality, wisdom, and fairness to which our legal system aspires."

In *The Black Flag*, one of the more recent books on the Sacco-Vanzetti trial, British author Brian Jackson writes:

> In researching and writing this study, I began, as I said, with a belief in their innocence. But at many later points in the work I doubted it, changed and rechanged my mind. What we can see, I think, is that Governor Dukakis was right. By the standards of today they did not have a fair trial. A "not proven" verdict is unavoidable, and the use of capital punishment ended whatever hope there ever was of learning more about the truth.
>
> Personally, though I retain some scintillas of doubt, I can only conclude that the State of Massachusetts executed two innocent men. Not perhaps the men whom their supporters presented to the public . . . [for] both had the touch of iron without which no revolution could pay the price for success. . . . Both were guilty—proudly so—of a cultural crime. They were foreign, working class, armed and anarchist. This clouded all judgments. In the end it was for this that the state executed them.[6]

In my book (and this is) the most egregious and unjust wrongful conviction of the century came in the "trial of the century" for the "crime of the century." The principal victim in this malicious miscarriage of justice fueled by bigotry and hysteria was Bruno Richard Hauptmann, who paid for it with his life in 1936. But there were other victims as well. One, of course, was the kidnapped Lindbergh baby, who was eventually found dead. The others were the child's parents, Charles and Anne Morrow Lindbergh, a distinguished couple who had to endure not only the loss of their child but also the indignities of Hauptmann's circuslike trial. Finally, there is Anna Hauptmann, who has fought for more than a half-century to clear her husband's good name.

In a nutshell, Hauptmann was convicted of felony, murder, and burglary, sentenced to death, and executed in 1936, still insisting on his innocence in the ransom kidnapping of Charles Lindbergh Jr. Bedau and Radelet summarize it well in their *Stanford Law Review* study of miscarriages of justice in capital cases when they conclude that:

Hauptmann's is a classic case of conviction based on an intricate web of circumstantial evidence, perjury, prosecutorial suppression of evidence, a grossly incompetent defense attorney, and a trial atmosphere of near-hysteria. The trial followed a two-year nationwide hunt for the kidnappers of the baby boy of "Lindy," the nation's favorite hero, whose wife was the daughter of the wealthy and socially prominent Morrow family. Hauptmann was the victim of overzealous prosecutors intent on solving the most notorious crime of the decade. Although Governor Hoffman believed that Hauptmann was framed, he chose not to halt the execution. There is no doubt that the conviction rested in part on corrupt prosecutorial practices, suppression of evidence, intimidation of witnesses, perjured testimony, and Hauptmann's prior record.

But that succinct summation doesn't begin to do justice to the injustice of this legal outrage. For that we must rely on Ludovic Kennedy, one of Britain's foremost journalists, who counts among his many books three that resulted in pardons for innocent people falsely convicted of murder: 10 Rillington Place, A Presumption of Innocence, and Wicked Beyond Belief. It had been Kennedy's stated intention not to write another book about a miscarriage of justice. But that changed one day in 1981, when he flicked on the television set in his New York hotel and listened to Anna Hauptmann for the first time as she declared with passion that a half-century had not eroded in the least her belief that her husband was innocent of the horrible crime for which he had been executed. Kennedy was so impressed that he contracted with the BBC to make an hour-long documentary on the case. But the highly successful film that resulted, Who Killed the Lindbergh Baby?, which appeared on the Public Broadcasting System in this country as well as on the BBC, failed to satisfy Kennedy's curiosity and growing sense of outrage. So he wrote The Airman and the Carpenter, a penetrating, thorough exposé of one of America's great miscarriages of justice. Using previously unavailable files from New Jersey, New York, and the FBI, and drawing on interviews with the amazing number of the principal actors in the drama who were still alive, Kennedy portrays a trial so tainted by perjury, blinded by withheld evidence, and prejudiced by public hysteria that it is hard for anyone to come away without the belief that, at the very least, Hauptmann did not receive a fair trial, and that, far more likely, Hauptmann was framed to satisfy the nation's blood lust.

Ironically, Kennedy shows that it was because Hauptmann had been the victim of Isidor Fisch, a con artist from his native Germany he had met at a German social club, that he became a victim of the U.S. injustice system. When Hauptmann, a frugal carpenter, discovered that Fisch had died during a visit to Germany and that the substantial funds Hauptmann had invested with him were nowhere to be found, Hauptmann compensated for his loss by spending the money he had discovered in a package Fisch had left with him for safekeeping. That was a fatal mistake. For unbeknownst to Hauptmann, the money was part of that used to pay the Lindbergh baby's kidnappers. Because the bills were marked, it didn't take long for police to be at Hauptmann's door. In short order, Hauptmann suffered open derision for his German heritage, a severe beating during a lengthy interrogation, and much, much more before his sensational trial, conviction, and execution. Kennedy concludes:

> If it was difficult at the time to believe in Hauptmann's innocence, it is impossible today to sustain a belief in his guilt. For not only do we know that the great mass of evidence against him was engineered, but if he was guilty—if with his own hand he kidnapped and murdered Charlie, wrote all the ransom notes, received all the ransom money—it seems inconceivable that he would have (a) agreed to readily copy out at Greenwich Street Second Precinct police station sections of the ransom notes with their uniquely peculiar misspellings, (b) agreed initially that he must have written on a board in his bedroom closet the [planted] address and telephone number which turned out to be that of the ransom money negotiator, Dr. Condon, (c) told the gas station attendant to whom he gave one of the ransom bills that he had a hundred more at home and (d), and most convincing of all, refused until death to admit any part in the crime despite the knowledge that in return for a confession the governor of New Jersey and attorney general had promised him his life and a newspaper had promised financial security for his wife and son after his execution.

As to who *did* kill Charles Lindbergh Jr. if Hauptmann did not, Kennedy says there are certainly some clues:

> The American minister in Vienna to whom Detective Johnson showed copies of the ransom notes believed they had been written by a southern German or Austrian, and on the first of two occasions when Hauptmann met Fisch on Hunter's Island [an outdoor social club] he was in the company of an Austrian. It seems also that there was an Italian element present (unless this was introduced to confuse the scent); an Italiante look-out was observed at Woodlawn Cemetery [where the ransom money was left]; on the telephone Dr. Condon heard one of the gang speak in Italian to another; an Italian woman approached him at a sale. Fisch's two partners in the bogus Knickerbocker Pie Company, Charles Schleser and Joe DeGrasi, could bear further investigation. An FBI report in which, just before Hauptmann's execution, a prisoner in Chicago named Spitz declared he had bought Lindbergh ransom money at 40 percent discount from two men in New York was followed by a further report saying the two men had been located; but after Hauptmann's death it was in no one's interest to follow this up. Maybe in the FBI files the names of these two still exist; but the difficulty in searching for the truly guilty men is that information at the time that pointed to anyone but Hauptmann was discarded and—for fear of opening up a whole new can of worms—may well have been destroyed since.[7]

Unsung Victims

For every famous victim of injustice like Hauptmann, there are, unfortunately, thousands of hapless individuals tried and convicted of crimes they didn't commit by unethical prosecutors with hardly anyone noticing—or caring.

One of the more tragic individuals to face that fate was Isidore Zimmerman. In 1937, the 19-year-old New York hotel doorman was convicted of first-degree murder and sentenced to death for providing the guns later used to kill a police detective. Zimmerman's appeal was unsuccessful, even though the court acknowledged that Zimmerman wasn't at the scene of the crime. Two hours before his scheduled execution in the electric chair at Sing Sing, with his head already shaved and his trousers slit in preparation of his electrocution, the governor commuted Zimmerman's sentence to life.

Zimmerman spent the next two decades trying to prove his innocence, with no success. Then an attorney became interested in his case and reinvestigated it. Based on the evidence he developed that showed the key witness against Zimmerman had lied on the stand with the full knowledge of the assistant district attorney prosecuting the case, Zimmerman's conviction was overturned by an appeals court in 1962. In 1981, the New York State Legislature finally passed a bill allowing Zimmerman to sue the state. One year later, the New York State Court of Claims agreed that the prosecuting attorney knew Zimmerman was innocent, suppressed evidence, and intimidated witnesses into falsely testifying against him. In 1983, Zimmerman—who had lost his right eye during a prison beating—was awarded $1 million in damages, of which he would net about $660,000 after lawyer's fees and other expenses. The genial 66-year-old then vowed to become a walking, talking argument against capital punishment. "There's a message in my story," Zimmerman said. "It could happen to anybody."

So, unfortunately, can unexpected death. Zimmerman died of a heart attack just four months later. "He bought a new car, he took a trip to the Catskills for a few days—that's about as much as he got to do," his attorney said. "He always said he had this black cloud over him."[8]

William Fisher, a contemporary of Zimmerman's, had an equally long struggle obtaining justice for his wrongful conviction and the eleven years he spent in prison in the same state. Fisher was arrested on January 28, 1933, when a friend and another man were killed in a shootout in a Harlem nightclub. Fisher said he had been stabbed in the leg, hit on the head, and carried out the back door before the shooting began. But he was convicted of manslaughter after the prosecutor produced two guns and said Fisher had used one of them. The prosecutor later admitted knowing that the gun he claimed was Fisher's had not been used in the slaying. In its 1958 ruling, the New York Court of Appeals ruled that the prosecutor had also suppressed evidence that clearly demonstrated Fisher's innocence. After several legislative setbacks, Fisher was finally awarded a $750,000 judgment for a state claims court in 1984, when he was seventy-four. "The loss of freedom, to say the least, is painful to any person," Judge Frank Rosetti wrote in his eleven-page decision. "That pain is all the more galling when accompanied by the realization that it was precipitated by a public official to whom society had entrusted the fair and just enforcement of its laws."[9]

But if it's "galling" to be unjustly convicted of a crime you didn't commit, imagine how it must feel to have it happen not once, not twice, but *three times*, as it apparently did to Clarence Boggie. In 1935, Boggie was convicted of the brutal blackjack murder of an elderly recluse on the outskirts of Spokane, Washington, and sentenced to life imprisonment. The case against Boggie was based on eyewitness testimony and Boggie's possession of the murdered man's coat. But Boggie told anyone who would listen to him in prison that he had bought the coat in a pawn shop, and that the eyewitnesses had lied. Two of the few to take Boggie seriously were the prison chaplain and another minister. Thanks to their entreaties, Boggie's case became the first to be investigated by mystery writer and Perry Mason creator Erle Stanley Gardner and his Court of Last Resort.

When Gardner first met Boggie in prison in Walla Walla in 1947, he immediately decided the man was not only unusual, but downright incredible. "I refer to him as 'incredible' because everything about the man was completely and utterly incredible," Gardner writes in his book, *The Court of Last Resort.*

> Virtually every time I talked with him I discovered some new facet of the man, some new twist of his background, some episode which seemed to be absolutely incredible, yet which turned out to be the truth.
>
> For instance, Boggie, a penniless prisoner serving a life sentence, with two previous convictions behind him, maintained stoutly that he had never been guilty of any crime. That, of course, seemed absurd. Yet subsequent investigations indicated the man's story might well be true. In each instance of a prior conviction he had received a pardon

apparently predicated upon the fact that an investigation showed he had been wrongfully convicted.[10]

Gardner eventually determined that Boggie was telling the truth once again when he and his associates turned up evidence that the testimony used to convict Boggie on a murder charge had been suborned by the deputy prosecutor who handled the case. They were also able to track down the likely murderer, but Spokane officials, already embarrassed for the mistaken conviction of Boggie, decided not to pursue the lead.

After twenty years in prison and a few false starts, Boggie adapted amazingly well to the outside world. He married his childhood sweetheart and then found someone willing to put him in charge of a logging crew. Before long, he was breaking all company records for log production and seemed to be headed for a happy, successful life. Within a matter of months, though, Boggie's two decades of confinement and poor prison diet caught up with him. He died of a heart attack at the age of fifty-seven, with far too much life to live. But any history of wrongful convictions is full of tragedies like his. It seems, for some strange reason, to come with the territory.

The condoning of perjury by prosecutors, as well as the withholding of evidence from the defense—both of which happened in Boggie's case—are gray areas of the law that vary by state. In the case of convicted murderer Walter A. Pecho of Michigan, these factors, along with others, led to his pardon in 1960.[11]

Pecho's ordeal began on the morning of June 9, 1954, when he notified Lansing police that his wife had committed suicide with a shotgun. When police arrived at the couple's home, they found Eleanor Pecho's body seated in a living-room chair with the gun pointing up toward her from between her legs. The shotgun pellets had hit her in the chest and forced her body back into the chair.

Pecho told the officers that the suicide occurred after an all-night quarrel, during which his wife had clutched the shotgun and continually threatened to kill herself. He even showed them a suicide note that she had written and then torn up at one point during the argument. The threats didn't unduly alarm him, he said, because she had made them many times before. Pecho said his wife had followed through on her threat this time, however, as he was walking out of the house.

But the local pathologist said it had not been suicide at all, but murder. He based his conclusions on the angle at which the shot entered the body, the fact that the victim had fallen backward rather than to the floor, and the fact that it had been impossible for her to reach the trigger while the gun was being held in that position. Pecho was tried and convicted of the murder in quick order and sentenced to fifteen to twenty years in prison. But then his attorney learned that the prosecution had concealed evidence showing that only Mrs. Pecho's fingerprints were on the gun. Based on that and other new evidence, the attorney filed a motion for a new trial, but it was denied. The discovery of even more new evidence also failed to gain Pecho a new trial. But in 1960, the parole board conducted its own investigation that confirmed the validity of the new evidence, and the governor granted an unconditional pardon, declaring: "This is a case of miscarriage of justice. . . . I am convinced on the basis of the findings, conclusions and transcript of testimony presented to me by the parole board that in this case, an innocent man was convicted."

Nothing happened to the prosecutor in that case, just as nothing happened to the perpetrator of an even more outrageous case of prosecutorial misconduct in California. In 1960, Robert Lee Kidd was convicted of first-degree murder and sentenced to death, but the state supreme court reversed the conviction a year later. No wonder: The prosecutor had prevented the defense from informing the jury that the coroner had told reporters that the alleged murder weapon, the victim's sword, could not have been used in the killing. The jury was also given the impression by a police witness that a three-page document he was holding was the defendant's "rap sheet," with the clear implication that he had a long series of arrests, which he did not. During the retrial ordered by the state supreme court, which ended in Kidd's acquittal, it was revealed that the prosecutor also had suppressed evidence that the victim was alive several hours after

Kidd allegedly had killed him! Further, it was discovered that police had evidence showing that the actual murder weapon was a revolver that had been used to beat the victim to death, and there was no evidence to connect the weapon to Kidd. In 1974, Kidd filed a $200,000 damage suit against the perverse prosecutor, but it was dismissed. Too bad the prosecutor wasn't.[12]

The same goes for the prosecutor who obtained the conviction of Eldon Miller Jr. in 1956 for the murder of a 7-year-old girl in Illinois. During the emotional trial, the prevaricating prosecutor introduced as evidence a pair of "blood-stained shorts" that supposedly belonged to Miller. He then called a chemist who testified that the blood on the shorts was the same type as the victim's. The defense attorney's request to examine the shorts, which Miller denied were his, was refused, and the jury convicted him, with the shorts being the only evidence other than a recanted confession. Miller's conviction was affirmed on appeal. During the next several years, Miller was granted a stay of execution *ten times*—once only seven-and-a-half hours before he was scheduled to die. In 1963, a federal court finally reversed the conviction after evidence was introduced that showed that the "blood" on the shorts was, in fact, *paint smears*, and that the prosecution *knew* this at the time of the trial. It was also shown that Miller's later-recanted confession had been extracted only after long ours of intense interrogation. Incredibly, the prosecution had the audacity to appeal the decision to the U.S. Supreme Court, which upheld the ruling clearing Miller, declaring: "The prosecution deliberately misrepresented the truth." Miller was released in 1967, after serving eleven years and three months for a murder he did not commit, allowing the real murderer to escape detection until the trail was too cold to follow.

The outrages don't stop there, either. Consider the cases of:

• James Hall, who was cleared of murder charges ten years after he was convicted of the 1973 strangling of Sarah Ann Ottens, a University of Iowa nursing student. Hall, a former football player at the university, finally had his conviction overturned in November 1983 after he had served six-and-a-half years of a fifty-year prison term.

In May 1984, another judge ruled that the original indictment of Hall should also be tossed out because of misconduct by the prosecution. The ruling cited "racial slurs" made by prosecutors before the grand jury. Hall is black, and the slain woman was white. The judge also found that the assistant Iowa attorney general who prosecuted Hall had failed to present evidence to the grand jury that pointed to other suspects in the case. Instead, Judge L. Vern Robinson said, the prosecutor slanted the evidence against Hall. Robinson also said a state investigator who worked on the case had lied to the same body about interviews he had had with Hall. The investigator testified that Hall had denied knowing the victim and that Hall had an attorney present during the interview. Both statements were false. Hall had admitted knowing the woman, which he said would explain why his fingerprints were found in her apartment.

A turning point in the case came in 1982, when Hall's attorney asked that previously sealed information be opened. The documents showed that prosecutors had other suspects, including one who had been identified in a photo lineup by a witness who testified at Hall's trial that the man she saw was Hall. Another suspect, according to a second document, "knew many unpublished details of the crime."[13]

• Robert McLaughlin of New York, who was convicted in 1981 of second-degree felony murder and sentenced to fifteen years to life in prison. Although the conviction was upheld on appeal, a judge in the state appellate division who believed the conviction "might have been a miscarriage of justice" asked that the case be reinvestigated. The conviction was overturned in 1986, when it was determined that prosecutors had deliberately withheld information contained in a detective's file showing that the suspect initially described by the only witness to identify McLaughlin at the trial did not even look like McLaughlin.

Subsequent investigation also suggested that the prosecutor had suppressed evidence showing another witness had given a description of the killer that differed greatly from McLaughlin's description.

In 1989, the New York State Court of Claims awarded a then-record $1.93 million to McLaughlin for the "devastating trauma" the wrongful conviction had caused him. The judge also praised McLaughlin's stepfather, Harold Hohne, who fought for years to have the case reopened. "He followed every lead, sought any available information, left no stone unturned to prove his son's innocence," the judge said. Too bad the prosecutors and police hadn't done the same.[14]

• George Merritt of New Jersey, a black man convicted of first-degree murder and given a life sentence for killing a white police officer during a "race riot." Merritt was one of twelve people charged with the crime. After winning a new trial on appeal, Merritt was again convicted in 1974, but the finding was reversed on appeal in 1976. The tenacious Merritt was tried and convicted a third time in 1977, only to have the conviction reversed once again in 1980, when it was revealed that the prosecutor had failed to disclose a report of a pre-trial police interview with the only witness to testify against Merritt, in which the witness said things completely at variance with what he said during the trial. Upon Merritt's release after serving ten years in prison, his attorney asked, "What would the proponents of the death penalty have to say if Merritt had been executed before the discovery of the concealed document?"[15]

• Terry Seaton of New Mexico, who was convicted of first-degree murder in 1973 and sentenced to life in prison. A state district judge ruled six years later that the conviction was based on perjured testimony given by another person in exchange for a promise from the prosecutor that he would get a lighter sentence on charges he was facing at the time. The judge said the state also had suppressed the confession of a third person. Rather than retry Seaton, the prosecutor dropped the charges. No need to wonder why.[16]

• James Creamer, George Emmett, and five others, who were convicted of first-degree murder and sentenced to life in prison by a Georgia court in 1973. Two years later their convictions were vacated after an *Atlanta Constitution* series of investigative articles revealed that the prosecution had suppressed evidence that would have totally discredited a woman who was the state's chief witness against Creamer and Emmett. Then the woman admitted she had committed perjury and another man confessed to the murders. New trials were then ordered for the other five men, and the charges were dropped.[17]

• George "Chiefie" De Los Santos of New Jersey, the first inmate to be freed through the efforts of the Reverend James McCloskey. When the two met in 1983, De Los Santos had already served seven years of a life sentence for the 1975 murder of a used-car salesman. McCloskey was skeptical of the inmate's repeated pleas of innocence, but he changed his mind after reading the trial transcript. McCloskey eventually discovered proof that prosecutors had suppressed evidence that subverted the credibility of their star witness. The same went for several others who testified against De Los Santos. The conviction was overturned in June 1983 by a federal judge, who said the testimony from the star witness, a cellmate who claimed to have overheard De Los Santos confess to the crime after his arrest, "reeked of perjury."[18]

• Earnest Lee Miller and William Riley Jent of Florida, who came within sixteen hours of being executed in 1983 for the 1979 murder of a woman. In 1987, new trials were ordered for the two men by a federal judge who said prosecutors and police had shown a "callous and deliberate disregard for the fundamental principles of truth and fairness." In 1988, they were released after agreeing, at the insistence of prosecutors, to plead guilty to second-degree murder even though evidence by then clearly showed that a man in prison on unrelated charges in Georgia was responsible not only for the murder they admitted to but a carbon-copy one committed while they were in prison.[19]

Jent and Miller later regretted to pleading to the reduced charge, and if they had had a good lawyer, the outcome might have been far more favorable. But, as the next chapter shows, good lawyers are hard to find.

Notes

1. "Man Revels in His Freedom," *Columbus Dispatch*, April 27, 1989, p. 2B, and, in general, Mark Lane, *Arcadia* (New York: Holt, Rinehart & Winston, 1970).

2. Defendant with an Alibi May Get a New Trial," *Miami Herald*, October 24, 1988, p. 1. Also, "Ohio Native Finally Cleared in Florida," *Columbus Dispatch*, September 5, 1990, p. 7A.

3. Raymond Moley, *Politics and Criminal Prosecution* (New York: Arno Press, 1974), p. 54.

4. *The Innocents*, p. 37, and Eugene B. Block, *The Vindicators* (Garden City, N.Y.: Doubleday, 1963), pp. 125–140.

5. See generally, Curt Gentry, *Frame-Up: The Incredible Case of Tom Mooney and Warren Billings* (New York: W. W. Norton, 1967).

6. Brian Jackson, *The Black Flag* (Boston: Routledge & Kegan Paul, 1981), pp. 139–140.

7. Ludovic Kennedy, *The Airman and the Carpenter: The Lindbergh Kidnapping and the Framing of Richard Hauptmann* (New York: Viking, 1985) pp. 6–7.

8. "Isidore Zimmerman, 66, Man Unjustly Jailed for a Murder," *New York Times*, October 14, 1983, p. 25. Also, "After 24 Years in Jail, a $1 Million Verdict," *Newsweek*, June 13, 1983.

9. Associated Press, January 14, 1986.

10. *The Court of Last Resort*, pp. 27–85.

11. *The Innocents*, pp. 40–44; *Stanford Law Review*, p. 151.

12. *Stanford Law Review*, pp. 134–135.

13. "Grand Jury Frees Man Convicted in Murder," *New York Times*, September 2, 1984, p. 29.

14. "$1.93 Million Awarded Man Wrongly Jailed," *New York Times*, October 19, 1989, p. B28.

15. *Stanford Law Review*, p. 147.

16. Ibid., p. 159.

17. Ibid., p. 104.

18. "Freed Lifer Wants New Murder Trial," *New York Times*, p. B6.

19. "Presumed Guilty," *Esquire*, March 1989, p. 178.

7

The Court Jesters

The law is a mighty machine. Woe to the unfortunate man who, wholly or in part innocent, becomes entangled in its mighty wheels, unless his innocence is patent or his rescue planned and executed by able counsel. The machine will grind on relentlessly and ruthlessly, and blindfolded justice does not see that the grist is sometimes stained with innocent blood.
—*Law Professor Edward Johnes*

The first thing we do, let's kill all the lawyers.
—*William Shakespeare, in* Henry VI

It is in part because the "able counsel" we all need in court is so hard to find that lawyers, as a group, are often held in such low esteem. While the number of incompetent, incapable lawyers is actually quite small, the amount of damage they do to their clients and to their profession is quite large.

Consider the damage done to the legal profession and the client in the case of Eddie G. Javor, who had his 1965 drug-possession conviction overturned by a California appeals court in 1984 because his attorney had slept through most of the trial. Javor served twenty months of a five-year sentence while fighting his conviction. He argued his own case before the appellate court and cried after learning he had won. "I'm so glad to hear it's over," he said.

Or consider the case of Francis P. Hemauer of Milwaukee, who unjustly served nine years of a sixty-year sentence for a 1972 rape of a 15-year-old girl. The district attorney asked that the charges against Hemauer be dropped in 1983 after the 60-year-old man's new attorney discovered that tests showed the attacker's blood to be of a different type than Hemauer's. The wrongfully convicted man later obtained a $500,000 settlement against the attorney who originally defended him, for his failure to note the blood-type discrepancy.

Or consider the case of a 29-year-old man who won a new trial on a rape charge in 1985 because his attorney had failed to note that he was impotent. "It's about time. I've been through a lot," said Joe Jerry Yrigoyen of Cypress, California, after the ruling by Orange County Court Judge James O. Perez that granted him a third trial. Yrigoyen was convicted after two trials of the July 1980 rape of a 20-year-old former neighbor. Yrigoyen had always proclaimed his innocence. But, out of embarrassment, he didn't mention his impotence, which was caused by meningitis at age five, until he was sent to the California Institution for Men at Chino. Prison counselors then told Judge Perez. Perez ruled that the defense attorney should have discovered the information during a proper background check on his client.

You can also imagine the impression Vernon McManus now has of lawyers after he was convicted and sentenced to death in 1977 for a murder he insisted he didn't commit, then watched in shock when, as soon as he was convicted, his defense attorney filed a divorce petition for McManus's wife, whom the attorney later married. McManus's conviction was reversed and the charges were dropped in 1983 because of insufficient evidence and his attorney's conflict of interest.

Fortunately, such cases are by far the exception rather than the rule. And when mistakes *are* made, they are usually the result of understandable factors, according to the Ohio State University study of wrongful convictions. "Such cases as appear in the literature and in our database do not generally show a defense attorney in league with prosecutors or working against the interest of the client," wrote C. Ronald Huff. "Rather, the counsel for the defense is more likely to have been inexperienced, harried, overworked, with few or no investigative resources. Sometimes the defense counsel is unreceptive to a client's wishes because of a belief in the defendant's guilt and in the futility, even self-destructiveness, of pursuing the line of defense suggested by the accused."

Among defense-attorney errors discovered by the Ohio State study were "failure to make discovery motions or to pursue them vigorously, using poor judgment in placing a defendant on the stand, allowing a defendant to take a polygraph exam (especially in the absence of the defense attorney), and failure to challenge vigorously contentions made by the prosecution in court."

Despite the relative rarity of inadequate counsel, Huff wrote, it has been a popular basis of appeal since 1932, when the U.S. Supreme Court ruled in *Powell* v. *Alabama* that the defense provided Ozzie Powell, one of the "Scottsboro Boys," was insufficient (to say the least, as we will see later) for a capital case.

"Such appeals are not easy to win," Huff wrote, "despite the fact that many attorneys are inadequately prepared for trial work. Collegial relationships within the legal profession, though pitting lawyer against lawyer as adversaries, stop short of promoting the idea of attacking colleagues for mishandling a case (just as doctors are not eager to testify against other doctors). Lawyers assigned anew, or on appeal, are not eager to pursue this line for a reversal, preferring to characterize as 'new evidence' that which had formerly been overlooked, for example."

Yet, as caseloads soared in the crime crackdown of the 1980s, evidence began to mount that inadequate counsel was becoming a more frequent case of mistaken convictions. And, ironically, it was found that the worst instances of deficient defense were in the cases of those who most needed an aggressive advocate—defendants facing capital charges.

"The problem is inadequate legal representation at the start," *New York Times* columnist Anthony Lewis wrote in a 1990 column. "Inadequate is indeed too weak a word. Most of the people who are on death row in this country got there simply because they had no effective lawyer's help at their trial or original appeal."

Lewis went on to relate the experience of Stephen B. Bright, a lawyer for the Southern Prisoners' Defense Committee in Atlanta. When Bright was teaching law in the nation's capital ten years ago, Lewis said, he was asked to help prepare an appeal to the Supreme

Court in a death-penalty case. Bright said he expected to find a huge trial record reflecting a conscientious defense. What he found instead was almost nothing.

"The students in our clinical program tried shoplifting cases better than this capital case had been tried," Bright later told a House Judiciary subcommittee. Bright said the defendant's court-appointed attorney made no attempt at all to present evidence favorable to the defendant.

"Many lawyers have had Mr. Bright's experience, coming in to represent someone already on death row and finding that crucial evidence was never presented," Lewis observed.

Three weeks later, the *National Law Journal* published a devastating study of the legal defense provided those facing capital punishment in six southern states known as the Death Belt, where 80 percent of the nation's executions have taken place since the Supreme Court reinstated the death penalty in 1976 and 40 percent of all death-row inmates now reside. Unfortunately, the problems unearthed there were even worse than many imagined. The study found that many poor defendants sentenced to death had lawyers who had never handled a capital trial before, lacked training in life-or-death cases, made little effort to present evidence in support of a life sentence, or had been reprimanded or disciplined, or were subsequently disbarred.

In effect, the *Journal* said it had found "that what the Supreme Court calls the 'main event' in the long march toward execution— the trial—is being played out in a sadly deteriorated arena."[1]

Among the respected legal weekly's key findings were:

• The lawyers who represented death-row inmates have been disbarred, suspended, or otherwise disciplined at a rate of three to forty-six times the average discipline rates for the six states studied.

• More than half the defense attorneys questioned said they were handling their first capital trial when their clients were convicted.

• Statutory-fee limits work out to about $5 an hour for many court-appointed lawyers, which discourages thorough trial investigation and preparation.

• Vague or nonexistent standards for appointment of counsel can result in lawyers handling capital trials as their first criminal cases.

• Capital trials in the Death Belt often end in one or two days, in contrast to the two-week to two-month trials in states where advanced defense systems for the indigent exist.

• The all-important penalty phase of a capital trial in the Death Belt usually starts immediately after a guilty verdict and lasts only a few hours. In one case, it lasted only fifteen minutes. And little effort is made at this time to present mitigating evidence.

• Judges regularly deny defense lawyers' requests for fees for expert witnesses or private investigators.

• The Supreme Court decision that lays out the test for ineffective counsel is itself ineffective, making it all but impossible for death-sentence inmates to challenge the performance of trial lawyers.

The study also noted that "studies by federal judges and legal defense groups in the past 10 years have shown federal appellate courts finding constitutional flaws—such as prosecutorial misconduct, illegally gained confessions, and ineffective defense counsel—in 40 percent to 73 percent of state death-penalty cases reviewed. . . ."

"Despite these estimates," the study continued, "there is a major movement in Congress, initiated by Chief Justice William H. Rehnquist, to limit federal review of capital cases, with an eye to bringing finality and order to a process that can be chaotic and lengthy."

If that happens, the burden will be pushed back on the capital trial itself, where justice is least likely to occur. With some of the lawyers who practice there, it is little wonder. Among the more pathetic examples the *Journal* revealed:

• In 1986, James Dukes, a Hammond, Louisiana, civil attorney with virtually no criminal-defense experience and absolutely no capital-defense background, was appointed lead counsel in the retrial of James Copeland for first-degree murder. His co-counsel was Gideon Carter III, who was just two months out of law school. In an affidavit attached to his post-conviction briefs, Dukes openly admitted the deficiencies of his defense:

I did not investigate the case outside the information received from the state through discovery, I did not attempt to have Mr. Copeland evaluated for competency to stand trial, I did not attempt to develop an insanity defense even though Mr. Copeland proceeded to trial under of plea of not guilty and not guilty by reason of insanity, I did not attempt to assess whether Mr. Copeland's drug and alcohol intoxication at the time of the offense would establish a defense based on intoxication, I did not attempt to have Mr. Copeland evaluated to determine if we could show any statutory mitigating circumstances relative to mental health, and I did not prepare to present witnesses and evidence relative to mitigation, except speaking with and presenting the warden of Livingston Parish Jail and a minister at the jail during the penalty phase. The reason for not doing any of the above is purely monetary; I did not have the money to spend to hire any of the persons necessary to perform such tasks as needed to provide competent representation.

Despite such an admitted poor defense, Copeland's conviction stands. He remains on death row.

• In 1987, an Augusta, Georgia, jury had the strange experience of having not only the prosecutor but the defendant's own attorney urge that he be sent to the electric chair. O. L. Collins told the jury that his client, Ernest Morrison, "has the right to choose and ask for [a death sentence] if he wants to," and it was his duty to "take [Morrison's] side of it." The state supreme court later ruled that Collins had acted properly. When Collins's performance at the 1975 capital trial of Billy Sunday Birt was questioned in a 1988 hearing, Collins was asked to identify any three criminal cases by name. Collins could offer only the Birt case, the Miranda decision and—wrongly—the Supreme Court's notorious pro-slavery Dred Scott case. "I don't go by names, I go by principles of law involved," Collins explained. Resentencing was ordered in the Birt case, but Morrison and another of Collins's clients remain on death row.

• During the capital trial of Millburn Wayne Bates Jr. in Louisiana, the prosecutor informed the court that he and Bates's public defender had dated in the past. What the prosecutor didn't say until a hearing on a successful motion to remove him from further involvement in the case filed by Bates's appeals attorney was that he and the defense attorney had gone beyond dating by the time of the trial and were actually living together. Bates, on the other hand, is now living with inmates on death row.

• Perhaps the most inadequate of inadequate attorneys discovered by the *Journal* was former Louisiana state Senator George Oubre. About the only good thing one can say about his background is that he can empathize with being a convict. In 1984, Oubre pleaded guilty to submitting a false statement to a federal agency, and received a three-year suspended sentence, plus 416 hours of community service as a volunteer attorney. As a result, Oubre ended up defending John Francis Wille, who had been charged in connection with one of the most horrible murders in local history. Oubre had never before tried a capital case, and he failed to tell the defendant of his conviction. At this writing, the state supreme court was considering whether Wille had had competent counsel.

• At 6 P.M. on a November day in 1987, the jury found James Wyman Smith guilty of murder. When the judge asked the defense and prosecution if they were ready to proceed with the death-penalty phase at that time, defense co-counsel Thomas E. Jones replied: "No, sir, we are not."

Clearly perturbed at having to send the jury back to a motel for another night, the judge asked why they couldn't get it over with. Said J. Michael Williams, the other defense lawyer, "Judge, I haven't even read the statute about it."

The judge then recessed the trial—but only until 8:30 A.M. the next day. Smith, needless to say, now resides on death row.

• The 1988 capital trial of Judy Haney in Alabama had to be delayed one day when the defense attorney showed up apparently intoxicated. The presiding judge ordered him to go to the courthouse law library for two hours to sleep it off. Upon his return, when the judge asked the attorney to explain his behavior, he was incapable of doing so and was held in contempt. After spending the night in jail, the attorney returned the next day to defend Haney against charges she had contracted for the murder of her husband. Despite such outstanding counsel, Haney was convicted. She is now on death row.

• In the 1982 trial of Jerry White in Orlando, Florida, the judge started each day by having the prosecutor check his opponent's breath for alcohol because of his odd behavior. The state contends that no alcohol odor was ever detected. But it could be that alcohol wasn't the problem. In a post-conviction affidavit, the attorney's own investigator said he had witnessed the attorney take cocaine during trial recesses. He said he had also seen him use speed, alcohol, Quaaludes, morphine, and marijuana after court sessions. Yet the defendant's request for a retrial because of inadequate counsel was denied.

• The attorney who represented condemned Georgia inmate John Young was arrested for drug possession soon after Young's 1976 trial. In 1985, the then-disbarred attorney signed a statement admitting he had been ill-prepared at Young's trial because of drug use, the recent breakup of his marriage, the discovery of his homosexuality, and extensive travel on business and personal matters. Four days later, Young was executed anyway.

Such obvious substance abuse would come as no surprise to officials at the State Bar of California. They say thousands of lawyers in that state alone come to court each day either drunk or high. As a result, the bar is going public with a high-profile campaign to battle substance abuse among lawyers.

"If you're in a high-stress occupation, substance abuse is greater," state bar president Alan Rothenberg told the Associated Press. "The legal profession is certainly a high-stress profession. If you're doing trial work, that's high stress. If you're in a criminal trial, your client's life or death is at stake. That's about as stressful as anything."[2]

But the problem isn't in California alone. Surveys conducted by the state bars in Washington and Oregon indicate that 15 percent to 18 percent of lawyers are alcoholics. The State Bar of Texas estimates the incidence of substance abuse among lawyers there to be 20 percent. That's twice as high as the rate for the general population.

To combat the problem, the American Bar Association in 1988 launched a Commission on Impaired Attorneys to serve as a clearinghouse for various programs.

Lawyers who turn to drugs and alcohol usually end up hurting their clients financially, although not before many have already been victimized by inadequate counsel. "We find that in a lot of cases, the person suffering from substance abuse is not handling business as they should," said Bill Davis, who handles complaints about attorneys filed with the ABA. "If the substance abuse gets worse, ultimately they're stealing clients' funds to support their habit."[3]

But the callousness and carelessness spreading through the legal community, whether caused by substance abuse, overwork, or a simple lack of care, can cost clients a lot more than money. It can cost them their lives.

It almost did exactly that to Larry Hicks of Gary, Indiana, who came perilously close to being executed for a murder he didn't commit because his obviously inadequate lawyer failed to file what should have been a routine appeal. Two weeks before Hicks's scheduled execution, he was getting truly worried about why he hadn't heard from his court-appointed attorney concerning an appeal or a stay of execution.

As the 19-year-old Hicks was being escorted back to his cell after visiting the chaplain, he saw attorney Nick Stanton, one of the state's best criminal appeals attorneys, who had just visited a client. Although normally shy, Hicks worked up the nerve to explain his predicament and plead for help.

"Just what I didn't need," Stanton later told Playboy magazine of his reaction to Hicks's plea. "An indigent slum-kid murderer who 'didn't do it.' But I promised to see about the stay and get back to him. That part sounded odd."

So Stanton checked with Warden J. R. Ducksworth, who confirmed that no stay had been issued and that he too was becoming concerned. Increasingly curious, Stanton checked further into the case. What he found amazed him. Although Hicks had grown up in crime-ridden slums, he didn't use drugs, rarely drank, had no prior criminal record, had lived with an aunt, and had worked steadily since his early teens. Despite a "low normal" IQ, Hicks had stayed in school and was about to become a senior at the time of his arrest. All of the adults who knew Hicks had nothing but praise for him.

After Hicks passed two polygraph tests, Stanton approached the Playboy Foundation, which often finances attempts to right a wrong, appealing for funds. "There is, I absolutely assure you," Stanton wrote, "an innocent man facing the death penalty in my state. . . . I urgently implore you to review the enclosed materials and get in touch with me as soon as possible. Larry Hicks is on death row for a murder he did not commit."

In January 1980, *Playboy*'s senior editor and an investigator with the magazine's defense team met with Stanton and reviewed the trial transcripts. They revealed that on a Saturday night in February 1978, Hicks had agreed to help two women neighbors move to a new apartment a few blocks away. Also helping were Bernard Scates, the boyfried of one of the women, and two other men. Before long, the helpers were doing more drinking than moving and were becoming quite quarrelsome. Hicks said he left in disgust around midnight, walked home, and spent the night with his girlfriend. When he returned to the women's apartment the next morning to retrieve some groceries he had left there, a girl in a neighboring apartment told him the two women and Scates had been picked up by police—no doubt, Hicks thought, because the party had got out of hand.

Hicks thought wrong. A few hours later, he found himself in jail, charged with stabbing the two helpers to death in the alley behind the building. Police based the charges on information provided by the two women, who said Scates and Hicks had killed the victims during a fight. Scates also blamed Hicks at first, but later told cellmates that Hicks hadn't been involved. A few days later, Scates died in his cell of what appeared to be a suicide.

Playboy picks up the incredible story from there:

> At his trial, the only significant evidence incriminating Hicks was the testimony of Scates's girlfriend, the other woman having changed her story so many times the prosecution moved to have her declared a hostile witness. The court-appointed attorney challenged none of the girlfriend's statements and ignored the prosecution's failure to present the blood-stained clothing she claimed Hicks had been wearing when he left. He did not call the alibi witness with whom Hicks said he'd

spent the night or present other possible witnesses to the events of the evening. He did not put Hicks on the stand in his own defense and virtually ignored the most important point of all: The county coroner, a witness for the state, testified that the murders had occurred not late Saturday night when the fighting supposedly started but sometime after six o'clock the following morning.

That last fact was merely stated in passing and apparently escaped the notice of the jury. After the verdict was read and the punishment phase began, Hicks asked to take the stand and had to be told the trial was over. He then asked the judge, "Your Honor, why did I get guilty?" A bit later, the following exchange occurred:

Court: It's your testimony that [the witnesses] were trying to frame you?
Hicks: They didn't try to frame me, they framed me.
Court: With the stabbings?
Hicks: They are the reason I'm here, that's all I can say.
Court: Is it your testimony you did not stab either person?
Hicks: I ain't stabbed nobody or nothing else. . . .
Court: Mr. Hicks, do you know why you are here this morning?
Hicks: Not exactly, sir.

In March 1980, Stanton successfully filed a motion to have the case reopened on the ground that Hicks—to say nothing of his grossly incompetent court-appointed attorney—hadn't understood the proceedings well enough to assist in his poorly presented defense.

To prepare for Hicks's defense in the retrial, Stanton obtained the help of an Episcopal priest, Martin Bell, who also was a licensed private detective. Bell and his partner, Carol Tewksbury, spent several weeks in Gary, during which they discovered, according to *Playboy*, that:

• The knife presented as evidence was not the murder weapon.

• Scates was the victim of murder, not suicide, in his cell.

• Police not only didn't find any physical evidence tying Hicks to the crime, but they also lost most of what they did find.

• Prosecutors had ignored a report by the chief homicide detective that the investigation had been totally botched.

• Other people who had visited the apartment that night hadn't been questioned by police.

• Witnesses to the removal of the bodies apparently had been threatened not to come forward.

• One of the victims hadn't been killed where Hicks's accuser said, and he hadn't been stabbed in the back, as the prosecutor claimed.

At Hicks's second trial, the prosecutor used just about every trick in the book to keep from having the new evidence favorable to Hicks introduced. The defense was nonetheless able to show that the prosecution had failed to present to police several possible leads that might have cleared Hicks. After deliberating for six hours, the jury returned a verdict of not guilty, and Larry Hicks was a free man once again—thanks to the Playboy Foundation and Nick Stanton, and no thanks to the original attorney who so poorly represented him and seemed prepared to let him go to his death rather than make the routine appeals.

Apparently, even the assistant prosecutor who had handled the case against Hicks with such relish realized deep down the injustice Hicks had endured. When Stanton remarked to her that the case should never have gone to trial, she replied, "I agree." Yet it did, apparently at the insistence of her politically motivated boss, who hated to admit a mistake had been made.

"Larry was one lucky slum kid, and it just makes you wonder how many unlucky ones will be going to the chair, or be locked up for twenty years," said Kevin McShane, Stanton's assistant. "And Larry was *clean*. I mean, he didn't do anything to deserve what happened to him, especially his years on death row, and that's scary."[4]

The Plea Bargain Rip-Off

What is also scary is the number of innocent defendants who, with the strong encouragement of their often lazy or inept attorneys, choose to avoid death row or twenty years in prison by pleading guilty to lesser crimes.

Since its introduction in the 1920s, plea bargaining—a defendant's agreement to plead guilty to a lesser charge in exchange for a lighter sentence—has become the most common way to adjudicate criminal cases. Although its acceptance varies across the nation, plea bargaining often is involved in more than three-quarters of the cases handled in a given jurisdiction. And while federal prosecutors have been less likely to plea bargain in the past, a 1989 study by a Syracuse University research organization found they now are relying on the technique more frequently to handle caseloads swollen by drug prosecutions; in fact, only 9 percent of federal criminal cases that year actually ended in trials.

On the surface, plea bargaining is an attractive option for all involved. It helps both the prosecutor and the defense attorney, to avoid a time-consuming and costly trial. It usually means a lighter sentence for defendants and, according to a 1990 Justice Department study, it greatly increases their chances of not going to prison at all. Of those defendants who plead guilty, the study found, only 65 percent are sentenced to prison. The other 35 percent are usually put on probation. Felony defendants found guilty by a jury or judge, on the other hand, are sentenced to spend time behind bars more than 80 percent of the time.

Beneath the surface, however, plea bargaining exhibits several flaws. The most important, says Peter Arenella, a law professor at Rutgers University, is that the presumption of innocence of a jury trial is replaced by the presumption of guilt that dominates the pre-trial stages.

"Since the pre-trial process does not require the government to present compelling evidence of factual guilt to an independent fact-finder or demonstrate that its evidence could satisfy the trial's formal proof requirements, prosecutors sometimes can and do get indictments despite insufficient evidence to support a conviction," Arenella wrote in an analysis of the pitfalls of plea bargaining.[5]

That tactic works well regardless of whether the charges are relatively minor or serious.

Concerning the former, the Ohio State study noted that:

A defendant who is unable to make bail and is offered, in exchange for a plea of guilt, immediate release with nothing more consequential than a minor criminal record (typically in a community where such records are not uncommon and not highly stigmatizing), cannot easily resist the lure of a guilty plea. That one will be found not guilty, although the defendant knows himself to be guiltless, is not at all certain. Alibis are difficult to establish; eyewitnesses can swear that they are confident in their identification of the defendant (even though they are often wrong); an assigned lawyer may not have the time or other resources for a good investigation; or an attorney unconvinced of his client's innocence may not proceed with enthusiasm, thus compromising the entire concept of the adversarial process.

In the subculture of the courts, the defense attorney, like the prosecutor, feels pressure to play the game of speedy disposal of cases. Unwilling to bargain in one case, he is offered little opportunity to bargain in another where he desires to do so. If his client has a criminal record, he informs him of the difficulty in placing him on the stand.[6]

Even when the charges are more serious, prosecutors often can still bluff defense attorneys and their clients into pleading guilty to a lesser offense.

As a result, people who not only might have been acquitted because of lack of evidence, but also those who in fact are truly innocent, will often plead guilty to the charge. Why? In a word, fear. And the more numerous and serious the charges, studies have shown, the greater the fear. That explains why prosecutors sometimes seem to file every charge imaginable against defendants. The know they are more likely to get some kind of guilty plea out of a frightened defendant.

This strategy first came under attack in 1968 in an influential *University of Chicago Law Review* article by law professor Albert W. Alschuler.

"When prosecutors respond to a likelihood of acquittal by magnifying the pressures to plead guilty," Alschuler writes, "they seem to exhibit a remarkable disregard for the danger of false conviction. This apparent disregard is not easy to explain. It might be supposed that when a prosecutor decides to charge a defendant with a crime, he makes a personal judgment concerning the defendant's guilt or innocence. Once the charge decision has been made, the prosecutors may regard trial as a technical obstacle standing between the defendant and the punishment he deserves."

But permitting the prosecutor to become judge and jury too has many pitfalls, Alschuler continues. "If trials ever serve a purpose, their utility is presumably greatest when the outcome is in doubt. The practice of responding to a weak case by offering extraordinary concessions therefore represents, at best, a dangerous allocation of institutional responsibility. And when even the minimal safeguard of a prosecutorial judgment of guilt is lacking, as it is in a significant number of cases today, the horrors of the guilty-plea system are multiplied."[7]

Consider the case of Howard Pearson of Denver, who spent three years in prison for an armed robbery he didn't commit. Despite his repeated claims that he was the victim of mistaken identification, Pearson's public defenders persuaded him to plead guilty to one of several charges he faced on a promise that prosecutors would drop the others. Later, authorities determined that Pearson was not the robber after all, and the understandably bitter Pearson was released.

Another problem with the plea-bargaining system is that prosecutors sometimes can't or don't keep their word to defense counsel. Tony Crews of Columbia, Missouri, learned that the hard way in 1981. Crews's fear began to mount when he first met with his skeptical court-appointed attorney. After going over the felony charges against him, which Crews said grew out of an attempt to coerce him to confess to a series of robberies he didn't commit, Crews's lawyer, the son of a local judge, approached the defendant's mother and informed her he wouldn't take the case to court unless her son pleaded guilty. "I'm here to represent your son to see he isn't convicted because his constitutional rights are violated," he told her. "I am not here to defend him."

Before the trial began, the attorney stressed to Crews that he would get a life sentence if he didn't plead guilty. So Crews followed his attorney's advice, expecting to get a ten-to-fifteen-year sentence. But the judge had a different term in mind: *three life sentences plus ten years*, which is a lot of lives.

The advantages to the defendant of a trial over plea bargaining were dramatically demonstrated in a highly publicized "gang rape" incident in 1983 in Massachusetts. The case concerned five men who pleaded guilty to raping a 42-year-old woman. The men received suspended sentences, which caused a huge public outcry, so the judge ordered them to either serve prison terms or stand trial. They decided to take their chances on a trial, and were acquitted by a jury whose members were not told of their earlier guilty pleas.

Something similar happened in Richmond, Virginia, in 1982. As Harry Siegler awaited the verdict of a jury that had heard the first-degree murder case against him, Siegler panicked, fearful that he would be found guilty and sentenced to death. Just minutes before the jury returned, Siegler desperately changed his plea to guilty to a lesser charge, only to learn—much to his surprise—that the jury had already voted to acquit him. Unfortunately, Siegler's guilty plea took precedence, and the judge sentenced him to sixty years in prison.

As Siegler's action demonstrated, the threat of execution often makes pleading to a lesser charge highly appealing to defendants, even if they are guiltless.

Among the death-defying examples on record:

• Jack Carmen, a severely retarded resident of Columbus, Ohio, who was mistakenly identified by eyewitnesses as the rapist-murderer of a 14-year-old girl in 1975. Apparently afraid of being sentenced to death, Carmen pleaded guilty to aggravated murder and was sentenced to life in prison. Six months later, the conviction was vacated on the ground that Carmen was mentally incompetent to enter a plea of guilty. At a second trial, in 1977, several alibi witnesses gave unimpeached testimony on Carmen's behalf—as did two members of the victim's family—and he was acquitted of all charges.[8]

• John Henry Fry of California, who was charged with the murder of his common-law wife in 1958. Because Fry had been too drunk to remember what had happened and was fearful of receiving the death penalty, he agreed to his attorney's advice to plead guilty to manslaughter and was sentenced to one to ten years in prison. The plea seemed like a bargain for sure until Richard Cooper, who was arrested in connection with another murder several months later, confessed to killing Fry's wife. A few weeks later, Fry was freed and pardoned by Governor Edmund G. Brown, and the State Board of Control agreed to compensate him with $3,000. Cooper was later convicted of both murders and executed in 1960.[9]

• Louis Bennett of Oklahoma, who said he pleaded guilty to manslaughter charges in the death of a friend because he feared he would get the death sentence if convicted of murder. Although he had been too drunk to remember his whereabouts at the time of the crime, Bennett still insisted on his innocence even though his fingerprints were found on the victim's door. Then, after Bennett had served three years of a thirty-five year sentence, a Texas prisoner confessed to the murder and details of his confession were verified. Bennett, who by then had remembered that he had painted the victim's door a short time before the murder, was released and given an unconditional pardon.[10]

Strange, yet true. But as French playwright Jean Giradoux wrote in *Tiger at the Gates*: "There is no better way of exercising the imagination than the study of the law. No poet ever interpreted nature as freely as a lawyer interprets the law."

Even more curious than an innocent person pleading guilty in order to avoid the death penalty is the rationale of Delphine Bertrand, who in 1944 pleaded guilty to manslaughter charges and was sentenced to ten to fifteen years in a Connecticut prison. Two years later, the two real killers confessed to the crime, and Bertrand was released. Both men were later convicted. So why did Bertrand plead guilty? Because, it turned out, she and a third man had been having sex in another part of the house at the time the killing occurred, and she chose to confess to the murder rather than to publicly reveal her sex life in court.[11]

Fear of a rape conviction and the urging of his attorney were reasons enough for Wayman E. Cammile Jr. of Delaware to agree to plead guilty to less-serious sexual-assault charges, even though it was *Cammile* who turned out to be the actual victim of a crime. Unfortunately, the truth did not come out until 1987—by which time he had served twelve years of his fifteen-year sentence—when his alleged victim recanted her story on her deathbed.

Here are the bizarre details: Cammile was arrested after police found him drunk and unconscious in the Middletown, Delaware, home of Alice Mock. Mock accused Cammile, who had a history of drinking problems, of rape. Just before her death in 1987, however, Mock confessed to a neighbor that she had enticed Cammile into her home, robbed him after he had passed out, and fabricated the rape to cover up her own crime.

The neighbor, Evelyn Burns, informed several public officials about the confession. But she couldn't find anyone interested in taking action until she got to the state Human Relations Commission, which succeeded in spurring an investigation that led to Cammile's release.[12]

Of course, there was in fact a logical—if unstated—reason that the legal system so readily believed Mock and so automatically suspected Cammile: Mock was white, Cammile was black. The next chapter shows just how sadly significant a person's race or ethnic origin still is in the execution of justice in the United States.

Notes

1. "Fatal Defense," *National Law Journal*, pp. 36–44.

2. "California Bar Brings Lawyers' Drug and Alcohol Problems Out of Closet," Associated Press, July 31, 1990.

3. Ibid.

4. "The Man Who Didn't Do It," *Playboy*, August 1980, p. 62. Also, "The Ordeal of Larry Hicks," *Playboy*, May 1981, p. 66.

5. "Protecting Defendants' Rights," *USA Today*, June 1981, p. 2.

6. *Guilty Until Proved Innocent*, pp. 17–18.

7. "The Prosecutor's Role in Plea Bargaining," *University of Chicago Law Review*, vol. 36:50, 1968, pp. 62–63.

8. "Carmen Cleared in Slaying," *Columbus Citizen-Journal*, December 20, 1977, p. 1.

9. *Stanford Law Review*, p. 116.

10. *The Innocents*, p. 154.

11. *Stanford Law Review*, p. 97.

12. "Deathbed Confession Frees Delaware Black After 12 Years," *Jet*, July 6, 1987, p. 16.

8

Bigotry Behind the Blindfold

Hitler's Final Solution for the Jews proved, if any proof was needed, that all too often law has little or nothing to do with justice.
—Judge Bruce Wright

The most certain test by which we judge whether a country is really free is the amount of security enjoyed by minorities.
—Lord Acton

America's history of injustice to the powerless in the name of justice for the powerful goes back to the days of its earliest white settlers. "The Pilgrim Fathers landed on the shores of America and fell upon their knees. Then they fell upon the aborigines," noted that famous phrasemaker Anonymous, whose "name" shows up so frequently in books of quotations.

By the time that injustice ended with the virtual extermination of the American Indian, white Americans began to turn their vengeance in a cruelly individual way on the nation's recently freed blacks and other strangers in their midst—many of whom were guilty of little more than being who and what they were.

While the emphasis here will be on the most serious racially motivated miscarriages of justice, it must be kept in mind that race-based wrongful convictions are a daily occurrence, though they rarely come to light. One that did took place in Madison, Wisconsin, when a white drifter, Jay Douglas Hoffman, accused two black men of robbing him at gunpoint. One of the two was acquitted. But the other, University of Wisconsin student Elwin Donaldson, wasn't as lucky. He was convicted and served two months in prison before Hoffman admitted he had made the whole thing up, apparently out of racial animosity.

Such miscarriages of justice, as serious and regrettable as they are, play a minor part in America's horrific history of bigotry.

Donal E. J. MacNamara, an associate professor of correctional administration at the John Jay College of Criminal Justice in New York, notes in the journal *Crime and Delinquency*:

> No discussion of convicting and executing the innocent would be complete without reference to the history of lynchings in the United States. During the nineteenth century and the early decades of the twentieth, literally thousands of Negroes and no inconsiderable number of whites, Mexicans, Indians and Orientals were surrendered to the fury of mobs. Often these men had not been charged or indicted, much less convicted of a crime; in several instances they had actually been acquitted; and in many cases the crime for which they were lynched was not capital in the particular jurisdiction. The records do not contain a single instance when any leader or member of a lynch mob was executed for the crime of lynching. On the occasion of these lynchings, there was not much of a cry for "law and order" by state and local officials and the press, or, until well in the 1930s, by Congress.[1]

Prejudicial justice was—and is—common even in the most sophisticated of states. Massachusetts Governor Michael Dukakis, for example, admitted that when he cleared the names of Irishmen James Halligan and Dominic Daley, who were executed in 1806 for the murder of Marcus Lyon in Wilbraham. "The historical record shows that religious prejudice and ethnic intolerance played a significant role in their arrest and trial, which resulted in the denial of their rights of due process and a miscarriage of justice," Dukakis said in a St. Patrick's Day proclamation in 1984.

Although the two Irishmen were in Wilbraham the day of Lyon's death, Dukakis said the evidence against them was "flimsy," and that an uncle of the key prosecution witness confessed to the murder on his deathbed years later.

The blurring of guilt and innocence, justice and injustice, criminal law and "lynch law" when it came to blacks and other minorities was clearly exhibited as late as 1934 by a judge running for governor of a southern state. According to an account quoted in Bedau and Radelet's *Stanford Law Review* article, the judge was accused at a political rally of favoritism toward blacks because he had sentenced an alleged black rapist to prison rather than death. He responded in all seriousness by explaining that he had helped secure a prison sentence instead of the death penalty only because he was convinced of the man's *innocence.*

"I shall have the blood of no innocent man on my hand," the judge told the crowd. "He was not guilty of rape; if he had been, the case need not have come into my court." The judge's implied acceptance of the lynching of guilty black defendants and mere imprisonment for innocent ones, the account noted, brought "the most enthusiastic applause of the afternoon."

The legacy of bigotry in the American system of justice, say Bedau and Radelet and many others who have studied the issue, continues to this day. As a result, 151 of the 350 defendants in the two researchers' list of those wrongfully convicted of potentially capital offenses this century are black. That equals 43 percent of the total during a period in which blacks averaged about 10 percent of the nation's population, suggesting that "blacks are much more likely than whites to be erroneously convicted of a potentially capital crime."

Bedau explained why in *The Death Penalty in America,* a book he edited:

> Suffice it to say that race is truly a pervasive influence on the criminal justice processing of potentially capital cases, one that is evident at every stage of the process we have been able to distinguish. It is an influence revealed not only in the movement from one stage to the next, but also in the decisions about circumstances, accompanying charges and sentencing findings within the respective stages of the process. And it is an influence that persists despite separate sentencing hearings, explicitly articulated sentencing guidelines, and automatic review of all death sentences.[2]

A 1990 federal study of more than two dozen research projects on capital sentencing came to the same conclusion about the influence of race on that aspect of the justice system. "In 82 percent of the studies, the race of the victim was found to influence the likelihood of being charged with capital murder or receiving the death penalty, i.e., those who murdered whites were found to be more likely to be sentenced to death than those who murdered blacks," the General Accounting Office said.

Laws making rape a capital crime, which were used almost exclusively in the South against blacks, have probably led to the execution of more innocent men than any other offense, according to Watt Espy, head of the Capital Punishment Research Project in Headland, Alabama. Of the 455 men executed for rape between 1930 and 1965, when the practice was stopped, 89 percent were black. Espy notes that no white man was ever executed in Alabama for raping a black woman, and only two white men were executed for rape in the state's entire history.

"If a black man was accused of rape there wasn't much he could do about it," Espy told an interviewer in 1984. "It is fairly clear that the death penalty was a racial weapon used by the white power structure, and a great number of blacks were systematically eliminated."[3]

But bigotry still knows no boundaries—including the defense table of Hispanics, a growing minority group that is now beginning to suffer the kind of prejudice that has plagued blacks for centuries. In a 1985 murder trial in Texas, for instance, one of Jose Moises Guzmon's "defense" attorneys referred to him several times as a "wetback," then advanced the novel argument that eyewitnesses couldn't identify him for certain because wetbacks "all look like that." To add insult to injury, Guzmon's other attorney apologized for his client's poor appearance on the witness stand by blaming it on "the attitudes of Latin Americans, wherein they can't take responsibility. They have to pass away everything as someone else's fault."

In its review of Guzmon's conviction and death sentence, the Texas Court of Criminal Appeals observed in 1987 that "it may have been difficult for the jury to realize whose side defense counsel were on."

When the court indicated it was contemplating overturning a capital case for the first time under current law because of ineffective counsel, Governor William P. Clements Jr. commuted Guzmon's death sentence to life in prison to avoid the precedent.[4]

But it isn't just blacks and Hispanics who have faced bigotry's legal wrath in U.S. history. In fact, one of the century's earliest and most outrageous convictions of an innocent American was that of Jewish businessman Leo M. Frank of Atlanta in 1913 for the murder of 13-year-old white employee Mary Phagan.[5] Ironically, Phagan's apparent murderer was a black who under normal circumstances would have been lynched with no question about his guilt.

But as O. L. Bricker, who was Phagan's minister and later one of Frank's staunchest defenders, later wrote: "One old Negro would be poor atonement for the life of this innocent girl. But when on the next day, the police arrested a Jew, and a Yankee at that, all of the inborn prejudices against Jews rose up in a feeling of satisfaction that here would be a victim worthy to pay for the crime."

Bricker's assessment has stood the test of time. As Leonard Dinnerstein relates in his excellent book, *The Leo Frank Case*, the judgment today of those who have studied the case is almost unanimous in the conclusion that, in the words of researchers Charles and Louise Samuels, "Leo Frank was the victim of one of the most shocking frame-ups ever perpetrated by American law-and-order officials."

The tragedy began unfolding in April 1913, when Phagan's body was found by the night watchman in the basement of Frank's pencil factory. The coroner determined that she had been beaten and strangled. Frank's trial took place in Milledgeville, with hysterical crowds outside the courthouse shouting "Hang the Jew!" It ended in a conviction and death sentence based on the perjured testimony of janitor Jim Conley, who apparently was the true murderer.

In 1915, Governor John Slaton commuted the sentence to life because of his doubts about Frank's guilt. After the announcement was made, a mob stormed the governor's mansion in Atlanta while a second abducted Frank from a Milledgeville prison. Chanting anti-Semitic slogans, the overzealous citizens lynched Frank near Phagan's home in Cobb County. In the anti-Semitic hysteria that followed, other Jews were attacked and many were forced to flee the state.

Debate over Frank's guilt or innocence continued for many years. Then, in 1982, Alonzo Mann came forward to say what almost everyone had concluded: That Conley had been the culprit. He said that, as a 14-year-old office boy at Frank's factory, he had seen Conley carrying Phagan's body on the first floor, where the murder had taken place. Mann said he had not come forward at the time because Conley had threatened to kill him if he talked, and his mother had also urged him to remain silent.

In 1983, when the Georgia Board of Pardons still denied Frank a full pardon, Mann said: "My conscience is satisfied. I did the best I knew how, and that's all I can do. The pardoning board is wrong."

In March 1986, one year after Mann's death, the board finally granted Frank a posthumous pardon "in recognition of the state's failure to protect the person of Leo Frank and thereby preserve his opportunity for continued legal appeal of his conviction, and in recognition of the state's failure to bring his killers to justice, and as an effort to heal old wounds."

The legacy of Frank's case, generally considered the worst single incident of anti-Semitism in the United States, became the catalyst for the formation of the Anti-Defamation League as well as for the resurgence of the Ku Klux Klan. After the pardon was issued, Stu Lowengrub, the ADL's southeastern director, said his organization's staff could "now finally close our files on our first case" with only one regret: "that Alonzo Mann did not live to see this posthumous pardon granted."

According to Leonard Dinnerstein, Frank's misfortune, which was mainly the result of current circumstances and past plights far beyond his control, left an important warning as well. "Above all, the Leo Frank case showed as clearly as possible that if the laws of civilization are to be respected, societies must eradicate the conditions which turn men into beasts," Dinnerstein cautioned in *The Leo Frank Case.* "For if they do not, other Leo Franks will continue to appear, and suffer punishment for crimes for which no single individual can ever be wholly responsible."[6]

Unfortunately, events from Frank's day to this offer little hope that Dinnerstein's warning has been or will be heeded. Legal lynchings and near-lynchings of innocent individuals convicted as a result of conditions beyond their command remain a major problem today, just as they proved to be in a town that would come to signify American racism: Scottsboro.

The infamous incident began in 1927 in this tiny Alabama town when nine black teenagers were charged with raping two white women of questionable background who made the allegation after they and the young men were found illegally riding a freight train together.

The women's sordid allegations enraged white Alabama to a fever pitch, which grew into what has been described as a "maddening atmosphere" after three white women from prominent families in Birmingham were abducted, allegedly by a black man, taken in their car to a remote area, raped, and shot. Two of the victims died. Several weeks later, the only survivor, Nell Williams, was riding through the downtown area with her brother when she excitedly pointed out a black man walking down the sidewalk as the assailant. Her brother, Dent Williams, pulled a gun from the glove compartment and took Willie Peterson into custody.

When police investigated the case, however, they discovered a number of problems. For one, Peterson didn't resemble in the slightest the description Nell Williams had given of the assailant. In addition, a half-dozen neighbors swore they had seen him on the other side of town at the time of the crime. At that point, Dent Williams asked if his sister could have another look at Peterson to make sure she was right. As soon as Peterson was brought into the room, the brother slipped his hand into his sister's purse, pulled out a pistol and shot him three times before he could be disarmed.

"Miraculously," Dan T. Carter writes in *Scottsboro: A Tragedy of the American South*, "Peterson recovered, but the aftermath of the shooting was a grotesque parody of southern justice. State officials, knowing full well that Peterson was innocent, went ahead and indicted and tried him as soon as he was able to leave the hospital bed. Peterson was eventually convicted and sentenced to die in the electric chair even though most admitted privately that Williams had 'picked the wrong Negro.' "

"Rather than humiliate Miss Williams by contradicting her story," Carter continues, "the state of Alabama was willing to convict an innocent man. The honor of one white woman was more important than the life's blood of a black man, said the *Birmingham Reporter*. A Negro accused of rape by a white woman had not the 'chance of a sheep-killing dog to establish his innocence or to get the benefit of any doubt.' "

Fortunately, reason prevailed—to a point. After pleas of mercy from many prominent Alabamians, Peterson's sentence was commuted to life—which didn't turn out to be that long. He died of tuberculosis several years later. Typically, Dent Williams was never indicted.

Amid this "fever heat" and ominous precedent, the nine teenagers accused in the freight-train incident—who soon became known as the "Scottsboro Boys"—were tried, over the objections of counsel, before an all-white jury. They were quickly convicted in assembly-line fashion, and all but one were sentenced to death. A retrial was ordered by an appeals court, however, and the first of the Scottsboro Boys to be tried was convicted again even though one of the two accusers had changed her story and testified that the attack had never occurred. At that point, the courageous trial judge, James Edwin Horton, set aside the verdict and ordered a new trial. In a strongly worded opinion that would cost him his job at the next election, Horton wrote: "History, sacred and profane, and the common experience of mankind teach us that women of the character shown in this case are prone for selfish reasons to make false accusations both of rape and of insult upon the slightest provocation or even without provocation for ulterior purposes." He said the testimony of the second woman, Victoria Price, was not only uncorroborated, but was improbable and contradicted by evidence that "greatly preponderates in favor of the defendant."

In a retrial before a different judge, however, the first two to go before the jury were convicted once again and sentenced to death. But those verdicts were overturned because of the unfairness alluded to by the defense attorney in the very first trial—the deliberate exclusion of blacks from the jury. In 1936, the first young man to be tried was again convicted and sentenced to seventy-five years. For good measure, he was also shot by the sheriff, and after the rape charges were eventually dropped, was sentenced to twenty years for the alleged assault that had led to the shooting.

In 1937, another of the Scottsboro Boys was convicted once again and sentenced to death. This farce continued, to the growing outrage of much of the nation, until, in the end, the nine had spent a total of 104 years in prison for a crime that even their prosecutors privately agreed probably had never happened. In 1976, the state of Alabama granted Clarence Norris, the only surviving defendant, an unconditional pardon based on the overwhelming evidence that all the Scottsboro Boys had been innocent.

"There had been many cases similar to that in Scottsboro and most of them had gone unnoticed," writes Carter. "But the number of participants, their youth, the stunning rapidity of their trials, and, most of all, the harsh sentences they received, roused a wave of protest from millions of Americans. It was a concern which the radical left would channel and direct until the name 'Scottsboro' became synonymous with southern racism, repression, and injustice."[7]

The first place the name "Scottsboro" was applied was in the case of "The Four Pompano Boys" who, from among a large number of black suspects rounded up, confessed after five days of continuous questioning to the 1933 murder of a white man. As the four were quickly convicted and sentenced to death, the case soon came to be known as "Little Scottsboro."

As it turned out, the highly suspect confessions were the only evidence presented against the defendants, three of whom pleaded guilty after receiving minimal advice from their court-appointed attorneys. When the Florida Supreme Court later heard reports that the confessions and guilty pleas had been coerced, it allowed the defendants to apply for a writ of error. When the writ was denied by a trial judge, the high court ordered that the issue be resolved by a jury. When the jury also decided against the four men, the high court reversed that decision as well on the ground of incorrect jury instructions. After a change of venue, a jury decided against the defendants once again, and the state supreme court affirmed the decision.

But that wasn't the end of the matter. In 1940, the U.S. Supreme Court ruled unanimously that the confessions were indeed coerced, and threw out the convictions on the ground of denial of due process. At that point, one of the four defendants was transferred to a mental hospital. The other three received a directed verdict of acquittal in 1942.[8]

At the same time these two nationally watched dramas were going on, an equally egregious case of prejudiced justice was beginning a long, tragic run in Oklahoma. In 1931, the same year as the start of the Scottsboro case, a black man named Jess Hollins was convicted of the rape of a white woman with whom he claimed he had been having consensual sexual relations for some time, and sentenced to death. As lynching rumors spread through Oklahoma City, Hollins, who did not have the aid of a lawyer, pleaded guilty. The conviction was reversed on appeal, however, because the plea was judged to have been made under fear of lynching. But Hollins was convicted once again, and this time the appeals court upheld the verdict. Just thirty hours before his scheduled execution, the U.S. Supreme Court granted a stay. It later threw out the conviction altogether because of the deliberate exclusion of black jurors.

So what did Oklahoma do? It tried Hollins before another all-white jury that convicted him despite the strong evidence presented by his attorneys that the alleged victim had regularly consorted with Hollins and had accused him of rape only when their relationship was discovered by her brother-in-law. Hollins's luck improved slightly, though, when he was given a life sentence rather than a death sentence.

Although many whites were beginning to believe in Hollins's innocence, and despite the obvious unconstitutional racial make-up of the jury, Hollins chose not to tempt fate by appealing only to end up with a new death sentence. He died in prison in 1950, a clear victim of racial injustice.

But Hollins was actually luckier than a contemporary, Roosevelt Collins of Scottsboro-incensed Alabama. Collins, like Hollins, was accused of raping a white woman, an allegation that inspired greater fury than murder among white men in 1937. As if to prove it, the alleged victim's husband pulled out a gun and fired at Collins after he had testified during his trial that the woman had consented to his advances, causing a near-riot in the process. Collins also came close to being lynched, and his defense seemed almost like an offense. The all-white jury, proving British cleric and writer Thomas Fuller's admonition that "a fox should not be the jury at a goose's trial," took all of four minutes to vote on Collins's conviction. Several of these upstanding citizens later admitted that they thought the woman had indeed consented to sex with Collins, but that he deserved the death sentence for the very audacity of "messin' around" with a white woman. The judge later said much the same thing. But that didn't help Collins. He was executed the same year he had been arrested and convicted.[9]

The casebooks are full of such examples in the system of alleged justice of that era, but they are all so shockingly similar that there is little use in repeating them. Suffice it to say that the United States was a precarious place for the black man to live before World War II. Unfortunately, it wasn't much better *after* World War II.

Take the 1945 case of Willie McGee of Mississippi, who was convicted of raping a white woman and sentenced to death after an all-white jury deliberated for a grand total of two-and-a-half minutes. The main evidence against McGee was a coerced confession given after thirty-two days of interrogation while being held incommunicado. An investigation by a young journalist by the name of Carl T. Rowan, later to become a syndicated columnist, disclosed that the alleged victim had been having an affair with McGee for four years and had made up the accusation after he told her of his desire to end the relationship. Rowan reported that blacks aware of this but were afraid to come forward and that the local whites considered the woman's consent either infeasible or immaterial: Black men knew sex with a white woman was a de facto capital offense. And that's what it proved to be. McGee was executed in 1951.[10]

Two years later, blacks Edgar Labat and Clifton Poret of Louisiana were convicted of the aggravated rape of a white woman and the robbery of her male companions and sentenced to death. After a series of failed appeals and stays of their executions, Labat and Poret were dropped by their attorneys and faced likely death in the near future. In desperation, they smuggled out an appeal that ran as a classified ad in the *Los Angeles Times*, where a sympathetic doctor who saw it hired new attorneys. As a result, the two men were granted their ninth stay of execution—with three hours to spare. Then one of three witnesses against them recanted and the second said he had been forced by police into perjuring himself. That left only the testimony of the supposed victim to challenge, which proved easy to do because of the inaccuracies and discrepancies it contained. Now supported by solid alibi witnesses whom the previous attorneys had failed to call and evidence that one of the defendants had been beaten into confessing by police, a new trial was ordered.

As is typical of southern states in particular, however, the courts seemed reluctant to admit that a mistake had been made. Instead, Labat and Poret were sentenced to the sixteen years they had already served and released in 1969. Incensed at the injustice of their treatment, Burton H. Wolfe writes in his 1973 book, *Pileup on Death Row*, that, "Although the details in news stories were vague, they were adequate for the public to see that if it were not for the long delays of executions brought about by the oft-damned 'legal loopholes,' these two men would have been executed 16 years before they were finally released, and their cases closed with nobody giving a hang that they had been unjustly convicted."[11]

But it is probably because somebody did "give a hang" that James and John Giles and their friend Joseph Johnson Jr. aren't dead. The legal odyssey of the three young black residents of Montgomery County, Maryland, began on the night of July 20, 1961. As was their frequent practice, the trio had gone fishing in the Patuxent River. By midnight, they were ready to call it a night, since they had to be at work the next morning. The picked up their generous gathering of fish and headed for their car. According to Giles-Johnson Defense Committee member Frances Strauss's book *Where Did the Justice Go?* the tired fishermen found, to their consternation, that their car was blocked in by one belonging to some parked lovers. According to the trio's later testimony, when they approached the car, a white boy inside, angry at the interruption, let loose with a torrent of racial epithets that finally caused the three blacks to respond. In a matter of seconds, the white boy was out cold on the ground and his girlfriend had fled into the woods.

When they came across her on their way toward the road, the girl seemed more than friendly. "I know what you boys want," Strauss quotes her as saying. "I've already had sixteen or seventeen this week and three more won't make any difference." She then took off her clothes, according to the three defendants' testimony, and pointed to John to start the fun. If John tried anything at all, he quickly changed his mind and disappeared into the woods. Joe Johnson wasn't so shy. He took his turn, then went home to bed. Then James took over, ignoring the entreaty of John, who had returned from the woods, that they get going. He also ignored the shout of the white boy that he was going to get the police. As James was lying beside the girl a short while later, he heard the police sirens and began running away. Then something the girl had said earlier began to worry him: that she was already in trouble, so if the police found her there, she would have to say she was raped. And that's exactly what she did.

The two Giles brothers and Johnson were all convicted of the rape of the girl, who turned out to be sixteen years old, and were sentenced to death. But Montgomery County, Maryland, was not Montgomery, Alabama. A number of the county's generally well-educated, articulate citizens saw racism in both the convictions and sentences, and decided to fight institutional injustice with individual justice. Before long the Giles-Johnson Defense Committee was formed, and an investigation of what really had happened that night was launched. Soon, enough new exculpatory evidence had been found that five of the jurors who convicted the three men wrote to the governor to inform him that if they had known about the new evidence at the time of the trial, they would have voted for acquittal. The governor then ordered his own investigation, after which he commuted the sentences to life. After the U.S. Supreme Court raised several questions about the alleged victim's credibility, it ordered new hearings in 1967. The prosecutors then dropped the case against the Giles brothers and they were released. Johnson was freed in 1968 after being granted a full pardon by a man who would have a much easier time in court a few years later than he and the Giles brothers did—then-Governor Spiro Agnew.

The case was history. But it left many wondering how one confused white girl could cause so much injustice to three young black men in Maryland, just as other such women had caused so much grief for the Scottsboro Boys, Willie McGee, Jess Hollins, the Four Pompano Boys, Roosevelt Collins, and hundreds like them.

"It would be hard to find more devastating proof of the awful fallibility of the American judicial system than the seven-year saga of three young citizens of Maryland" notes CBS Radio commentator Edward P. Morgan in his introduction to *Where Did the Justice Go?*:

> The sexual element in racism seems to bring out the worst savagery of prejudice. Perhaps we have passed the time when a black man can be convicted of molesting a white woman by simply casting a glance in her direction. But when a Negro is suspected of the craven but titillating crime of rape, he is automatically presumed guilty unless and until he can prove his innocence. In the past this has been well-nigh impossible because the whole machinery of society was geared against the accused. And, as it was put by one of the dedicated attorneys who donated countless man-hours to the defense without fee, Joe Forer, "Innocence is a relatively irrelevant factor of the American law."[12]

The Focus Changes

Ironically, just when someone was willing to openly raise the sexual element of the racism that had led to so many miscarriages of justice in the United States, it suddenly no longer seemed to be an issue. After the Giles-Johnson case, Americans seemed far more concerned about the political and physical threat of increasingly assertive blacks to society in general than about their threat to white womanhood in particular.

One of the first miscarriages of justice to result from this change had its origins in 1963, two years after the start of the Giles-Johnson case. On August 1 of that year, Freddie Pitts was a 28-year-old pulp cutter, and Wilbert Lee a 20-year-old Army private on leave. That night, along with a woman and several other friends, they stopped at a service station in the small Gulf Coast community of Port St. Joe, Florida. When they discovered that the station had a "whites only" policy on the use of its rest rooms, the two black men argued with the two white attendants, whose bullet-riddled bodies were found three days later.

Their woman companion soon accused Pitts and a soldier other than Lee of the crimes. When the Army proved that the other soldier had a firm alibi, the woman accused Lee instead, and the two men were arrested and charged with first-degree homicide. Although there was no physical evidence to link them to the crimes, the two were convicted of murder and sentenced to death after they pleaded guilty at the urging of their court-appointed attorney, who told them there was "no other way" because of the detailed confessions they had provided.

Pitts and Lee insisted those confessions had been beaten out of them and that they were innocent, but no one seemed to take them seriously. A few days later, however, a black parolee was arrested in Fort Lauderdale for the murder of a service-station attendant under similar circumstances, and in 1966, after his conviction on that charge, he told a cellmate he was also responsible for the Port St. Joe killings.

Word of the confession reached *Miami Herald* reporter Gene Miller, who would later win the 1967 Pulitzer Prize for an exposé that resulted in the exoneration of Pitts and Lee. Miller's articles on the case soon attracted the attention of the American Civil Liberties Union, which filed a motion for a new trial on the two men's behalf. They got the trial in 1972. But the confessed convict refused to testify when the prosecutors refused to grant him immunity, and Pitts and Lee were convicted once again.

Meanwhile, unbeknown to the defense, the woman who originally identified Lee and Pitts as the murderers had recanted her accusation, claiming she had been forced by police into "naming somebody."

When the governor's chief legal aide read about this suppression of evidence in Miller's soon-to-be released book on the case, *Invitation to a Lynching*, he persuaded Governor Reubin Askew that there was serious doubt about the two men's guilt. Askew ordered an investigation that culminated in the granting of an executive pardon signed by the governor and three members of his cabinet. "The evidence which was not available at the trial and now available is conclusive," Askew said. "These men are not guilty."

Thus ended, after twelve years, one month, and nineteen days, what the *New York Times* said many had branded "the saddest, most blatant miscarriage of justice in Florida's history." The two men's volunteer appellate attorney put it rather bluntly when he said Pitts and Lee, "although totally innocent, were convicted because they were black."

As the two were finally released on September 19, 1975, Lee turned to Pitts and asked softly, "Is it over, Eddie?"

"It's over, man," Pitts replied as they walked through the Florida State Prison gates near Starke together. "It's really over."[13]

But not completely. Starting in 1979, after each had settled in Miami, where Pitts became a respected owner of a small petroleum-products business and Lee a social worker, the two men began seeking financial compensation from the Florida Legislature for the twelve years the state had wrongfully taken away from them. And each year since then, the never-say-you're-sorry legislature has found a way to turn them down. And so it was again on May 14, 1990, when a House committee rejected by a vote of six-to-four a bill that offered a relatively modest $250,000 to each of the two men.

"The Pitts and Lee case," the *Miami Herald* editorialized three days later, "is an outrageous example of a system that has denied justice based on race for twenty-seven years! . . . But the legislature can still redeem the state on behalf of Mr. Pitts and Mr. Lee this session. It merely has to do the right thing."

Once again, though, it didn't.

The state of Massachusetts came a little closer to compensating one of its victims of racial injustice when a bill introduced on behalf of Lawyer Johnson passed both houses of the legislature but died in a conference committee. Johnson himself could have died at the hands of the same state after he was convicted by an all-white jury of the first-degree murder of a white man and sentenced to death in 1972. The state supreme court reversed the decision, however, saying a government witness had withheld evidence and the court improperly limited Johnson's chance to cross-examine witnesses.

In 1974, Johnson was convicted of second-degree murder rather than first-degree murder by an all-white jury, and sentenced to life in prison. Johnson and his attorney contended that both convictions came about because of racial tensions and the tainted testimony of the state's principal witness, Kenneth Myers.

They were proved right on the latter count, at least, in 1982, when a previously silent witness came forward and identified Myers as the actual killer. Dannielle Montiero, who lived in the housing project where the 1971 slaying occurred, said she didn't speak up earlier because she was only ten years old at the time and feared reprisal by Myers. The prosecutor said he was forced to drop the charges because Myers, who was then in prison on unrelated charges, suddenly decided he no longer wanted to testify. It isn't hard to figure out why.

"I feel better, but I could have felt a lot better if it was ten years ago," Johnson, then thirty, told the *Boston Globe* after he was freed. "I'm bitter as hell that it took all this time."

Johnson's attorney agreed. "A totally innocent man would have been executed, killed by the state," Michael Avery said. "As it is, he lost ten years of his life. . . . We can't give that back, but if he had been executed, we certainly could not have given him his life back."

Nineteen-seventy-two also marked the introduction of wrongful convictions of blacks not just because of their color but also because of their politics. One of the first such victims was Harllel B. Jones, the controversial leader of a Cleveland black nationalist organization called Afro Set. Jones was convicted of second-degree murder and sentenced to life in prison for allegedly ordering random shootings in retaliation after a security guard shot and killed an Afro Set member. The chief witness against him was the admitted triggerman, who had more serious first-degree murder charges against him dropped in return for his testimony against Jones.

The only problem was that two others who were present at the shooting said Jones had nothing to do with the crime. Even more important, another co-defendant's written statement about the murder didn't mention Jones at all. But both that statement and the agreement to drop the charges against Jones's chief accuser in return for his testimony were concealed from Jones's attorneys. When Jones later found out about the suppression of the exculpatory evidence, he filed a petition for habeas corpus and was released in 1977 pending a new trial. A year later, all charges against him were dropped.

Jones, who by then worked for a Cleveland interfaith group, repeated his claim of innocence after the charges were dismissed. "I wouldn't order anybody to do something like that," he told the Cleveland Plain Dealer. "I would still take a lie detector test to prove that I didn't do it." That, of course, is the worst way to prove one's innocence. But the polygraph myth is hard to overcome.

Like Jones, Frank "Parky" Grace was a political activist. His first brush with activism came when he became involved in the anti-war movement after serving in Vietnam in 1967. In a 1984 interview with the Boston Globe, Grace said his Vietnam experience had radicalized his views on racism as well as on the war.

When he became friendly with some of the locals in the area where he was stationed, Grace said, "They used to tell me, 'Ho Chi Minh, number one.'

"I used to say, 'No, no, he's a Communist.'

"Then they asked me, 'Why are you here?'

" 'Fighting for freedom.'

"They say, 'You have freedom at home?'

"Through them I started seeing I didn't have any freedom."

When he returned to his native New Bedford, Grace said he was exposed to the writings of Che Guevara and Malcolm X by the white radicals with whom he demonstrated against the war.

Soon, according to records later obtained by his attorneys through the Freedom of Information Act, the FBI had put Grace under surveillance and kept him there as he began to organize an arm of the Black Panthers in 1970.

Not coincidentally, the New Bedford police began regularly arresting Grace on a variety of charges. "Harassment," Grace told the *Globe*. "They arrested me over forty times and never convicted me of anything."

Until 1974, that is. That's when Grace and his brother, Ross, were convicted of first-degree murder by an all-white jury and sentenced to life in prison. In 1983, however, an evidentiary hearing was ordered after an investigation by the New England American Friends Service Committee showed that "he was arrested [for the murder] by a police officer who had a longstanding antipathy toward him, . . . he was sentenced although there was no evidence to convict him, and he remains in jail although proof of his innocence abounds."

Then, in 1984, one of the key witnesses for the prosecution admitted he had been forced by police to falsely identify Frank Grace as the killer during the original trial. "Frank's brother, Ross, shot [Marvin] Morgan," Jasper Lassiter said in an affidavit. "I saw Frank Grace for the first time at his murder trial. Before my testimony, police officers told me that Frank would be sitting next to Ross in the courtroom and that I should testify that Frank fired the gunshot which killed Morgan."

At the same hearing, Ross Grace testified that it was he and not Frank who shot Morgan.

"Morgan and [Eric] Baker had kidnapped me a month earlier and stole $800 from me," Ross Grace told the *Boston Globe* in an interview after the hearing. "So I decided to get a gun in case I ran into them again." Ross Grace said his brother had been across town at the time of the shooting.[14]

In January 1985, Superior Court Justice Elizabeth J. Dolan overturned Frank Grace's conviction and set him free for good because the new evidence revealed at that hearing appeared "so grave, material, and relevant as to afford a probability that it would be a real factor with the jury in reaching a decision."

But more than facts enter into how a jury makes a decision. Racism has long been suspected as an additional factor, but that has been hard to prove because of the traditional secrecy of jury proceedings.

That secrecy historically extended beyond the trial itself. But some jurors in recent years have been increasingly open in discussing the inner workings of the panel after the decision was rendered.

Spencer Allen, now of Columbus, Ohio, is one of them. And he offers some rare insight into how racism entered into a jury's decision in 1974 to condemn a man to death for a murder in Tampa. The man was eventually cleared after fourteen years on Florida's death row.

Joseph Green Brown, who had no criminal record before his conviction—although he admitted he was "no angel"—was sitting in the death-watch cell only thirty feet and fifteen hours from the electric chair at Florida State Prison in Starke when a federal judge stayed his execution. Then, in March 1986, the U.S. Circuit Court of Appeals reversed his conviction on the grounds that the prosecutor had knowingly permitted and exploited false testimony from the state's key witness.

That witness had long since recanted his testimony, leaving prosecutors in Tampa no choice but to drop the charges against Brown and release him. "Welcome to the free world," his lawyer said with a smile as Brown walked out of the Hillsborough County Jail. It would have been nice if it really was a free world, because Brown had only seventy-five cents to show for the fourteen years of grief and pain he had been through.

Although it couldn't begin to compare with what Brown endured, Spencer Allen had been through some grief of his own since serving on the all-white jury that condemned Brown to death. Allen's concern began as soon as the jury convened to decide whether to recommend the death sentence.

"It was then that the vehemence of the jurors whom I had, until then, respected came out and I began to question on what motives they found Brown guilty," Allen told me fifteen years later. "They said things like 'This nigger's been doing this since he was fifteen,' and, 'He probably did this all the way down from South Carolina.' "

"I was stunned, numbed," Allen said. "The gross, vicious prejudice made me, and still does to this haunting day, wonder on what facts or evidence others based their decisions. . . . I sat powerless in my misery while the majority voted to recommend death and it came crushing down on this black man because he'd 'been doing it since he was fifteen.' "

In 1983, Allen finally tried to give a statement to Brown's attorney regarding the jurors' prejudice. But the prosecutor obtained a court order prohibiting him from doing so. Then, in 1986, it all came out that Allen's suspicions had been justified.

Among the factors that entered in the appeals court's reversal of Brown's conviction was evidence that:

• The star witness had first tried to recant almost immediately after giving his testimony, despite threats of a life sentence by both the judge and the prosecutor, but was not allowed to do so.

• The prosecutor had suppressed an FBI report concluding that the bullet found in the murder victim's body did not come from Brown's gun and that the victim's rapist had a different blood type than Brown.

• The state had changed the estimated time of the murder to fit the facts of its case against Brown.

• A second key witness also admitted he had given false testimony against Brown in return for having charges against him dropped.

• After Brown's release, Allen was given a chance to apologize to the wrongfully convicted man on ABC's "20/20" a few weeks later. But he remains disturbed by the entire experience.

"I used to be a firm believer in the American justice system, but now I have my doubts," the social worker said. "I used to believe in the death penalty, but now I don't. I also believe prosecutors who mislead juries should be severely punished."

Did anything happen to the prosecutor in this case? I asked.

"As a matter of fact, yes," Allen replied with a look of disgust. "He was elected judge."

Given his performance as a prosecutor, the good judge will probably fit right in with Circuit Court Judge Thomas Shands, who helped the local police and prosecutor railroad a black former divinity student and aspiring writer from Chicago right onto death row the same year Brown was being shipped there.

Delbert Tibbs wasn't your typical murderer-rapist, which is what Florida officials accused him of being. At his first trial, attorney Anna Langford, a member of the Chicago City Council, described Tibbs as "a concerned, conscientious, gentle young man." And the Reverend Charles Mack, a professor of Cardinal Mudelein College in suburban Chicago, recalled his "concern for theological studies and creative writing."

After being honorably discharged from the Army, Tibbs had become heavily involved in community activities on Chicago's South Side while also attending Chicago City College and the Chicago Theological Seminary. He worked as a youth counselor, supported drug abuse programs, and became involved in politics. He also began gaining a reputation as a writer, and had his poetry published in several publications.

It was Tibbs's interest in creative writing that took him to Florida; he was hitchhiking around the country gathering material for what he had hoped would be his breakthrough novel.

On February 3, 1974, the same day Tibbs claimed to be in Daytona Beach, a heavy-set, dark-complected black man driving a pickup truck 400 miles to the southwest offered a young white woman and her male companion a ride. According to police, he then drove them to an isolated area outside of Fort Myers, shot and killed the man, and raped the woman.

The "woman" turned out to be Cynthia Nadeau, a 16-year-old habitual runaway and admitted drug user who had smoked three marijuana cigarettes that day. She gave police a confusing, often contradictory account of what actually had happened. She was shown approximately two-hundred photos of black men, but could identify none as the attacker.

Four days later, Tibbs was stopped by police in Ocala as part of a statewide search for the assailant. Since the tall, slender, light-complected Tibbs in no way resembled the man described by the victim, police took some photos of him, gave him a "safe conduct pass" so he wouldn't have to go through the same inconvenience elsewhere, and sent him on his way. Tibbs's photos were sent on to Fort Myers police, who, against normal procedures, showed them to Nadeau by themselves instead of in a group of photos. And although he didn't match the description she had given, Nadeau identified Tibbs as the killer-rapist. Nadeau was apparently already well-acquainted with racism by sixteen; she had shown an ability to lump all blacks together during her first interview, when she initially described the attacker as "a nigger with wooly hair, like they all have." So, under that description, at least, Tibbs qualified.

Tibbs was arrested near his aunt's home in Mississippi, where police had known to look for him because he had given the Ocala cops his itinerary—just like any man on the run would do. Confident that the confusion would be cleared up quickly, Tibbs cooperatively waived his extradition rights and was taken to Fort Myers, where his photo had been all over the newspapers. Nadeau easily picked him out of a lineup. Case closed.

Enter the judicious Judge Thomas Shands. When he opened the trial on Wednesday, December 11, 1974, Shands expressed hope it could be concluded by Friday, implying the case seemed cut-and-dried. And so it appeared. The only major witness was Cynthia Nadeau, who reconciled Tibbs's light complexion with her description of the assailant as being "very dark" by saying simply: "Maybe he changed colors." The thought that a young white girl such as Nadeau might be changing her story apparently hadn't crossed the minds of the members of the all-white jury.

The only other witness against Tibbs was the usual jailbird willing to claim, in return for a shorter sentence or some other incentive, that the defendant had confessed his guilt while in jail. These informers apparently are so good at getting people to confess that one wonders why they didn't go into police work or the priesthood. The latter field might be particularly appropriate for Sylvester Gibbs, because he testified that he performed the miracle of getting Tibbs to confess to him on a date *three weeks* before Tibbs was in the jail.

George C. Howard, a top defense attorney from Chicago hired by the Delbert Tibbs Defense Fund there, immediately noticed the inconsistency and bluntly asked Gibbs if he was lying.

"Right," a sheepish Gibbs replied after considerable hesitation.

Then came the prosecutor's surprise evidence: A card made out in Tibbs's name at the Salvation Army mission in Orlando, 150 miles from the crime, and dated the day after the crime occurred. While the card hardly put Tibbs at the crime scene, it did contradict his claim that he was in Daytona Beach. A furious Tibbs and Howard contended the card was a forgery, and later tried to call handwriting analysts to testify that the signature was not in Tibbs's handwriting. But Judge Shands refused to admit their testimony.

Despite the flimsy evidence against Tibbs, it took the white jurors only ninety minutes to find him guilty and recommend his execution.

George Howard pulled no punches in his remarks to reporters afterward. In his fourteen years of criminal practice and three hundred murder trials, Howard said, he had "never had a case resulting in this kind of conviction where there was absolutely *no* evidence against the client. But this case is a very dangerous thing. It means those in authority can rig any kind of case against a person, and the law doesn't mean a thing. It's the oldest trick in the country—a 'nigger' did the killing—and the citizens of the United States and the State of Florida bought it."[15]

The Florida Supreme Court, fortunately, did not. In an extraordinarily strong opinion, the court expressed "considerable doubt that Delbert Tibbs is the man who committed the crimes for which he has been convicted" and ordered a new trial. One justice even argued that Tibbs should be set free without a second trial.

But Tibbs's prosecutors weren't about to do that. So they ended up going all the way to the U.S. Supreme Court to overcome defense arguments that a retrial would be double jeopardy, and won in 1982. But then the state announced that the case would not be reopened because the police investigation of the crime "was tainted from the beginning . . . and the investigators involved knew it." In a rare case of magnanimity, the original prosecutor announced that if there was a retrial, he would testify as a witness for Tibbs. That kind of open-mindedness probably precluded the prosecutor from ever becoming a judge.[16]

As outrageous an example of racism as Tibbs's case was, Clarence Lee Brandley's may be worse. What makes it more frightening is that what the courts themselves eventually admitted was an egregious ex-ample of racism wasn't corrected until—and may still be litigated in —the supposedly enlightened decade of the 1990s.

Brandley's tribulations began in 1980, when he was convicted of raping and strangling a teenager at the Houston-area high school where the 38-year-old black man worked. After a ten-day hearing on a motion for a retrial in 1987, a retired state district judge fi-nally gave Brandley and his numerous supporters some hope when he ruled that the evidence presented showed that Brandley was in-nocent and shifted suspicion to two other school janitors, both of whom happened to be white. Brandley's attorneys also presented evi-dence to show that, incredibly—well, maybe not, considering that this was Texas—that the district attorney and the trial judge met secretly to discuss the case.

Retired State District Judge Perry Pickett agreed with all defense claims in an order that recommended a new trial. And he didn't mince words in doing so:

> In the thirty years this court has presided over matters in the judicial system, no case has presented a more shocking scenario of the effects of racial prejudice, perjured testimony, witness intimidation, an in-vestigation the outcome of which was predetermined and public offi-cials who for whatever motives, lost sight of what is right and just. The continued incarceration of Clarence Lee Brandley under these cir-cumstances is an affront to the basic notions of fairness and justice.[17]

With such an impassioned plea, you might think that the Texas Court of Criminal Appeals would move quickly to consider the case. But things don't work that way in Texas. So it was another fourteen months before the court got around to a hearing, during which Brandley's attorney stressed that blood tests made only after the state attorney general entered the investigation revealed that foreign Type A blood was found on the girl's body. Brandley is Type O. The two white janitors implicated in the crime are both Type A.

It took the appeals court until December 1989 to finally get around to overturning Brandley's conviction, saying his prosecution was marked by "blatant unfairness." In a six-to-three decision, the court said the state's investigative procedures "lacked the rudiments of fairness," noting, among other things, that another janitor who testified for the state was allegedly coerced into doing so by a Texas Ranger police officer and that the state suppressed evidence that could have implicated someone else.

"The principles of due process embodied within the United States Constitution must not, indeed cannot, countenance such blatant unfairness," Judge David A. Barchelmann Jr. wrote in the court's decision. Even then, however, the court declined a request to have Brandley freed on personal recognizance bond. Brandley, who once came within six days of being executed, was finally freed on $75,000 bond in January 1990. But his trial appeared to be far from over. Calling Brandley a "continuing threat to society," District Attorney Peter Speers vowed to take the case all the way to the U.S. Supreme Court to get the ruling reversed.

But—and here's the typical escape hatch for tough-talking prosecutors in such cases—Speers added that it was doubtful he would retry the case because of the lapse in time. This was another way of saying he knew he could never win, while still heaping on Brandley a burden of doubt—and, in the minds of some, guilt—to live with.[18]

A recent, unfortunate side-effect of such racially tinged and widely publicized miscarriages of justice, along with highly politicized trials like that of Washington Mayor Marion Barry, is what has been called "race–based denial"—the belief among many blacks that the white-dominated legal system is rigged against them and that many blacks it judges to be guilty are in fact innocent.

In an article following the racially divisive Central Park–jogger trial in the summer of 1990, the *New York Times* noted that as this argument gained credibility among blacks during the late 1980s, it damaged the credibility of many black leaders and perpetuated racist stereotypes. "Yet the denial of culpability is fueled by two potent factors," the *Times* article added. "One is that practitioners of race-based denial are sometimes proved correct. Moreover, evidence in a criminal case is often reduced to a credibility contest between the official version and the defendant's. This premise brings two fundamental legal tenants into conflict: the presumption of innocence, and the popular acceptance of a verdict once jurors conclude that guilt has been proved beyond their reasonable doubts." The other factor behind blacks' distrust of the system is what black sociologist Shelby Steele described as "a clinging, at all cost and beyond reason, to a victim-focused identity. . . . We have been locked into victimization as a source of power for so long now we're reluctant to give it up. But it inadvertently means not taking responsibility."[19]

And not taking responsibility will only make crime seem more excusable to some, escalating the nation's crime rate, and the suffering of people of all colors that crime causes, to new heights—or, more accurately, new depths.

Avoidance of more cases like that of Clarence Lee Brandley and Delbert Tibbs, which reinforce such feelings of victimization, would be a good place to start reversing this trend while we still can.

Notes

1. "Convicting the Innocent," *Crime and Delinquency*, 1969, vol. 15, p. 61.

2. Hugo Adam Bedau, ed., *The Death Penalty in America* (Oxford: Oxford University Press, 1982), p. 220.

3. "Et Al.," *Student Lawyer*, April 1984, p. 45.

4. *National Law Journal*, p. 34.

5. " 'Our Willie' and the Leo Frank Case," *Christian Century*, October 9, 1985, p. 807.

6. Information on the Frank case come from "Georgia Pardons Victim 70 Years After Lynching," *New York Times*, March 12, 1986, p. A16, and from Leonard Dinnerstein, *The Leo Frank Case* (New York: Columbia University Press, 1968).

7. Dan T. Carter, *Scottsboro: A Tragedy of the American South* (Baton Rouge: Louisiana State University Press, 1969).

8. *Stanford Law Review*, pp. 104 and 127.

9. Ibid., pp. 106–107.

10. Ibid., pp. 145–146.

11. Burton H. Wolfe, *Pileup on Death Row* (Garden City, N.Y.: Doubleday, 1973), pp. 296–298.

12. Frances Strauss, *Where Did Justice Go? The Story of the Giles-Johnson Case* (Boston: Gambit, 1970).

13. " 'It's Over' for 2 Wrongly Held 12 Years," *New York Times*, Sept. 20, 1975, p. 1.

14. "A Murder Conviction Overturned After 11 Years for Former New Bedford Black Panther Leader," *Boston Globe*, January 16, 1985, p. 19.

15. "The Delbert Tibbs Case," *The Nation*, December 18, 1976, p. 654.

16. *Stanford Law Review*, p. 163.

17. "Texas Is Often Slow to Admit Mistakes," *Columbus Dispatch*, March 1, 1989, p. 9A.

18. "Brandley's Still a Threat, D.A. Contends," *Dallas Times Herald*, December 15, 1989, p. A-1.

19. "For Some Blacks, Justice Is Not Blind to Color," *New York Times*, September 9, 1990, p. 1C.

9

Grave Injustice

Listen to the voice of justice and of reason. It tells us and tells us that human judgments are never so certain as to permit society to kill a human being judged by other human beings. . . . Why deprive yourselves of any chance to redeem such errors? Why condemn yourselves to helplessness when faced with persecuted innocence?
—Robespierre, three years before his execution

Captain George Kendall, who in 1608 earned the dubious distinction of being the first person executed in America, may also have been the first innocent person to suffer that fate. Kendall, a governing councilor in what is now Virginia, was supposedly shot for spying. But Watt Espy, the nation's leading researcher on the history of capital punishment, says the evidence indicates Kendall was actually framed by opponents so upset with his policies that they decided to get rid of him for good.

Espy, who has documented close to 16,000 executions dating back to Kendall's, estimates that a total of about 22,500 people have actually died at the hand of the state since colonial times.

The Alabama researcher says he had no strong feeling either way about capital punishment when he started his project as a hobby in 1970. But the dozens of executions of innocent people he has uncovered has changed that. Espy now believes the documented cases of mistaken executions are the most powerful argument against capital punishment. "To my way of thinking, nothing can be more horrible or repugnant than that the state, with all its power for good or evil, should deprive one of its citizens of life for a crime committed by another," he wrote in 1980.[1]

Each such case is filled with tragedy and irony, but some particularly stand out in Espy's mind.

One involved the father of Supreme Court Justice Lucius Quintius Cincinnatus Lamar. A brilliant Milledgeville, Georgia, jurist in his own right, the senior Lamar once sentenced a Methodist minister to hang for the rape-murder of his sister-in law.

"The judgment of the court was duly carried out," Espy says, "and several years later Judge Lamar was in his office when he was informed that a message had just arrived from Mississippi that a man, hanged there for another crime, had confessed from the gallows to the crime for which the minister had been executed. So hurt was the judge that he locked his office, walked to his home, kissed the members of his family, including the future Supreme Court Justice—who was then but a small child—goodbye, and shot himself through the head."

Espy also tells the tragic tale of the execution on January 7, 1898, of Jack O'Neill, one of the last persons to be hanged in Massachusetts before the state began using the electric chair. O'Neill, who claimed to be the victim of the anti-Irish bigotry then rampant in the Bay State, had been convicted of the rape-murder of a Buckland woman a year before. As he stood on the gallows, O'Neill's words rang out with unusual passion. "I shall meet death like a man," he vowed, "and I hope those who see me hanged will live to see the day when it is proved that I am innocent—and it will some day."

O'Neill was right, albeit dead right. A short time after his execution, a member of the Massachusetts Militia, who was dying of wounds received in Cuba during the Spanish-American War, confessed that he had raped and murdered the woman in Buckland, and furnished details only the actual killer could have known.

"I concede that most of the people who have been executed in this country have been guilty of the crimes for which they were convicted," Espy says. "However, there also have been plenty of inno- cent people, subsequently proven innocent beyond a shadow of a doubt, to have been deprived of their lives by due process of law.

In addition to those proven innocent after their execution, there are others, I am sure, who were innocent but have never been proven to be so, because law enforcement officials and prosecutors will not investigate a case once an execution has been held. The case is closed for them, and it is probably too much to expect them to go out and try to prove that they have executed an innocent person, no matter what the evidence."

Through his hundreds of thousands of hours of research over the past twenty years, Espy has become convinced that no state that has had a number of executions hasn't taken the life of an innocent person. Of the 681 people executed in his home state of Alabama by 1984, for example, Espy says at least ten were innocent.[2]

One of the more bizarre executions in U.S. history was that of poor William Jackson Marion of Nebraska, who protested his innocence until his last breath as he was hanged on March 25, 1887. It turned out that Marion was telling the truth when his alleged homicide victim turned up alive four years later. For what it was worth to Marion, the governor and the Nebraska Board of Pardons granted him a very-posthumous pardon on the hundredth anniversary of his hanging.

(The Board of Pardons wasn't nearly as magnanimous the following year to Darrell Parker, a living victim of injustice in the Cornhusker State. Parker had been convicted thirty-five years earlier of murdering his wife after giving a coerced confession. By the time another man's confession to the crime was released by his lawyer after the man's death in 1988, Parker had been out of prison for nineteen years. His conviction had been overturned because of the coerced confession, but he had never been officially cleared of the crime. Despite the new evidence of Parker's innocence, the Board of Pardons refused to clear his name.)

As for Marion's conviction for the murder of a man who turned out to still be alive: That was then and this is now, right? That could never happen is a sophisticated age like ours, right?

Wrong. Just ask Merla Walpole and Antonio Rivera. In 1975, Walpole and her former husband were convicted of murdering their

3-year-old daughter in 1965. Nine months later, their convictions were set aside and they were granted a new trial in which Defense Exhibit A could have been their then-13-year-old daughter, who was very much alive. But it never came to that. In November of the same year, charges against them were dismissed and they made plans for a Christmas visit from the San Francisco teenager their attorneys, a district attorney's investigator, and the judge were all convinced was the daughter they were convicted of killing.

Walpole and Rivera had insisted throughout their trial that they had abandoned their daughter, Judy, in a San Francisco gasoline station because she was seriously ill and, because of their dire financial condition, they believed her only chance for survival was to be found and taken care of by someone who could afford her treatment. In 1973, however, bones of a girl were found in a primitive grave about ten miles from where the couple had lived at the time of the girl's disappearance. Hence the trial. Hence the all-so-certain conviction, even though the defense presented as evidence an article in the *San Francisco Chronicle* about a 3-year-old girl matching the couple's daughter's description who had been found abandoned at a Bay area gasoline station on January 16, 1965, which was exactly when the couple said they had deserted their daughter.

After the guilty verdict was set aside on one of the "technicalities" people complain so much about, the DA's investigator set out to track down "Judy Gasse," as she had been referred to in the article because she had been found at a gas station. The detective finally found her in October 1975, living with a woman who had adopted the child after she had spent two years being cared for in a San Francisco hospital.[3]

Another California case shows just how easy it is to get wrongly convicted of not one, but two potentially capital offenses. The unfortunate but not totally blameless victim was Robert Williams of Long Beach, who admitted he was an 18-year-old "punk kid" when he slapped his girlfriend during an argument and ended up in a state juvenile correction camp in 1956. When Williams got word that his girlfriend was planning to marry someone else and his other attempts to reach her to ask for forgiveness and reconciliation failed, Williams decided the best way to get back to Long Beach was to confess to the unsolved murder of a motel owner that had taken place there sometime in the past. "I knew the cops would bring me back to Long Beach for questioning and I figured I could get in touch with my girl once I got there," Williams explained to reporters later. "I figured I could never be convicted because I knew I hadn't done it."[4]

That was a poor assumption. Williams was convicted of first-degree murder and sentenced to life in prison. But he still hadn't learned his lesson. After two years in Folsom Prison, he decided to confess to a 1955 Long Beach murder as well.

"I was subscribing to the Long Beach paper . . . and I saw this article on the Burgess case, which was an unsolved murder," Williams said. "I figured that if I could convince them I had done the Burgess murder, just using the details from the newspaper, that would prove I could have made up the first conviction too." So, as five convicts looked on, Williams wrote out a confession that merely repeated the details in the newspaper article. He had planned to call the inmates as witnesses at the trial but, to his consternation, was prohibited from doing so. Williams was duly convicted of the Burgess murder and sentenced to another life term. He spent the next seventeen years in prison contemplating his stupidity—as well the fact that his predicament was all the result of an attempt to reconcile with a girlfriend from whom he had never heard one word.

When he was paroled in 1975, Williams set out to clear his name. Finally, he came across a record showing he had been in police custody at the time of the first murder. That was evidence enough to convince the man who had prosecuted him for the murder that Williams was innocent after all. By then a judge, Lynn Compton, testified in Williams's behalf at a hearing that released Williams from life parole.

"We never came up with a gun or fingerprints or witnesses or anything," Compton said. "We had the bodies, the circumstance, him confessing and exhibiting certain knowledge, and the jury figured he was the guy. But there's no question that his mouth got him into trouble, because that was all we really had—the confessions."

Williams later wrote an aptly titled book about his case: *Backfire*. "I must have been-half crazy to do what I did," he said. "But I figured the justice system would take care of me because I knew I wasn't guilty. That's one of the things I want to say—it won't."[5] Judgment affirmed.

But Williams, Rivera, and Walpole were among the lucky ones who didn't pay the ultimate price for a crime they didn't commit. The following were among the twenty-three innocent Americans who did, according to Bedau and Radelet's *Stanford Law Review* study, but whose cases haven't been covered elsewhere in this volume. (Additional sources are noted in citations.)

• Everett Applegate of New York, who was convicted with his mistress, Frances Q. Creighton, of murdering his wife with arsenic in 1936. He was executed the same year. Creighton, who had been acquitted on two similar charges twelve years before, confessed that she had killed the victim, but only at Applegate's urging. At the same time, she also confessed to one of the other murders she had previously been cleared of. Because no other evidence against Applegate turned up and Creighton varied her story several times, the governor asked the prosecutor to support a grant of clemency. But the prosecutor refused, and the governor dropped the idea.

• Thomas Bambrick of New York, who was convicted of murder in 1915 and executed the following year. Evidence was discovered while he was on death row that another man had committed the crime, but Bambrick, who knew who the murderer was, went to his death rather than "squeal" on him.

• Charles Becker and Frank "Dago" Cirofici, who were executed in New York in 1915 and 1914, respectively. Becker was a police detective accused of gambling by the murder victim, a gambling house operator, just before he died. Becker was convicted amid extensive newspaper coverage of police graft and on the testimony of a rogue's gallery of gamblers and ex-convicts. Cirofici was one of the four alleged hit men, but the other three insisted to the end that he had nothing to do with the crime.

• Vance Garner, who was executed for murder by Alabama in

1905 without benefit of any appeals of his conviction. When Garner and his alleged accomplice, Jack Hunter, were hanged, Garner maintained his innocence from the gallows while Hunter admitted his own guilt but also insisted Garner was innocent.

• Stephen Grzechwiak and Max Rybarczyk, both convicted of murder in New York in 1929 and executed the following year. A third co-defendant insisted both were the victims of mistaken eyewitness identification, but he refused to name his true accomplices. In their final words, Grzechwiak and Rybarczyk still maintained their innocence, and so did the admitted murderer.

• Joe Hill, who was convicted in Utah for the murder of two storekeepers and executed in 1915. The conviction was based on sketchy circumstantial evidence and collusion between the judge and prosecutor in an atmosphere of anti-unionism. Hill, a native of Sweden, was later described by labor historian Philip S. Foner as the Industrial Workers of the World labor union's "most accomplished, most famous and most prolific songwriter." Hill claimed he was the victim of a frame-up, and his lawyers seemed to agree. "The main thing the state has against Hill is that he is an I.W.W. and *therefore* sure to be guilty," they wrote in the I.W.W.'s *Solidarity* magazine after his conviction. Despite pleas for clemency from President Woodrow Wilson and thousands of people from around the world, the gifted folk singer was executed by a firing squad using dum-dum bullets—which cause large wounds by expanding on contact—on November 19, 1915. An estimated 30,000 people marched in Hill's funeral procession in Chicago.[6]

• Harold Lamble, who was convicted of a 1920 murder in New Jersey and executed in 1921. The governor refused demands for an investigation of the case despite what the *New York Times* called a "rather widespread fear" that Lamble was "deprived of his life unjustly." His attorney was later disbarred for his poor handling of the case. The main evidence against him had been the discredited testimony of an alleged accomplice. Subsequent hearings concluded that the determining factor in Lamble's conviction was his admission of guilt in *previous* convictions.[7]

• Maurice F. Mays, a black convicted of killing a white woman in 1919. The Tennessee National Guard had to be called out to prevent his lynching, but several other Knoxville blacks were indiscriminately killed by white rioters. Mays was executed in 1922, insisting on his innocence to the end. Four years later, *a white woman* confessed to the murder. She said she had dressed up as a black man to kill the victim, who had been having an affair with her husband.

• Albert Sanders, who insisted to the day of his execution in 1918 that he was innocent of the murder for which he and another man were convicted in 1917. His alleged accomplice admitted to the crime and said Sanders had nothing to do with it.

• Charles Sberna, who was convicted of the murder of a police officer in 1938 and executed the following year. His co-defendant said Sberna was innocent. The detective who handled the case told the co-defendant that he also knew Sberna was innocent, but would clear him only if the co-defendant identified the real accomplice, which he refused to do. The same detective was later implicated in the wrongful conviction of Isidore Zimmerman.

• R. Mead Shumway, who was convicted of a 1907 murder in Nebraska and executed in 1909. One juror committed suicide after leaving a note expressing misgivings about the conviction, which was based on weak circumstantial evidence. The victim's husband confessed to the murder on his deathbed a year later.

• Charles Tucker, who was executed for murder in 1906 even though more than 100,000 Massachusetts residents had signed clemency petitions. The county coroner had been replaced because he had insisted the medical evidence supported Tucker's claims of innocence, and a minister said one of those who had testified against Tucker had confessed to him that she had perjured herself.

Now back to the future—well, the present, actually. There was a relatively slow return to executions since the practice was given the go-ahead again by the U.S. Supreme Court in 1976 after a four-year legal lull; then experts feared that executions in Illinois and Oklahoma during the same week in September 1990 would set off a new flurry that would cost the lives of several innocent individuals in the coming years.

Based on the ratio of twenty-three mistaken executions among the seven thousand carried out in the United States since 1900, it is estimated that seven or eight of the twenty-four hundred people now facing execution could be proved innocent after it's too late to correct the mistake—as four states were able to do in 1989 by releasing once-condemned inmates whose innocence was established to the satisfaction of embarrassed officials. By mid-1990, an inmate who had once come within six hours of execution in Texas was released after being exonerated by two different courts.

Edward Earl Johnson of Mississippi, Willie Darden of Florida, and Jimmy Wingo of Louisiana weren't so lucky. Since Johnson and Wingo went to the electric chair for murder in 1987 and Darden followed in 1988, questions about their guilt have continued to mount.

It would hardly be a surprise that Florida would have made a mistake in Darden's case. The "Sunshine State" executed the last three men on the *Stanford Law Review's* list of innocent Americans executed since 1900. Florida also has been forced to release eleven condemned inmates in the past decade who had either been proved innocent or were denied a fair trial at which their guilt was proved beyond a reasonable doubt.

Darden's case attracted international attention, including pleas for clemency from Soviet physicist and Nobel Peace Prize winner Andrei Sakharov, politician Jesse Jackson, actress Margot Kidder, and others who claimed his conviction resulted from an unfair trial in which race had been a major factor. The Nobel Peace Prize–winning group Amnesty International also claimed that Darden's strong alibi was ignored, and that the prosecutors had engaged in professional misconduct.

Amnesty International has also expressed "serious doubts" about Edward Earl Johnson's involvement in the murder for which he was executed in Mississippi's gas chamber. Johnson, who had had no prior criminal record, was arrested in Walnut Grove in 1979, when he was eighteen. He was convicted the following year of murdering a white police officer who had been investigating a call about a burglary and attempted assault. Johnson was arrested along with several other black men who lived in the area and brought before the white woman who had made the initial call to police and had witnessed the shooting. The woman, who had known Johnson all his life, said he was not the murderer. She described the assailant as being heavily built and having a beard. Johnson was slim and had no beard.

Two days later, Johnson was arrested again and eventually signed a confession. He later claimed that police had taken him to a wooded area and threatened to shoot both him and his grandparents if he didn't confess to the crime. Johnson recanted his confession at the first opportunity. "I was scared," he said in explaining why he had signed the document. "I was convicted before I even went to trial." Johnson didn't see a lawyer until after he had been brought to court to be charged.

By then, however, much damage had been done. After hearing of his confession, the burglary-assault victim, who had at first insisted Johnson was not the murderer, changed her story and identified him as the man who had attacked her in her house and killed the officer as he attempted to escape.

Before his trial, the prosecutor offered Johnson a life sentence in return for a guilty plea. But his attorneys mistakenly told him he would be sentenced to life without parole if he accepted the offer, so he turned it down. In actuality, he would have been eligible for parole in 1986—the year before he was executed.

Johnson's lawyers apparently made a number of similar mistakes during his trial and early appeals. When he finally got a top-notch attorney, it was too late to rectify those errors or to conduct a proper investigation. Johnson, whose final days and execution were the subject of a haunting, emotional BBC documentary about capital punishment, died proclaiming his innocence. The documentary, *Execution: Fourteen Days in May*, was later shown in the United States on HBO.

A week after the execution, his last lawyer located a woman Johnson had claimed all along he had been with at the time of the murder. None of the court-appointed attorneys who had represented him previously had made any attempt to find her, Amnesty International says. The woman, a black, said she had gone to the courthouse on her own in an attempt to testify at Johnson's trial, but was told by a white police officer to go home and mind her own business.

Jimmy Wingo was executed for a 1982 double murder even though his common-law wife came forward on the eve of his execution and admitted that she had lied at his trial five years earlier because a sheriff's deputy had threatened to put her in jail and forever separate her from her children if she didn't say what he told her to say in court.

If the pace of executions quickens, at least two men who had exhausted their appeals by the time of this writing could face death in a matter of months, even though substantial doubt exists about their guilt. One of the two is Virginia inmate Joseph M. Giarratano, about whose guilt even conservative columnist James J. Kilpatrick, among many others who have studied his case, has expressed doubt.

The well-read, highly articulate Giarratano made a passionate plea for all those in his situation in a widely circulated news-service article in early 1990. Noting that the U.S. Supreme Court recognized in 1989 that there is a "high incidence of uncorrected error," in capital cases, Giarratano urged that, "where life is at stake, we must ensure our judgments of death are correct. If we must have a death penalty, then we cannot let our anger and frustration blind us to our own fallibility."

But that, unfortunately, seems to be what Americans have too often done. In their rush to judgment, they have forgotten the wisdom of a Spanish proverb: "He is always right who suspects that he makes mistakes."

The best, albeit imperfect, solution to that dilemma is to determine how those mistakes can be minimized and, for those that aren't, corrected before it's too late.

Notes

1. "The Death Penalty in America: What the Record Shows," *Christianity and Crisis*, June 23, 1980, p. 193.

2. *Student Lawyer*, p. 45.

3. "Girl to Visit Pair Accused of Killing Her," *New York Times*, November 23, 1975, p. 42.

4. "Convict Says Confession to Killing Was Only Ruse," *New York Times*, December 24, 1978, p. 22.

5. Ibid.

6. Philip S. Foner, *A History of the Labor Movement in the United States* (New York: International Publishers, 1987) pp. 152–155.

7. "Afraid They Made a Mistake," *New York Times*, August 30, 1921, p. 14.

10

Doing Justice to Justice

Injustice anywhere is a threat to justice everywhere.
                              —*Martin Luther King Jr.*

"Could this happen to *me*—now?" author Eugene B. Block asked rhetorically in the epilogue to *The Vindicators*, his 1963 book about those who have aided in the exoneration of innocent people who "through no fault of their own, have been caught in the web of circumstance, prejudice, or police bungling."

Block's answer—"that it still could, but that it is far less likely than ever before because of the many safeguards . . . that have been set up in recent years to prevent such miscarriages of justice"—was obviously over-optimistic.[1]

To correct a problem, we must first admit we have one. I hope this book has demonstrated that the American system of justice still has a serious problem with the number of innocent people it unjustly convicts, imprisons, and sometimes executes.

Although the victims of such injustices are usually poor and less-educated than the average American, mistaken convictions still afflict people from all walks of life—doctors, lawyers, business executives, devoted parents accused of child abuse, and well-to-do teenagers included.

Regardless of the economic status of the victim, wrongful convictions are a wrong that must be righted—for the sake of the victim and of society as a whole. For these all-too-common miscarriages of justice do far more than destroy the lives of the innocent. They also give new life to the guilty. And, convinced that they can beat the system, the guilty often commit the same or even worse kinds of crimes in the future while someone else pays for those of the past.

The resulting loss of faith in the system by both the innocent and the guilty is a prescription for disaster when mixed with all the other toxins now invading the body politic.

That's why Americans must recognize the conviction of the innocent as both a *moral* problem and a *morale* problem that must be cured. Fortunately, it can be. Most of the causes of wrongful convictions are as correctable as they are recognizable. All we have to do is open our eyes and our minds.

The best way to do that is to review the major causes of wrongful convictions and then consider how they can be avoided.

Let's start with the keystone: cops. That's where much of the problem lies. If innocent people aren't charged, they can't be convicted. To avoid that problem, police departments should do three things.

First, obtain—and *maintain*—a better mix of officers who can look at problems from a variety of perspectives. A recent Claremont Graduate School study showed that merely hiring more black, Latino, and female officers doesn't necessarily achieve that goal. The study, based on a survey of more than 1,000 members of the Los Angeles Police Department, found that they all had similar opinions about their lives, jobs, and ideals—regardless of their sex or race.

"Bringing all these women and minorities onto the force has not made and significant change in the way police perform," said George T. Felkenes, a criminal-justice professor at the college. "Once they get into the department, they're shaped and molded into what the department wants them to be."

To avoid that, departments must not only recognize the problem, but take steps to ensure that all officers don't march to the beat of the same drummer. Otherwise, they will all *think* to the beat of the same drummer when it comes to fighting crime. That's why investigators tend to lock in on one suspect and consciously or subconsciously twist the evidence to match that person.

Attempts to avoid that mindset should begin in the police academy, where different thought processes should be encouraged, the danger of "decision traps" discussed, and the case histories of wrongful convictions studied.

Second, police departments should improve the accuracy of criminal records and emphasize that previous arrests and/or convictions do not mean automatic guilt.

Third, they should make the detective bureaus and crime labs part of a greatly altered prosecutor's office, where the presumption of guilt so common among police officers would be discouraged.

To help ensure that is the case, the prosecutor's office should be transformed into a subsidiary of an investigating magistracy similar to those that exist in almost all industrial nations other than the United States. The advantages of this are obvious, as pointed out by Harvard University law professor Lloyd L. Weinreb, in his book, *Denial of Justice*:

> Transfer of investigative responsibility from the police to a legally trained judicial officer allows unification of the independent investigations of the prosecution and defense into a single investigation, the outcome of which is a careful conclusion supported by the evidence. . . . The declared purpose of the investigation should be to find out what happened, not to develop a case for either side.[2]

A second advantage of such a system would be limitation of the uniquely American adversarial process that turns trials into time-consuming pitched battles between lawyers over issues that are greatly irrelevant to the question of guilt or innocence.

A third advantage, Weinreb adds, would be to eliminate the rubber-stamp grand jury, which even its originators in England did away with in 1933. "In place of the bare indictment or information unsupported by any official record of evidence that we have now," Weinreb writes, "a magistrate who has conducted a thorough investigation in which lawyers for the defendant and, if the prosecutor's office wishes, the state have participated will be able to make serious recommendations for disposition of the case."[3]

That in turn, would lead to a far speedier trial, because few facts would be in dispute. Neither would be most judgments, which is why wrongful convictions in nations that use such systems occur far less often and are generally treated as national scandals when they do.

Also under this system, government crime labs would be encouraged to analyze scientific evidence without pressure and would file all results with the defense as well as the prosecutor. Employee qualifications and salaries would be raised to meet those of private forensic labs to ensure high-quality work.

Use of polygraph exams and hypnotically enhanced questioning should be greatly discouraged, if not banned. If deemed necessary, they should be conducted by crime-lab specialists, and treated as a secondary investigative tool only.

Because costly appeals would be less likely under this approach, state-supported public defender's offices could be beefed up so the defendant can get help when it is most needed and where most mistakes are all but set in concrete—at the trial itself.

Emphasis would also be placed on the development of physical evidence rather than eyewitness testimony. When eyewitness testimony would be used, juries would be presented cautionary instructions on the high rate of inaccuracy of eyewitness identifications and when errors are most likely to occur.

That brings us to the courts, where we should:

• Give judges a more active role in the trial by permitting them to give more frequent guidance about testimony, evidence, and the reasons for their rulings.

• Restrict the much-abused, time-consuming system of *voir dire* or "jury vetting," through which attorneys seek malleable jurors who often lack strength of character and independent judgment.

• Encourage the selection of jurors with expertise in fields relevant to the case at hand.

• Give jurors a more active role by permitting them to ask a limited number of questions of or through the judge.

• Establish policies to ensure that defendants are protected from pleading guilty when the prosecution has little evidence of "factual guilt." Develop other safeguards so that a presumption of guilt does not replace a presumption of innocence in the plea-bargaining process.

- Establish a quasi-judicial "Court of Last Resort" as an adjunct to state supreme courts to consider the question of innocence of those who claim to have been wrongfully convicted, through investigation if necessary, rather than the question of legal error through argument to which most appeals courts are limited. If the evidence warrants it, a new trial could be ordered.
- Establish disciplinary procedures for any officer of the court who violates prescribed rules of conduct on the presentation of evidence and argument.
- Establish a compensation fund from which those judged to have been unjustly convicted would be paid according to general guidelines. This would ensure at least some form of remuneration for the damages caused by the state and avoid costly and time-consuming judicial or legislative remedies.

Some twenty-five hundred years ago, the Athenian statesman and lawmaker Solon was asked how true justice could be achieved in Athens. His answer, Chief Justice Earl Warren told the World Conference on World Peace Through the Rule of Law in the same Greek city in 1963, was that "justice could be achieved whenever those who were not injured by injustice were as outraged as those who had been."

With several thousand innocent Americans being needlessly convicted of serious crimes every year; with thousands of families being destroyed and dreams being shattered by the nightmare of mostly avoidable miscarriages of justice every year; with several innocent individuals unnecessarily sitting on death row every year, it is high time for America to be outraged.

Notes

1. *The Vindicators*, p. 267.
2. Lloyd L. Weinreb, *Denial of Justice: Criminal Process in the United States* (New York: Free Press, 1977), p. 132.
3. Ibid., pp. 134–135.

Index